'We Can Mind t[ ]

Memories of Craster People

Edited by Colin Biott

Drawings by Mick Oxley

Published by Craster Community Development Trust

'We Can Mind the Time'

Memories of Craster People

Copyright © Craster Community Development Trust

ISBN 0-9550859-0-X

First printed 2005
Craster Community Development Trust
Cartref,
South Acres,
Craster,
Alnwick,
Northumberland
NE66 3TN

Our Funders

To whom go our thanks and appreciation for making this all possible.

Local Heritage *initiative*

Heritage
Lottery Fund

Nationwide

The
Countryside
Agency

'We can mind the time'
Memories of Craster People

Contents

Introduction

Part One: Memories of Working in Craster

1. Fishing 9

2. Fish Curing And Kippers 29

3. Shops, Trades And Taking In Visitors 41

4. Quarrying And Pipe-making 56

5. Farming 62

Part Two: Memories of Living in Craster

6. A Place To Live 72

7. Childhood And Schooldays 78

8. Pastimes And Social Life 89

9. Lifeboat And Coastguards 107

10. Church and Chapel 114

11. Wartime 118

12. Some Village Characters: 'they are the people you miss' 131

Part Three: Context

i) Medieval Craster, Craster Tower and the Craster Family by Mary Craster 152

ii) Changing Maps Of The Village 157

iii) Glossary 159

'We can mind the time'
Memories of Craster People

The inhabitants, no longer so numerous as formerly, maintain themselves and have many characteristics, which distinguish them from the agricultural people of the neighbouring villages.
A stranger will receive a pleasing impression from the fisherfolk. He will observe their fine physique, their rugged but handsome features, and the peculiar softness of their speech. These traits, in some measure due to the simple and healthy occupation of the people, have been developed by their manner of life. The similarity of their names (and it would be hard to find a Craster man who was not an Archbold or a Simpson) shows that the inhabitants of Craster, as of other fishing villages along the coast of Northumberland, are a colony apart.

Bateson E (1895) A History of Northumberland, Volume 2, p167, Andrew Reed Publisher

Introduction
'It's good we're getting these things written down afore it's too late'

Craster folk have been saying for some time that the village is at risk of losing its community memories. As a Church Newsletter reminded us after the death of Howick Scar farmer Willy Curry in 1995, *'when an old friend dies, a library is lost' (1.)* Unless we do preserve our local social heritage we will forfeit a thread of continuity which connects generations and links past, present and future. Shared memories are especially precious in rural villages as population patterns change and more and more homes are bought as holiday houses.

Fortunately, the experiences and stories of older villagers were valued enough for the Craster Community Development Trust, with Michael Gibbs as a driving force, to make a bid for funding to The Countryside Agency, which had launched a national scheme to support heritage projects run by community groups. A small, local-history group was awarded £12,175 from the Local Heritage Initiative Fund to finance the Craster Village History Project, which has run from January 2003 until March 2005.

Over the past two and a half years, the project has run a series of participative, community events and collected an archive of personal stories and memories of life and work in the village. Six events have been held: a launch meeting at which children performed plays based on stories told by elderly villagers; two further drama performances drawing on the archive and involving story-telling and music; an exhibition of old film, photographs and scrapbooks; a 1940s dance with a pooled supper and a final celebratory presentation and performance.

Stories have been gathered from group discussions and narrative interviews with 'memory-bearers' (2), who carry with them the history of the village (see list below.) We asked people to tell us about their lives in their own ways, with only a few questions to help the story along. We tried to be attentive listeners, but not to get in the way

Throughout the project the 'memory-bearers' have been co-researchers as well as contributors. The first step was to hold a meeting of interested villagers in the Memorial Hall. Those present told us what aspects of Craster's social heritage should be recorded and who should be interviewed. Following this, we carried out interviews, all of which were taped and transcribed. Once we had established a provisional structure of the book, we selected quotes, vignettes and stories, prepared draft thematic chapters and gave these to villagers who were quoted within them. They were invited to comment on the overall impact of the chapters, to identify errors or weaknesses and to suggest further topics and/or sources. They were also asked for permission to use their contributions. Following this we conducted a further set of interviews and added new material. The whole, re-drafted text was read by a small group of volunteers and further modifications were made.

The book is divided into three parts; *Memories of Working in the Village*; *Memories of Living in the Village*; and *Context*. We want to emphasise the importance of villagers' voices, and we invite readers to enter the book, as they would the village, from any direction and to eavesdrop on these stories, in any order. The book does not have a linear, narrative or chronological structure and it has no commentary

For readers who do not know the village, we have outlined its historical background in Part Three and included a set of maps. Documentary material and a selection of old photographs, loaned by villagers, are also included throughout the book. We do hope, however, that this collection of evocative memories contains sufficient background information to contribute cumulatively towards an understanding of the changing times through which Craster people have lived.

We chose the title – *'we can mind the time'* – because of its double meaning of 'calling to mind' or remembering and of 'minding' or looking after. It catches the essence of the project through a much used conversational idiom, as in - 'we can mind the time when we all walked up the hill to school.' It also reflects, in its other meaning, our attempt *'to mind,'* to preserve a community's stories of what it has been like to have lived and worked in the village for many years.

Accounts of dramatic and noteworthy incidents are mixed with insights into the daily round of village life, and humour is never far away. Early in the project we kept saying that we were 'making a living history' and that is how it has felt for us, both in special events and in helping to gather these memories. At times the project has opened a community story-chest of familiar, ready-to-tell stories from a thriving oral tradition connecting Craster families. At other times, especially in group discussions, I have listened to old friends help each other to dig down into the past and awaken dormant memories. Together, they have reached back to shape new ways of seeing incidents, sometimes at the point of utterance.

Colin Biott (Editor)

March 2005

1   Newsletter No 76, The United Reform Church, Embleton, June 1995, p4
2   *We have used the term 'memory-bearers' as Daly (1993) uses it to refer to long term feminists, who carry with them the history of the modern women's movement. In our sense the memory bearers carry the history of their village.*

   Daly M (1993) <u>Outercourse; the bedazzling voyage,</u> *London, Women's Press*

Thanks to the generosity of our sponsors – The Heritage Lottery Fund; Nationwide; and the Countryside Agency-each home in the village will receive a free copy of this book.

A selection of source materials used in the preparation of this book can be accessed on the project web-site www.crasterhistory.co.uk. The material on this web- site may also be added to in the future.

The Project Team

Colin Biott (Project Director and Editor); Sue Chapman (Community Arts Programme Leader); Michael Gibbs (Chair and Project Administrator); and Angus Tait (ICT and Design Leader)

Interviews: Colin Biott; Doris Clarke; Joe Flegg; Rosemary Gibbs

Documentary Sources: Joan Angus; Mary Craster

Design and ICT: Mick Oxley; Angus Tait   Drawings: Mick Oxley

In addition to specified roles listed above, all members of the team have contributed to the general direction and progress of the project, and to the running of community events.

Audio Typing was done by Moira Anderson and Jennifer Doherty.

We also acknowledge the specialist support given at community arts events by Peter Brown, Andy and Margaret Watchorn and Robert Whitehead.

The Memory Bearers

Joan Angus; Ada Archbold; Willie Archbold; Winnie Banks; Jack Browell; Martin Browell; Doris Clarke; Marjorie Clarke; Les Crate; Bill Curry; Adam Dawson; Alan Dixon; Rosemary Gibbs; Carol Grey; Eddie Grey; Geordie Grey; Jimmy Hall; Violet Hall; Dougie Hogg; Winnie Hogg; Billy Lumsden; Marjorie Lumsden; Garth Lowerson; Willy Mitford; Vera Mitford; Alison Newbigin; Iain Parker; Michael Robson; Neil Robson; Joyce Shaw; Jimmy Shaw; Lena Shell; Edwina Simpson; Gladys Simpson; Mary Smail; Fred Stephenson; Eleanor Venus; Ken Venus; Dennis Williams; Eddie Williams; Keith Williams; Maggie Wilson; Isabel Young.

We thank Jimmy Shaw for the loan of additional documentary evidence of village history, and also Mrs. Harrison (daughter of Adam Dawson), Marion Gallon, Gerald Sables and Wilfred Taylor for photographs and documents.

In chapter 10 we have quoted from Donald Leslie (1980) *One Hundred Years On: Craster Methodist Church 1880-1980*, printed by Coates of Alnwick

We have been pleased to include notes written by the late Eva Archbold in 1957. She had an enduring passion for village history and in an introductory paragraph she wrote:

This does not pretend to be a concise history of Craster but only notes taken at random. When complete, I may reconstruct them. If I do not, perhaps someone else will. Should this fall into the hands of someone who cares nothing for these matters, or who has no interest in them, I trust it will not be treated lightly but given to someone who will appreciate it. This is the earnest wish of the writer: (Signed) Evangeline Archbold, Craster, 1957.

Chapter 1 Fishing

Craster Haven (taken from Eva Archbold's collection, and labelled 'the oldest photograph of Craster.')

Carol Grey

During the 60's when the North Sea was open to the herring, the cobles went out from Craster, and we used to stand at the harbour sometimes till 2 or 3 o'clock in the morning and of course when you looked out to sea it was just like a street, all the lights from the fishing boats.

One night Billy Smailes came in and the boat was 'full to the gunnels.' If there had been any movement on the sea he would have sunk. The scales used to be on the sides of the boats. The people on the north side on the 'Tatie grounds' never used to have any peas those nights 'cause we used to sit and watch the boats coming in and eat the peas, and the rocks below us used to be covered in pea pods and we used to have to clear them up in a box to destroy the evidence. It was a lovely time, the nights seemed lighter then. I couldn't live away from the sea. Some people prefer to be in the hills and some prefer the sea.

Eddie Grey

When I was young I used to go with the boats here. Billy Smailes and Bartie Dawson used to fish for herring and I went with the Silks a few times - nighttime drifting with the cobles. It was like Piccadilly Circus out there 'cause you used to get the ring-netters, the Scotch boats, going backwards and forwards. They had it off to fine art how they used to work their gear. In fact, when you think back, you weren't safe there in a coble, the lights they used to have were just like a jam jar with a bulb. There was no navigation like there is now. The Scotch boats had the white lights and what not, but the cobles were pretty primitive, the rig that they had. It was quiet weather when we went out. It was still, but we could hear when the ring-netters were going steaming about. You could hear the wake coming off them, you couldn't really hear the engine, just the wake off the boat and they used to come steaming close past you.

I remember the first time I was there. I was with Billie Smailes. I'd never been to the herring fishing before. I can remember him hauling the nets. I think there was about five or six cran, I can remember the herring coming over the side and they were squeaking, like a mouse. When you see them in the water it's like fire in the water, they shine.

One night I was with the Silks and I think we had about 17 cran. We had these Polish pellets, they were roundy, but more oblong and I can remember shooting off the Castle. Eric Archbold was there. We hadn't been shot very long, and I can remember Eric saying, 'It's time we had them nets aboard.' The pellets were standing on end and the nets were full of herring. We didn't get all the nets back. They burst away with the weight of the fish. I was pulling on the oar keeping the boat steady to the net as they were hauling. They had about 17 cran, and the boat was sitting right down in the water. I had just left the school then.

We used to go down at night and stand at the harbour wall waiting on the local boats coming in. The horizon used to be a mass of lights and where the herring were they would be steaming around looking for a shoal to shoot the nets on and you could see a searchlight going and all the boats seemed to congregate and there was one big mass of lights. It was a fascinating sight. We used to raid the gardens, time we were waiting for them coming in. We used to pinch the apples and the peas and everything.

Some Craster Boats

Joan Angus

The boats and cobles had wonderful names - The Lizzie Buist Rennie, a herring boat bought from a fisherman in Newbiggin for £90; The Verbena; The Lady Fanny; The Margery Banks; The Elizabeth & Mary; Charles William; Mayflower; The Water Lily; The Annie & Nellie; and Isabella. I can remember cobles with names like: Our Girls 1 & 2; Our Brother; Thankful; Silver Spray; Supreme; Just Reward; Eleanor Dawson; Jane; Unity; Anne B. Smailes; Anne B; Thomas H; Marian; and Star Trek. I think Dodie Archbold had Silver Spray, John W. Dawson had The Thankful and Ralph Martin Archbold and Jack Hall, The Isabella. Buist Rennie belonged to Bob Smailes and the fishermen called it 'Lizzie Bust Rennie.'

Extracts from the Shipping Register – Craster Boats 1920s

Archbold
Thomas W	PROVIDER	Built 1922, sail and motor, lost 22.3.23
Ralph	ANNIE & NELLIE	lug sail, motor installed 13.8.23
Martin & Ralph	OUR BROTHER	lug sail, foremast & jib
J N K	HERO	lug sail, mizzen mast, condemned 5.1.25
Joseph Tait	JANE	lug sail, motor added 8.12.22, to N Shields 23.6.28
Thomas Nesbit	MARY	lugger, foresail & jib
J	BOY WILLIE	sail fore & aft, lug & jib
Adam	OUR GIRLS	sail fore & aft, motor added 10.2.20
William	NAOMI	lug sail, foresail and jib, went to Blyth 25.2.25
James	OUR LADS	sail, lug, foresail & jib

Dawson
Sep & George	EBENEZER	sail, lug, broken up 31.12.28
J W	SHAMROCK	sailing lug
George	OLIVE LEAF	sail, lug, foresail and jib
Henry	GUIDE ME	coble, lug sail, condemned 31.12.27

Septimus	ROBERT & WILLIAM	broken up 30.12.26
Grey		
William	VERBENA	sail, lugger, foresail and jib, transferred to Blyth 13.3.29
Smailes		
Robert	ROBERT & JOHN	sail, lugger, foresail & jib
Stephenson		
James	UNITY	coble, sail & lug
William	TRANSVAAL	coble, sail & lug, condemned 31.12.27
Taylor		
R, G & W	THANKFUL	motor
Robert	LEAD ME	coble, sail lug

Willy Archbold

About 1939, when I was about four years old, there were about seven fishing cobles. My father's boat was 'The Brighter Dawn,' - Dawson's boat, 'Our Lads,' - Smailes' boat, 'Our Girls' - Ralph Archbold (Harry's father) 'Isabella,' - Dodie Archbold, 'Silver Spray,' - Taylor's boat, 'The Thankful,' - Archbold family, 'The Onward.' The herring fishing had finished then, the keel boats, but my father went with the coble, herring fishing. His crew were Archbolds. Another crew went with the Silver Spray and they were the only two boats that fished for herring in the summer during the War years. They were pretty successful. The other boats kept to the crabbing and lobster. In 1945 the number of cobles reduced because the Taylor family had all retired or died and Ralph Archbold retired and lived to a fair age.

Working at sea

Eddie Grey

To be a good fisherman is mainly just practice. You pick it up as you go along but I served my time with Billie

Fishing Coble.

Smailes. When I started originally, I went with Billie when he had a trawler 'The Germania.' We fished out of Seahouses. I went with him for three year there and then I got a coble of my own; I wanted to be back here. I didn't think much of the trawling. As Billie said to me, 'You're better off in Durham Jail, as doing that job.' I hadn't been married that long and I had two young children and I never used to see them when I came home at night - I used to see them at the weekend, like. They were in bed when I got home - sometimes it was 9 o'clock when I got home and I was away again at midnight, they really didn't know me. I wanted to be back here. My heart was here. I wanted to go lobster fishing. I love cobles.

I always wanted a coble of my own. I applied for a white fish grant and I was lucky enough to get one. Me and Edward Dawson started together, then Edward wanted a boat of his own so we went our separate ways. Then Billie was about to finish with 'The Germania' and he came back here and went with me. I learned a lot from him. He had been at it all his life. The best years of my life were going to sea with him, 'cause he was funny and you used to get some laughs. He was a good fisherman and I learned a lot from him, marks and that and where we caught a lot of lobsters. I can always remember him saying to me when things were hard 'Never let nowt beat you – when times diven't gan right just keep your heart up and soldier on, they'll come right for you.' Aye, he says, 'Never let nowt beat you.' It takes a bit doing, sometimes like. He was a great friend to me.

My coble was built by Dawsons at Seahouses. She was started in 1979, say 1980 - she's 25-year-old now. There's none being built now. That's a shame all the yards are finished, and Harrisons at Amble laid down a lot of cobles but they're all finished now, nobody makes cobles any more. I hope my coble sees me out. I'm 55 now. I hope I get another ten years out of it. There's one at Beadnell, she's still lying on the beach, she's knackered now, but she's 60 year old now, but she hadn't been looked after in the latter years. You can put them right, you can get them re-nailed or get a plank put in. It's a dying art now 'cause a coble's just built by the eye, there's no set plan for them, it's just sort of handed down. There's going to be nobody left. It's a shame if they'll be like a keelboat, a thing of the past, everything's fibreglass, now. If you want a boat now, you've got to go all the way to Cornwall, to get a lobster boat, it seems ridiculous. Fibreglass boats are all right but they're not like a wood boat. I know you haven't got the maintenance with them but they're lively in the sea and they are not designed for the likes of Craster. It's not a safe harbour; you have to haul the boats up. The way they're designed is for a harbour where they're afloat all the time.

I keep my boat at Beadnell in the winter. I fish out of Beadnell in the winter 'cause there's not the men here to help hauling up and down. It's easier on my boat to keep it in Beadnell if I kept it here it would be knackered by now, hauling it up and down, the nails would go and everything. There's not the men to work on launching them. When I started there were nine or ten of us. Sometimes it was a day's work getting them into the water, especially in the winter mornings. The beach was never the same two days running. If you got a bit of sea on, the weir washed up and it was hard work, especially when the seaweed gets deep and it gets boggy. It's heavy going. We used to have what we called a 'Haak,' like a rake with a shank on and we pulled the heaps down to cut a way down, it was a day's work sometimes. You were lathered with sweat and by the time you got steamed off to where your gear was, you were frozen, on winter mornings when it was frosty and that. It was heavy on the boats and that's why I keep my boat at Beadnell. It's just tied up against the pier and it's easier on the boat and it's easier on me. I'd rather be here but that's just the way it is.

I sell my fish to Swallows at Seahouses and it goes to Bergens at Eyemouth. We get our stuff weighed there. He's got a big processing plant there now. He exports the lobsters to the Continent mainly, I think, Belgium and France, there's a big market for them there. He's got a big processing plant for the crabs, which is a good thing for us, 'cause years ago when Kenneth (Robson) used to get them I think they went to Hull, Roach of Hull, I think. He had one or two buyers but I think a lot of them were family firms and I suppose they just died out. After Hull, there was a chap from Shields used to get them, but Bergen always took the lobsters.

In the 1970s there were about nine or ten used to fish from here. Bartie was there, Billy Silk, Billie Smailes, Albert, Billy's father, was still going to sea, but then he retired. Billy Silk and I used to have some laughs pulling each other's legs, and Jackie Browell. There's no characters left now. I suppose Dougie (Hogg) will be a character. There were some grand old people. Dougie's grandfather was a grand old fellow, Adam Scotty. Some of the older men at Beadnell used to call him Big Adam.

Working at the capstan, hauling up the boats.

Jack Browell

I took a bloke called Jamesie Smailes' berth, when he packed up. The boat was called 'Just Reward,' a coble. There was Bartie Dawson and Vincent Morris and myself. That time of year we were working three to four miles of track, fishing 8 by 30 pots. A fleet of lobster pots consists of 30 pots. Later on we were fishing for lobsters. I got pushed into steering the boat. I had to learn all this and I used to get pointed out the landmarks. I used to have to take compass readings, pocket watch time – I used to have to carry a pocket watch, which I still have, that was my job. You were told once and you had to remember, you were never told a second time. We used to work right on the five mile track and about Christmas time we used to cut the fleets back to six, land the newest nets - as long as you got Christmas in, the lobsters was good then - you were doing well. It was hard graft because there was no such thing as self- haulers then. Everything was done by hand. We had a central bollard with a wheel on. That was my job, working the hauler in the middle, which you couldn't leave. You were on the whole time. We worked right through till Christmas time. We worked round the Craster Carrs, (five miles east of Craster.) Bartie was a good fisherman. Then there was 'Berried Hen Law': we had to put the lobsters back with berries on. This was a breeding lobster. There was a breeding ground off there.

We used to get up, sometimes 2 o'clock in the morning, put the boats down, sit in the winch house, which at that time was all whitewashed out, we used to have chairs there. We would then get on to the boats and drift around till daylight. Some mornings at that time of year, when it was frosty, we used to carry a flask of coffee. Once we got down the harbour, we never went back home, this was a superstition.

Our gear was a sou-wester and a smock. We used to wear a blue or yellow smock. We didn't wear gloves. You worked with bare hands all the time, for a better grip. You get used to the cold. We had an air-cooled engine and if we were steaming between fleets, we used to warm our hands. You got hardened to it. I'm sometimes affected by arthritis now.

I remember once we were coming home when a gale came up about five minutes from the shore and the sea had broken astern of us and she ran away, she was running right above the cover and once a coble runs away that's it, but she was a good sea boat. It was the first boat Bartie had. The coble was designed on Viking boats. There is a difference in build between a Yorkshire coble and a Northumberland coble, the Northumberland coble is finer built and there's never two the same. You just tell the boat-builder what you want, if you want it laid out more.

Dougie Hogg

I was out of my time (as an apprentice joiner,) I come home one night and I said to the wife 'I've had enough of that mind, I'm going to build a boat and I'm going fishing.' She just laughed at us and about six months later I packed the job up and the gaffer come to us and says, 'You know, you should have stopped here, you'll be alright, we would look after you,' but my mind was made up and I went to the sea. I was making about £10 a week and was about 20 years old.

When I eventually got some pots shot - cos it had been a bad few years for the fishermen, they weren't catching much, - but I was lucky when I started. There were loads of lobsters and I made a tremendous wage the first week. I couldn't believe it. I was making about £150 a week, the first week I fished with that boat. It just had an outboard and I put an inboard engine in it and did a lot of work on it, put bilge keels on it and pulled her up and down the beach.

I used to gan myself and there was one day I was fishing just beside the Castle and I got a rope around my leg and it pulled me over the top of the engine box and my hand landed on the gear stick, otherwise I would have been ower the side and away. So I got somebody after that and we done away quite well, but when the weather broke in September time, we always used to lose our gear, cos we couldn't get to the nets as the lobster pots were falling about as the boat wasn't big enough. I had to go back to joinering.

There was a storm and we lost all the gear. The fishermen down there give me a hard time, because they thought I should have kept fishing, but I couldn't because I had no gear. I found this hard to understand - my grandfather had been a fisherman down there. They give me a bit grief like. They thought I was just going to fish there in the summertime, but I had no intention of doing that. I was going to go full time when I got properly established. My dad used to sort them. He came down to the harbour wall one day and the boat was pulled up and I was doing some work on it, they were all there giving me some grief and he came down and sorted them out.

The fellow who first had the coble (I had bought,) came from Newbiggin and he died in the stern of it and one day we were out at sea, I was with Peter Browell, he was one of my crew. It was a lovely day and the engine started to rev up and down and Peter looked at me and I looked at him. I said 'he's come back.' It had done it loads of times; the engine was revving out of control and to tell you the truth we had the wind up, we didn't know what was going on and we got a look, it was a big crab under the floorboards and it had hold of the throttle cable and was pulling it every now and again. We were relieved after that.

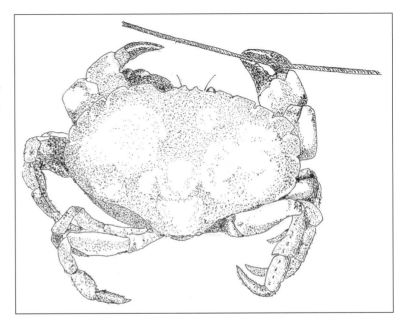

My friend, Ian Banks bought this hull, it was a Dory and he asked me to do it up, 'cos I was a joiner to trade. So I done all the joinery work for him and we done a good job, he put the engine in, 'cos he was a mechanic. I thought, 'well, I'm going to have one of them 'cos when I got a look, there was no maintenance, they were fibreglass.' I was just lucky then - there were grants to get help to buy the fishing boats - so I saw this Cornish Dory advertised, which was bigger than Ian Bank's boat. It had a hell of a beam on it, so I got the whitefish fellow to come down and I told him what I wanted and I got it sorted out and I think I was the last around here to get a boat with a whitefish grant. The fellow asked me why I was going all the way to Cornwall to get one of them, he asked why I just didn't get a coble, I told him I had helped to do my mate's boat out and could see the benefit of fibre glass, so I ordered the boat up, it was Port Isaac in Cornwall. We were looking forward to it coming, but my Dad died at the Christmas and he had been looking forward to seeing it, it was a bloody shame, so we named the boat after him, Thomas H.

The Bon Amy (current boat) originally came from Dartmouth and somebody from Fishguard bought it and I bought it off him. We got it transported from there and I had a lot of work to do to it. It needed bilge keels on a metal plate around about and Jimmy Hall come along one day when I was busy and he asked if I wanted a hand and it was the best thing I ever done, his welding's fantastic, me and him got on fine and I was doing fibre-glass and he was welding, we just got on fine together, if I had just had my sons helping, we would have been fighting all the time.

The Fishing Year

Eddie Grey

You used to have seasons, crab fishing come the spring and then the lobster fishing, but the seasons seem to have changed now. Everything seems to be back to front. You get crabs nearly all the year round, lobsters too. I don't know what's happening, whether it's caused by global warming or what. A few years ago you couldn't catch a crab. We thought the crab fishing was finished. About 10 or 12 years ago, we couldn't get a boxful.

There was no crab fishing in the spring like there used to be. About three or four years ago we started fishing further out, about five or six miles out and there were plenty of crabs. They were a Godsend really 'cause we were nearly on our backsides then. The crabs were maybe there years ago but we couldn't go out that far, we daren't go because you used to get the Scotch boats fishing for haddock and whiting and that. Your gear wasn't safe. You used to keep it further in. We used to make our new gear and mend our old gear, paint the boats and that getting ready for the spring.

Jack Browell

Lobster fishing started July working very close to shore - 'The Rock Ends' - working eight fleets of 30 pots per fleet. We had catches of sometimes up to 100 to 200 pounds of lobsters at the start of fishing. As the months went by and nearing December we would be off to 5 miles and deeper water. Some winters were very poor and we use to lose some pots if it was really rough.

January & February we landed our lobster pots (trapnets) and prepared for the crabbing season. Crab pots were different to lobster pots. We shot 8 fleets of 40 pots on the 20 fathom depth about the end of Feb. If the weather was reasonable, by March & April time we were working about 15 to 20 minutes from home in an easterly direction. We'd catch anything between 60 and 100 stones of crab per day, but as time went on we used to be put on quota of 10 to 15 stone per crewmember.

The ropes weren't like they have now, our ropes were tarred. You used to tar and bark them, your hands got all tar and you used to get spikes off them with running through your hands. What we used to do when we came home at 12 o'clock, the catch had to be in then to get away to the market, we used to try to get in between 12 – 1 o'clock, then we used to come home, have our dinner and then back to the shed where we used to knit covers – our goal for the year was to knit 100 covers and wood for 100 bottoms, knock them up, bore them and stack them and then go away and cut ash sticks for the bows, bend them and shape them. That was the performance for the year, used to hang them up, bend them, tie them at the bottom with string and then have a session cutting a box of wedges and that was it. Used to get stones, it's all metal now, used to use different shaped stones for to tie your pots. You didn't get much break.

About February we used to shoot the crab nets, which is an entirely different pot to a lobster pot. We used to start crabbing then on the 20 fathom mark, somewhere about the 3 mile track. We worked in and worked in until about March time when you were about 10 minutes off the shore. We used to work 8 x 40's. We didn't board them every day, we used to just over run them, (didn't keep them on board just baited them, take stuff out and then throw them away.) Some days with the big tides you were flat out. I've seen us just stripped off, just a shirt on, going flat out. Crabs had to be landed around 12 o'clock for Mr K Robson to transport them by wagon down to Hull and he used to fetch our crab bait on the return journey, cod heads which had to be cut up into pieces for next day.

We used to come home and go to bed sharp and that was it, up early in the morning again. Then when the crabbing really started, there were always crab, once you started getting loads of crab, I'm talking about 80, 90 a 100 stone. Crab was everywhere. What used to happen was they put a quota on – 15 stone a man. You were then very limited as to what you could get. We used to catch a lot of crabs then, but it was a hopeless job because time you had them in boxes on the pier, if the sun got them or they were laid in the harbour. You can imagine if they were all boxed up and nailed, you had to keep the claws tied as they used to fight. By Monday morning a lot of them were dead.

That was the crab season and then we started with the lobsters again in July and August, around the weirs. We used to work 8 x 30s lobster pots. The worst thing that ever came out was self haul and the steel pots. When we worked, we had to watch the weather. We didn't want to lose our gear, so you worked off the shore. The steel pots were never out of the weir, amongst the rocks, they leave them in now - the ruination of fishermen. The self haulers took all the hard work out of fishing.

The herring fishing came about in September. We had a bash at that. The Scottish driftnet men all used to come down to this part of the coast, and we decided to go with the cobles. We used to work with seven herring nets, used to go away about 7 o'clock at night working at the west end of the drifters: Bartie Dawson, myself, Vincent Morris and we had an old fellow, called Geordie Norris. We used to carry flasks of soup and coffee. We used to put a little winkie (floating light) on one end and we used to drift on the tide and watch what was happening. One night, Geordie was with us and we had a small searchlight, which we used to put on the nets to see how they were and they were getting deep in the water and this night Bartie said it was about time we had them hauled. Geordie kept saying 'no, no, there's not enough in yet.' So we had a drink of coffee. After another fifteen minutes we put the light on again. What a sight, every net was on the top of the water solid silver full of herring. They were full from end to end, so we started to haul them. What a job we had, we couldn't shake them out because they were mashed from both sides, one mass of silver, so we had to heave them on board the boat. So anyway, we had them on board and realised then, we hadn't much free board, it was a fine night and that was a good job as we only had about a plank and a half above the water. We must have drifted well away out to the east that night with the driftnet men.

Never mind, coming home, we spoke to old Billy Silk, Albert Silk and Eric Archbold, they had to cut two nets away and leave them, so we came home together. They used to leave the lights on in the harbour so we could see the landfall. Understand it was black dark at two o'clock in the morning. I was steering the boat, leading the way with the Silks' coble behind. Now the Dunstan Steads Farm had the same lights on their barns as our harbour. We were right away down, I would say nearly to the Farnes. We mistook the lights and it was a good job the moon broke through the clouds and we saw the Castle standing to the south of us, otherwise we would probably have been ashore. What a job we had to get around about. Never mind, we came into the harbour and we turned the boat around about, but we didn't realise how much depth of water we drawed with all the herring aboard. So Vincent Morris jumped over the side as normal when cobles are beaching and with the extra depth he was up to his waist in water. We hauled the boat up to the top of the harbour to discharge the herring. I believe we had 28 cran that night. We had boxed herring; I think we had about three boxes forward, as much as we could to balance the coble. We had them all out by 4 o'clock in the morning, everything washed down and hauled the boat back to sea to haul our pots. What a way to make a living.

I went with Billy Smailes one night, and Eric, (Vincent wasn't keen on nighttime fishing.) We ended up at the back of the Farnes and it came away a northerly gale. Tom Dawson, who had the Providence then, says to Billy, 'I'll run you home to see that you're all right, not much doing,' so he came with us. This was a big seine-net boat. We were coming to what they call the Castle Holes, about 3 mile off. We had been about nine miles off the back of the Farnes when it turned poor. We had an echo meter on and Eric and myself were lying on the engine box and Billy was steering the boat and all of a sudden the echo screen went black and we eased the boat back and Billy came up and said 'that's herring,' so he waved the torch to Tom who was just behind us in the Providence and we then shot the nets out and I think we had 12 cran that night, hauled them out. I think the Providence had a good shot, he shot on and we came home. That was about the tail end of the herring fishing. The year was approximately 1962 – 63.

We carried on with the lobster pots in September time, right through the winter and of course there were some poor, poor winters and we lost a lot of gear sometimes. Had to go away and cut boat sticks once or twice a year, these were to haul the boats up and down on. These were mostly ash and oak and we used to soak them with water. We could haul them down a long way then but we used to get a lot of seaweed piled up in the harbour, after very heavy seas and we couldn't get out of the harbour some days. Sometimes we used to have to get the tractor down from the South Farm to get a lot of seaweed away. They then brought the bulldozer down, but that made it a lot worse, it took the bottom out. It was just like a runway and lasted two or three days and a heavy sea put it all back to normal again. The seaweed in those days was terrible, much worse than it is today. Alongside the harbour used to be covered. It would be hanging off the piers. We used to have to pull it down and make a runway and lay the sticks down before you go out in the morning. I've seen us pull Billy Smailes boat right down to the harbour mouth, on sticks. There was a gang of men then.

Danger at sea: 'I was thankful we got in alright'

Willie Archbold

About 20 years ago, it was one day it came away very bad and he (Dougie Hogg) had his nets right in at the rocks and at that particular time, he had all the nets he had at sea, he had none in reserve on the beach and if the sea had come really bad, which it was mekking, he would have been cleaned out and had to pack up. So he asked me if I would gan to sea with him, because his mate was away for the weekend. So I said yes I would gan and it was a pretty rough day, I'll tell you, and we went away and there was one fleet north of the Muckle Carr rock and we went in as far as we could and we saw that it was going to be dangerous and we just left it. Now that fleet, later that day was washed clean ashore and they were nearly all right, on the beach, the whole lot. We went to the back off the Castle where he had two fleets and we got them out. It was a poor day and after that we went away south and we got two fleets in off Cullernose and we got them out and then we turned home and it was high water and that helped the situation 'cause it's dangerous coming into the harbour, when it gets shallow between the two rocks and it was a big tide which helped as well. I was thankful that we got in alright.

Another day, I wasn't out with Dougie, it was about 1984 and it come bad and when he was coming into the harbour, he was coming in all right, coming between the Carrs but just outside the pier, this sea come from nowhere and there was three in the boat, Andrew, Dougie and Dick and it broke underneath the boat and had it broken right on the stern I think she would have foundered and sunk just outside the pier, but fortunately it broke under the boat and he was lucky. He had gone out in pretty good weather and then it just broke. That harbour is a good entrance to come in but if it's an easterly sea, it's not so easy. It's a good boat. I wouldn't have liked to have been in a coble on that day. The coble can stand a lot as well, but it can't empty itself, like that boat, it hasn't got the scuppers. I'm not saying that his boat couldn't come to grief either because if it took a massive sea, it wouldn't get out the scuppers quick enough and that could founder an all. It could happen to any boat, even the lifeboat.

I was out on another occasion when it come bad. We went away, it wasn't ower good, but we knew the tide and when you know the tide and that, we thought we'd get the work done before the tide turned 'cos the wind was out the south-east and of course the tide was ebbing. We went away at 8 o'clock in the morning and the tide would ebb nearly till about 1 o'clock, so it was going the same way as that wind and that was not ower bad, but we knew as soon as it turned there would be a very sharp sea and we wanted to be in afore that. So we got the work well done and we were on the last fleet and the tide had turned and there was some massive lippers and one come aboard the boat and give we a bit of a fright and one of us said that was enough, so we just finished off and come in and it was pretty bad when we come in. The tide had turned. A lipper is a wave, a white horse, they get bigger with the wind and the tide. I've just described the wind as south-east, now the course of the tide on this coast is that when it's ebbing, it's running north and when it's flowing it's going south. At this particular time when we went out, we knew it was going with the wind, on that occasion, everything was all right but when the tide turns against the wind, you get a very sharp sea and the boat could founder and you see one worse than another. If you get into a trough and you're going forward, your boat's right down. There's been about six cobles lost on this coast and an old fisherman, who died in 1945, told me and my father that they were all lost in a forward sea, not into the wind, it's the worst sea oot, 'cos your boat's down with the engine going.

In those days we didn't wear lifejackets, and had no wireless. Engines had just come in, two or three years previous. Dougie has satellite navigation now, but he treats it with care. I asked him one day, 'if you were approaching the rocks in the fog, do you use it?' And he said he didn't, just in case there's a mistake. When he thinks he is about half a mile off the rock, he slows down and puts someone on the head looking out. Look what happened with the Titanic, it's easy for me to condemn him, but if I'd been on that boat and was told about an ice field, I would have been gannin very slow because there was no boat unsinkable. They said it was unsinkable, it tore the side oot, if he'd been gannin at half speed it would have been half the hole and that boat would have remained afloat, or he could have stopped the boat all night and just drifted and if he had hit it drifting, it wouldn't have harmed it much. She went down in two and a half hours. I think they told him she was unsinkable, when she left the shipyard. The very best ships have gone wrong.

When I was a laddie there was an old house, they've pulled it down now, you had to line up with to get into the harbour. It was on the hill, next door to ours. If you're coming in there you've got to be a little bit southward of centre, not north of centre 'cause of Little Carr. Now nearer Muckle Carr is deeper, although it's still a dangerous place.

In 1958, my father was going to sea, but just part time, he had finished the big fishing and he got a small boat and shot a few lobster nets. He had two little fleets in. He was about 68 years old. He went down to go out about

6.30 in the morning. The other boats had been away about an hour and they were right out, it was about July/ August. There was a fishing coble came from Newton and they saw a Polish boat had been fishing for herring and there was nobody on it and they shouted at my father to tell the Coastguard there was a boat ashore and he came to tell me and me and him were the first down, but the boat had come ashore then and the tide had ebbed and we could walk right around it at low water and they fired the rocket line across. It had come right up and sunk on the stones, it was a total loss. The crew, of about nine, went away on a mini-bus to Newcastle.

My father told me when it was a foggy, when he was at the herring, about 20 mile out, he wouldn't go to sleep. He would stay out all night on the deck just in case a boat run him down, 'cos there was steamers then. In 1910 when he was fishing, before he went to the First War, there was steam drifters as well, from Scotland. He wouldn't go below, like the others did.

Jack Browell

One morning I went away in the dark with young Harry and young Eddie, the rest of the boats were tied to the pier and were waiting till daylight. We had no GPS, just watch, compass and a torch. I had a good idea where the last fleet was and we steamed her off, hit the bow, perfect, hauled the fleet aboard. We were going to steam a bit further off and of course, silly me, there was an easterly sea on and the throttle was up in the engine box. There was nothing back aft, the gear-stick and everything was up there and the two lads were sitting there and I'm back aft and we went over double sea and threw me straight out, straight up in the air, right over the side. A double sea slopes instead of going up with another one behind. The boat dived and threw me off. I hit my face on the side of the roller. On the coble is a strip of wood round the stem and I held onto that. They didn't know I'd gone over the side, I had an oilskin on and an oilskin apron and was full of water. I just hung on.

When they realised I had gone, they stopped her and threw the first net they got hold of, which was full of weights, then they got hold of me and turned me upside down and emptied the water. I had been trapped. I took everything off, rung them out and then put them back on again. They were ready to go home but I wanted to carry on and fish.

I can always mind a poor day we were very lucky. I was with Bartie and Vincent and Billy Smailes. That morning, we came into the harbour and the sea was that lively, you could smell like sulphur in the air. We got into the harbour, hauled up and everything. Old Billy Silk, Albert and Eric had trouble up north. The wind came through with a bank within about half an hour and we thought they would have made it to Newton.

Next thing we saw them coming round the Castle point - what a fright they got - we had to stand on the pier and throw ropes to them to hold the boat's head up. That very afternoon, same gale, Seaham Harbour Lifeboat turned over with a whole crew. The crew of the coble was lost as well. There were six or seven on the Lifeboat and two or three on the coble.

One year (in the 1970s) we worked the coble, 24 hours around the clock. We were at the salmon, never stopped, from Monday morning till Saturday dinnertime. I used to do the nightshift. I would go from 7 at night till 7 in the morning with Eddie Armstrong and old Eddie went with Harry through the day. One Friday there had been a gale all day. I was a bit of a hothead then and I went down and said it seems to be dying way, so I said to Eddie that we would get ready and go to sea. The others thought we were mad. We did well. We went to about the 3 mile track and then fished out of the road of everything and that night about half past ten or eleven o'clock it started to blow. We were the only boat in sight. The Providence had been fishing, but had gone away home. Eddie said 'what are we going to do? We should we go home.' I said that no way were we going ashore in the dark, we couldn't see anything. We had a big bridle on and we made it fast and let the nets go all night and she was riding like a little duck ahead of the wind, she was just riding the big rope, which held all the time. The seas were coming right over the cover. We had to keep pumping her out. We were sitting with a canvas cover over our legs, had to put up with the freezing cold, to make a living. For nighttime fishing you wore as many clothes as possible and your oilskins - wore big sea boot stockings and boots. That night the wind fell away and we carried on fishing and I think we ended up with 67 salmon. When we came ashore, they were all standing out in the summerhouse, next to the pub - that was the first house built in the village, was built for the Squire - they were standing watching for us, they had all hauled their boats up — we got 'played war with' for not coming ashore, but things had got so bad that there was nothing else we could do but get shelter within the Inner Farnes.

Dougie Hogg on the Thomas H coming into harbour on a rough winter's day.

Dougie Hogg

One day we were hauling lobster pots around the Castle in the Thomas H and there was a little bit of a swell on and I said to Dick 'you'd better hang on here mind' and he says 'what for?' and the sea went right over the top of the wheelhouse. I had to shout again and another one come over the wheelhouse and we were up to our waist in water and with it being a decked boat it cleared all the water. If it had been an open coble, we'd have been thrown over. We had no lifejackets on, as it wasn't a bad day, just a big lazy swell.

There was another time when Billy's son was at sea with us, we got up to go to sea and there was quite a bit swell on and we launched the boats and the other lads turned back and we kept on going 'cos I really had no fear then like, I was bloody wild. One of them down there said, 'you'll never make a fisherman.' I think that was the worst thing he could have said 'cos then I was determined to show them. We kept going and we went 5 mile offshore to the lobster pots and by that time the swell was tremendous and we couldn't even pick the bells up. They were disappearing with the swell and we heard on the radio that the Seahouses boats were heading in. One of the boats going into Seahouses got swamped, one of the big trawlers - it got in, the Lifeboat was there. So we headed back for the harbour. When we came to the back of the rock, it was horrendous. I lay there for about an hour at the back of the rock and I got the chance to get in and I gave it full throttle and that's when a holidaymaker took a picture of the boat surfing in between the piers. I'll give you that picture, when I can find it. We turned in around the South Pier and got a rope up and then the bloody sea came right over the pier and filled the boat, so it was bad like.

Disasters at sea

Friday 10th February 1928

CRASTER VICTIMS.

(1) William Stephenson. (2) The three victims aboard the Provider, hauling in their nets. Stephenson, senior (formerly one of the crew) is in the foreground. (3) James Sanderson. (4) A group of Craster fishermen, with Archbold on the extreme right.

Cutting from Journal and North Star Monday February 13th 1928

There follows an extract from the article 'Three Lives Lost at Craster' in the 'Northumberland County Gazette and Guardian' for Saturday February 18 1928.

A Neighbour's Story.

Mrs Simpson of Heugh Crescent, wife of Mr Thomas Simpson, was baiting the lines with mussels for the next day's fishing when we called upon her. Indeed all Craster is engaged baiting hooks before the boats start on the morrow, so far as its female population is concerned.

'I went over to Stephenson's (a knoll' in the village) to get a bag of mussels that had been left there for me,' Mrs Simpson told us. 'That was about half past seven on Friday morning. I saw William Stephenson come out of his mother's house. He mentioned my name Esther and spoke to me about a pain in his hand. He had his oil skin hat on his bended arm and his food in it, and a cap on his head. He then spoke a few words to Mrs Smailes at the Post Office door and passed on, His two friends were waiting in the boat for him in the channel. I said 'Gan on they're waiting for you, Bill' and he went down to the boat. That is the last time any of us ashore spoke to him.'
Then turning to our reporter, Mrs Simpson remarked, 'If ever a Coastguard has done his duty it is Mr Abbs. I feel for him, he is properly worn out.' This we found truly interpreted the feeling not only in the bereaved homes but throughout the village. All the missing men were relatives of Mrs Simpson.
'When my husband came in when the boat had not returned he said to me 'I doubt they will never come more back,' sorrowfully concluded Mrs Simpson.

Gallantry of 'Our Girls' Crew.

Deftly picking Dutch mussels from a tub and attaching them to the hooks on a long line which passed rapidly and methodically through his hands, Mr E. A. Smailes sat in his shed while he related to us in homely manner the following account of the brave and gallant service he and his men did by going back into a dangerous sea on a rescue mission:–

The two boats 'The Provider' and ours ('Our Girls') proceeded to the fishing ground in the morning. Other three boats were along the shore closer in with their lines shot. We went out about a mile and a half further than they did to cast our lines.

There was a good strong wind up as we were going out. While we were fishing 'The Provider' was about three-quarters of a mile away shooting on the south side.
After our lines had had about half-an-hour's tiding—that is lying at the bottom we started to haul again. The wind was gradually freshening all the time and a few drops of rain came.
When we had got about half hauled my mate Adam Archbold still saw 'The Provider' hauling her lines. That was the last we saw of her. It was very hazy, and with the motion on the surface of the water it was bad to see a boat that distance away.

We never thought there was anything amiss when we were returning, because we had been to sea only a week before that on a worse day. Friday was not what one would call an extremely bad day but it was a day that required a bit of caution.

Having hauled our lines we made for home about twenty minutes past eleven in the forenoon. Arriving inshore we proceeded to take our fish out of the boat in the harbour and to get them weighed. We did not suspect any mishap then. We kept looking out to see if the boat was coming in as we often do – to see that a boat is not stopped with her gear. 'The Provider' still never turned up.

Then we heard two maroons go off, the signal for the Boulmer Lifeboat to launch. I said to one of our men 'They're launching the Boulmer Lifeboat.' Shortly after that the wind drew into the west and there was good visibility. We could see about seven miles off. It was a heavy gale when the wind drew into the west. We saw the Boulmer Lifeboat going to the scene.

My mate, Adam, suggested that we should go and see if we could see anything of the missing boat. I said 'Right, O.' And so went off to the scene where both 'The Provider' and we had been, fishing, but we did not see anything there. Then we came to the north and inward and we saw a lot of gulls feeding. 'That's the fish out of the boat!' I exclaimed to Adam. It was very rough then and blowing hard.

'Getting among the gulls, we saw some fish floating — codlings. We picked up a cap. Adam says 'That's Bill's cap,' meaning William Stevenson's. Close by there was his sou'wester and the top of the engine box. We also picked up one of the swills for carrying lines in, a tiller and a compass box. We knew whose the tiller was. We could see that everything was over and thought we had better get ashore ourselves as it was very rough where we were searching.'

'People were standing ashore waiting to see what we had got when we came back. Mr Hugh Stephenson the Secretary of the Lifeboat, was there and Mr Abbs. When we told them we had got the caps, everybody's hope fell.'

The crew of 'Our Girls' consisted of Messrs Robert A. Smailes (skipper): Adam Archbold and James R. Smailes.

Willie Archbold

My mother's brother's boat, 'The Provider' with two other fishermen from here, Tom Archbold and James Sanderson and my uncle, William Stephenson and they went to the long lines. It was 1928, Friday, 10th February. There would be about 9 to 10 fishing boats from Craster then and my father said it was a pretty good morning when they set off. It was flat calm, but there was a red sky and they didn't like that, but never mind the boats went away. They shot the lines and as the day wore on, coming up to 11 o' clock the wind blew up from the southeast and the boats were fishing south east of here. They had to come forward, which is very bad for a coble - they are better coming into it and they had to come into Craster and my father was the last in, bar the one that never returned. He was with the two Smailes brothers - Billy Smailes father and uncle. And my father told me that they were still hauling the lines when they passed the boat that never returned and they seemed OK when they were off Cullernose about two mile out, coming in.

There was a tremendous sea had started the back of them, what we call a south easterly lipper and they saw it coming towards them and one of them in the boat asked if they were going to turn the boat to head up to it 'cos they were stern onto it and they said no, in case it caught them broadside on and that would be a bad job. They put the boat's engine out of gear and, when they were hit, the boat was nearly stopped and when the sea hit them there were two or three bucketfuls came into the boat, but one of them seas had hit the boat that never returned. It just took one, that's what they thought and I'm sure they were right, but my father said they never got another bad one like that, for a good job and they just put her into gear again and put her in the harbour. They got in about 11 o'clock and they reckon the boat was lost about 12 noon.

There was an old fisherman on the summerhouse, they called him Simpson. He died in June of that year. He was 88. He wasn't getting out with being old and he was looking out of the window and there was a man called Bob Taylor, he was going back and forward asking him if he could see it, 'cause everybody was watching for it. About 12 noon, he must have seen out the window and he said, 'if that boat's not in now, it'll never come back' and he was right. The sad thing about it as well, the Boulmer Lifeboat was sailing then and my uncle's father, his brother, was the coxswain of the lifeboat and it was sad for him, because it was my uncle who was in the boat.

There was only one motor lifeboat then on the Northumberland coast, between the Tweed and the Tyne and that was at Holy Island and they fetched it out and it came right up here and they asked the shipping to look out. As the day wore on the wind turned to the land and my father said that about 2 o'clock, he asked for volunteers and the two Smailes volunteered and they launched the coble and they found a hat and an oar and some dead fish, not exactly where the boat had sunk. They did know exactly where the boat had gone, 'cos there was oil and that winter it broke up on the bottom 'cos there were bits coming in. There were three crew lost, my uncle, William Stephenson who was 31, Tom Archbold, the skipper was 51 and James Sanderson, he was about 39. They were all bachelors at that time, although my uncle was courting.

Work Ashore: 'it's just like an aircraft - it's the ground crew that keeps them up a height.'

Willie Archbold

I served my time with Appleby at Embleton to be a bricklayer and after that I started with Harry's firm. He and his brother went into partnership as builders. The man I served my time with was a mason and I learned to do a bit of stonework as well. My dad died in 1963, he was finished with the fishing then, we sold our coble. I came back to the fishing for a brief period in 1966 but it was a bad year and me and my partner sold the boat and then I went back to the building trade for quite a while. I fell off a roof and hurt my back and I got a job mending the nets for Dougie and I finished up with that. I told him I wouldn't go back to sea with my back being bad, but I said I would mend the gear and that, which I did, so when they came ashore, they had no gear to mend 'cause I mended the whole lot. It's just like an aircraft - it's the ground crew that keeps them up a height.

Billie Lumsden

'There would be about three men to a boat then. They were all cobles then, there were none of the bigger boats like Dougie has now. They were like Eddie Grey's. They told me, well I didn't know 'cos I've never gone to sea, but they used to pull them up with the capstan. There were two capstans down there and they used to put the long bar through and they would all walk round and round and that's how they used to haul them out of the harbour. Adam Archbold's son-in-law came up from Liverpool and he brought a little winch and a Bedford engine and that was the first winch they ever had (1947.) They reckon, I don't know if it is true mind, but they tell me all he got for his bother was two boxes of fish. He was an engineer and he thought it was terrible that men had to walk round and round just to haul boats up. I think it was Clarke Chapman gave them a winch, that one that's there now. They got a Ford engine onto it. Then they built the winch house. When you come to think, eh, - having half a dozen cobles to have to pull up with this capstan thing, after you'd done a day's work at the sea.'

Adam Dawson

After all the herring fishing was finished, the fishermen had to preserve their nets. So they used to use a solution, which was called Bark, in what they called the Bark Pots. The Pots were filled with water and the bark was melted in there. The nets were dipped in to preserve them and they used to hang them out to dry. They stored the nets in the top of their houses. The fishermen in Craster used to store their nets in a false roof, where it was nice and dry. They were aired ready for the next season. It was on the Burn Hill, North Craster, and they were there for years because when I was going to school we used to play in them. They were wrecks then of course. That was in the 1800's when they were there.

My father, George Dawson had a big herring boat which had a crew of five men - the boat was called the Morag. I think he bought her from Eyemouth and his brother Sep, was one of the crew. My father was very, very young in them days, in fact he wasn't married. That was in the 1800's. I can remember an Eyemouth boat called 'The

Holly' bringing a hundred barrels in. In them days the herring boats had no motors and I can remember they used to use a lot of horses and carts to cart the herrings away. The North pier was full of barrels, but they were empty. They would fill them up with herrings and go to the herring yards and get them ready for going to Russia. They worked all night on that job and the horse and carts used to ferry them off. They went to the herring sheds to be cleaned and packed in the barrels to be sent abroad.

Baiting the lines

Joan Angus

Fishermen's wives had a hard life. From October until March lines were baited with about 700 hooks to each line and each fisherman had two lines. The wife was involved in 'skenning' the mussels out of the shells and limpets were used as well to bait the hooks. This work went on when the boats came ashore and if the boats were late she would be busy until late evening.

Marjorie Lumsden

My mother said she had to go and get some limpets off the rocks and she only had me and she says I was asleep. They mustn't have had a cot, 'cause I was asleep in the bed and she said she had to pile as many blankets and cushions on the floor in case I rolled off when she went down to the rocks to get a pail of limpets. She said when she got back I was lying on the blankets on the floor.

Willie Archbold

They used to go to the long lines in the wintertime. Each man had two of these lines and one line was 700 hooks, so each man had 1400 hooks to bait every day. This fishing went on from October to March of the following year. They were fishing for white fish, codling mostly but haddock and a little bit plaice but the bulk was codling. Everybody in the house was involved 'cos you had to open the mussels in the morning and as soon as the boat come in, about dinnertime or 2 o'clock, the boats were hauled up and emptied out of fish, anything from 50 to 80 stone they used to fetch in and they were good quality fish and Tom Grey took them at the bottom. He was Eddie Grey's grandfather. He operated at the bottom shed. The last boats fished with the lines about 1953. That was the last of the lines 'cos the younger womenfolk wouldn't do it because they were working as hard as the men, to get the mussels out and as soon as the boats came in they had to bait the lines and it took about two to three hours, to have them ready for the next morning. Sometimes the women would go into the hut in the morning to open the mussels and it would take from about 7 o'clock till 12 noon, they would get something to eat and by that time the boat was coming in and they had to get the line hung up into their sheds and start doing it again for the next day. If the boat was late in, this could go on till 8 o'clock at night but generally they were finished about seven.

The lines went on till about 1953 and I was 18 year old then, I was fetched up with the lines. They used them in the winter from October till end of March. They used to get some good catches of cod and few flat fish. The fish was especially good at Christmas time and in the New Year. The womenfolk won't do that now - it was hard work - they were doing more work than the men really because they were at the line huts in the morning, opening the mussel shells and it took nearly to dinnertime, by when the boat was coming in and these lines had to be started. Some days if the boats were late, it was late getting these lines done and they had to go to Budle Bay, it was a right cold job that.

There was sometimes you had to muck the lines because you didn't get in the sea and they got stinking, that was an awful job, the bait was wasted. Mussels were £1 a bag then, if you didn't get the bait from Goswick. The mussels used to come by train into Little Mill Station and were fetched down with a lorry. The fish and crabs all went from Little Mill when I was a laddie.

Looking to the future

Eddie Grey

I can remember Bartie Dawson saying to me when I first started the sea – he said 'Well, I've getten my time out of it, but I think you'll have a job getting yours.' I'm still here yet, like. I often wondered if he'd be right, 'cause I can remember Eleanor, his wife saying that he used to look out of the window and he used to say, 'one day there'll be nowt to catch oot there.'

With the salmon you get good years and bad years. Drift netting, the last couple of years I was at it, you never made a fortune, you made a living. Back in the '60's there were a lot of fish caught here, drift netting right up the coast. They blame us for the decline in the salmon, but that was a lot of Tommyrot. I think they were caught in other places before they got here. I think they used to trawl for them in Greenland and that - the Japanese and that. The amount of net we used to work with, 600 yards of net - as somebody once said, 'it's just like shoelace in Wembley Stadium' - it was nothing really. People thought when you were fishing for salmon that you came in with boat loads every day, which wasn't the case. The most I ever caught in one day was 50 odd. You could go the next day and perhaps get two or three – very hitty missy. Salmon fishing was 75% luck. You had to be in the right place at the right time. I don't know how we could be blamed for the decline.

Of course, farm salmon knacked the salmon fishing, price wise. There's a difference in the taste. They're a different looking fish, a wild salmon has a swallow tail, the farm fish have a blunt nose as well, you can tell the difference when they're lying side by side. The wild fish is a bluey, silvery colour – they're bonny. Neil (Robson) tells me that these farm fish are better for smoking, but they feed them on prawns and that which makes the flesh pink, otherwise they're just white.

The sea trout have been poor, quantity wise, the last couple of years. There has been more salmon on the beach, obviously 'cause the drift netting has stopped. There's only 15 boats left drift netting further south - Blyth, Shields way - nearly all the fishermen gave them up. I really didn't want to give my licence up. I was going to keep it, but I thought I was going to be the only one left, but the ground is saturated with pots and you cannot get driven for lobster pots.

The seals as well are a problem. You tell people about them and I think they think you are making it up. They're a pest. You wouldn't mind if they just took one or two fish and left you, but it's relentless. The last year I was fishing for salmon, David Hogg was with me and we shot off Boulmer, close in, and we put the kettle on and had a cup of tea and I think David was nodding off and I went to the net and there was two big oily patches. Seal had getten the fish. We hauled them and shifted off and the damn thing followed us and I think we shifted three or four miles into sea and we shot again. I don't know if it was the same one, but it was there and we shifted all over the place. We came close in for the slack tide, that's when the fish are supposed to rise and were going to shoot the net and I sees this bloody seal on the stern of the boat. There was about an hour to go before the tide eased and we went and lay close in below Tully's House along at Howick. A cup of tea and we were sitting and there was a seal lying at the stern of the boat and another lying at the head waiting on us shooting. They chase you away off the fish as well you know. We steamed away north off the Castle and we got shot down off there and we got one fish over the slack tide. I wouldn't like to see them become extinct, but it wouldn't bother me if I never saw one again. The sea's full of them, they are taking the bait out of the pots now, you cannot beat them. They're not stupid.

I can remember Billie Smailes telling me once being at the salmon and they had Lister engines in the boats, air-cooled noisy things. They would start the engines and they would look over the back of the pier and there would be two or three seals bobbing their heads, waiting for them coming out. They reckon they could hear the engines. He told me once they were being pestered by the seals and they caught some whitings and they had baited a hook with these six whitings and they had a plastic ball on and they shot it close to the nets and thought, 'this'll fix them.' They sat and watched it for about an hour and it never moved, the ball, and when they went to get it there wasn't a whiting left. It had taken the lot. They'll take fish out of the nets - rive a great big hole in it. They peel, skin, the salmon before they eat them. Some days, you know he's there, but they keep a low profile, they're wily. Some days they just lie against the net and take the fish out. Some days there are two of them working the net. If you get them you have them all week and other days you never see one, which is lovely, then they come back with a vengeance. They seem to get their fill and then they leave you.

I can remember one day we were lying at the salmon, having another cup of tea and there was a seal lying against the net, beside the pellet and there were a couple of corks and I said I thought there was a fish there and we went and there were two big salmon lying together and the seal was only yards from them and he never touched them. Aye, it left them, Maybe it was because they were dead. I think if I remember rightly he got the next one.

They take the bait out of our lobster pots now. We used to have a trap net and now we've done away with them and they still get their head in and they take the bait out of the bait bag, I've seen them burst them. We started putting a bait bag in, you put the bait in and tie it tight and it's fitted into the pot, it was alright for about a week or two, but they can get into that now.

Willie Archbold

I think the herring's still there yet but the reason there's no herring fishing off here, I can't see any boats going to it as they would have to spend a load of money on new nets. The men haven't got the nets and I think it would cost nothing less than £20,000 to get started and you don't know if you're going to get it back. I reckon there's definitely herring out there. They just stick to the trawling. I'm not against the foreigners, but this is an island and we had an exclusion zone and it should have remained. If they had kept to the old methods, like the driftnet, when the fish went into the mash, instead of trawling them, the small would have got away and there would never have been a scarcity. They've altered the mash of the cod net of the trawlers now, to let the small away but it will take a few years for the fishing to build up but it's a good thing that. Line fishing will never come back because it was hard work.

Dougie wouldn't survive if he didn't do the fishing trips. The winter of 2003 was one of the worst because if they get bad frosts the lobsters 'hole up.' They must react to the cold like us. There's been a pattern over the years, if you get a very severe frost it jinxed them for getting catches for the rest of the winter and if you get a moderate winter you can survive but last winter sometimes they weren't sharing out 'cause by the time they got their expenses but thankfully he has the trips. Another factor is, he has to do all his mechanical work himself, which helps because he wouldn't be able to afford to get a mechanic. A lot of folk see him coming in with a good catch and think they get that all the time. Lately some of the crews have been reduced in other places, I've heard that some boats in Seahouses are going out with just one. My father said he would sink the boat rather than go with no crew.

Dougie Hogg

'The Fishing Policy doesn't affect us much. (Now) we just go for crabs and lobsters and with having the fishing trips. They let the Danes fish for sand eels and cod feed on sand eels and there just isn't any feed out there for the cod and the cod we are catching now are just full of little crabs and that. When I first started fishing 25 years ago, the sea was absolutely full of sand eels. You hardly ever see the birds diving out there now. It's not properly managed out there, we should have a 200 mile limit, where it's possible, to keep the foreigners out. There's only a 12 mile limit now and what's supposed to happen is they're going to open it up to Spaniards and that and they could fish outside the 12 mile limit, ridiculous, there's not enough fish for us, never mind them. We have no quotas. At Seahouses there was a big fishing fleet but there's no fish coming onto the banks now like they used to. There was Seahouses Middle Bank and that would be solid with sand eels and the cod were feeding on them. There's just no fish coming 'cos there's no sand eels. The Danes fish for them to feed the salmon in the fish farms. When we are hauling lobster pots, I would say the birds are that hungry that they would come aboard the boat and knock boxes over to look for food. It's not properly managed, these educated folk should know better than to take part of the food chain away. The fishing is good for the Norwegians and that.

I think I'll get my time out of the fishing, but I think Andrew and David [sons] will have to struggle 'cos the trawlers have all packed in at Seahouses and they've bought potting boats and there's thousands and thousands of lobster pots out. There's nowt, and the ground never gets a rest.

Chapter 2   Fish Curing and Kippers

Herring Lassies (from the left) Ethel Watson, Annie Jane Norris, Belle Straughan, Bessie Archbold, Georgina Renwick. Brian Park is in the background.

Eva Archbold – from written notes 1950s

Craster has earned worldwide fame for its kippers. This may sound exaggerated, but it is perfectly true as we have had proof from South Africa, America and Denmark. I am told Craster kippers were first made by a man called Jack Mason, who came from Tweedmouth. This Jack Mason married Mary Archbold, my grandfather's aunt. They lived in Coquet View.

Willlie Mitford

Sir John (Craster) used to come down with his own little box and he got to pick his own kippers from the rack. When he got his Knighthood, he took kippers down for the Queen. The Queen came up to Holy Island and he took her some kippers then.

Rosemary Gibbs

I remember my uncle saying that some visitors came as a boat was coming in and asked if they could have some fresh kippers straight from the boat!

Marjorie Clarke

I was born in Coquet View where my mother still lives. My father was the Fish Merchant, Kenneth Luke Robson and he continued the business from his father, Luke Robson, who died in October 1948. Dad had come home from the war and he and Alan went into business together to continue fish curing. I was an only child and Alan has a son called Neil.

As a child, I was always given a new pair of black Wellingtons to work in the yard. I was probably about 5-7 years old. In those days my mother used to sell the kippers which were so many pence a pair. She worked with Bill Seager and he also worked for my grandfather together with Robert Stephenson. On a posting day, she would be doing the post and I would be helping to carry the boxes from table to table in the shop, it was all done in the shop then. My other job was to hose down the big wooden boxes that the herring came in. Towards the end of the day when everything was finished I used to hose Garth Lowerson, Neil and then everyone ended up being soaked. My father used to go mad but I always managed to have a little bit of fun.

In those days the herring came from North Shields. Occasionally 'The Paragon' would come into the harbour with herring. Dad preferred that, it saved him going to North Shields. Sometimes I would go with him, he would get up just before dawn. We went in the fish wagon, there would be no other traffic on the roads. He used to stop at a horrendously smelly factory which recycled all the guts into fish food. The gut barrels would be emptied and then we would go down to the quayside and find out which boats were coming in and when and then we would go to the Fishermen's' Mission and have big, hot, steaming cups of tea from huge white cups. This was fascinating for me as a child, 'cause there would sometimes be Polish sailors there, different nationalities. Then you would have a lovely, thick bacon sandwich. Then we would go back to the quayside and look at the various herring and then go into a little room, which was where the herring was auctioned. It was done so quickly, they would mention the name of the boat and Dad always went for certain boats and then they would start bidding. Dad just used to push his cap up with the point of his pencil, or his finger. He then suddenly got up and went out. He then would go and get the boxes and then telephone back to Alan to get the women out for 8 o'clock. He then went to the Ice Factory, which was a very tall building with chutes coming out of the top. He would reverse the wagon and from these chutes would come the ice, to be scattered over the boxes to keep the fish as fresh as possible. Put the tarpaulin over, rope it and off we would go.

By the time he came into the village, the women would all be lined up waiting for him, at the harbour wall. There were about 8 -10 women working at the time - Belle Straughan, Vera Mitford, Isabel Young, Annie Jane Norris, Lizzie Sanderson, Mrs. Wilson, Lena Shell, Ena Renwick. It was very hard work, the women used to split the herring. There was a machine came about 1956, Alice Shell used to work on it. It was a gutting machine. It was a marvellous machine. It saved a lot of work. I was the one that had to keep that clean and also the baskets, which were interwoven willow. They were grand because the water gushed through the gaps and then I used to swing one away across to the brine tub and then get another one ready for the herring to come slipping down to the machine again. Then they went into the brine for about 20 minutes and were lifted out and then just pushed and slid down over the water, in the baskets, down to the tentering troughs, where the women would be gathered and they would put them up on the tentering hooks. Vera always calls them 'trows.' Then they went straight into the smokehouses where they were hung. Once it was full. Dad would set the fires away by about 4/5 o'clock, then he would check them again about 10 o' clock, then he would let them get well down before he would build them up again, you had to be very careful they didn't get too hot. The sawdust and the shavings were in huge barrels and Dad just used to roll them with one hand and he had a special scoop and once he built up the shavings pile, he had a little metal scoop and he would use that to sprinkle the sawdust on the top. He would be up again about 3 o'clock in the morning to re-set them. In the latter years he didn't go to bed, he had a bed in the living room and he would sleep there. At 7 o'clock in the morning the whole process would start again. Alan and he took turns to go to North Shields.

My mother used to make a drink for him to keep him going. It was a very tall glass, in which was milk, raw egg and brandy. That used to be his 11 o'clock drink.

The sawdust used to come in wagons. We always had a tremendous amount kept at the Yard. It was never allowed to go down, there was always plenty kept. The season started in June, through to September, there was always great excitement at the beginning of each season. Dad relied on certain boats, possibly because they knew the best areas of the sea to get the fish. He always checked the herring. He knew what sort he wanted. In that day there used to be seconds. Later Dad hit on the idea of cutting them up and using the meaty sides of the kippers and they were called portions, these were very popular..

The kipper boxes for post were wooden. Bill Seager used to make those. When demand increased, Neil and I, or whoever had spare time during the summer, used to go into the workshop which was where the restaurant is now, it was a huge workshop and in there we used to have stacks of wood and we used to make the quarter box, the half box and the full box . There was a work bench and there we had to stack these boxes up and what we used to do, particularly before posting day, either Wednesday or Thursday, to ensure the kippers got to their destination before the weekend and we always had a rough idea how many we would need and then we would count how many had been made and try to get the correct number ready for posting. They all went by post. In fact when there was a shop and post office in the village, the post office was underneath the shop, the basement. There was a door where the current letter box is and the door led down the stairs and we had to carry the boxes down there and we used to stack them in a blue van, called The Tilly and I used to sit at the back to make sure the boxes didn't tip and we would pull up at the side of the shop and carry these boxes downstairs and Edward Grey used to be ready to stamp them and sort them ready for collection. When that closed, the next best thing was to have them collected by the Post Office van that came into the yard. We had them already stamped and they would go into the Post Office van and go to Alnwick. They went all over the country. In the '70's, waxy cardboard became the norm, they were flat packed and had to be folded and stapled together. Bill Seager used to stamp the lids on the wooden boxes with the Robson name. The workshop was then closed down and the restaurant was built in 1973. Dad got the idea of opening a restaurant, because he used to go on holiday to Jersey and they visited some place or other that used to have a cafe so he thought that if people came for their kippers, they may come for a cup of tea and kippers. In 1974, this was extended to provide the bar and the coffee lounge.

When Little Mill station was open, we used to pack crabs into kegs, again made by Bill Seager. They weren't very large kegs, the crabs were stacked in them at the bottom yard, then they were covered with seaweed, they had to be kept alive, if possible, so they were stacked straight from the boxes when caught. They were then covered in damp newspaper, then hessian was put on top of that and the hoops would be hammered down really tight, they were loaded into the wagon and taken to the station. If you look on the left as you come to Little Mill, there's a gateway with a slope and then the platform. Dad used to drive it up there and then they were rolled along the platform, the train came and off they would go to Billingsgate. I would only be about 7 years old when Little Mill closed. This happened on a daily basis, about ten kegs each day. Dad used to telephone Billingsgate to say they were on the way. We would go there when we were in London on holiday and Dad used to meet up with some of his contacts.

Every night the floor was washed, caustic soda was put down and the floors were brushed thoroughly.

At the end of September, October time, there was the herring trip and everyone used to go on the Herring Trip on the bus and they went to Edinburgh, York or Harrogate, then it came back to Newcastle, parked outside the Theatre Royal. Dad would give all the ladies a box of Dairy Box and then they would go and see a variety performance, get home in the early hours of the morning. It was a fantastic day, everyone enjoyed it. Dad loved it, he felt like Santa Claus. Following that we used to go to the Saddle Grill at Alnmouth for a dinner and a dance. After Dad died that was the end of that.

In the spring, before the season began there was the job of preparing all the equipment, the sticks were all cleaned and any hooks that came out had to be replaced, then they were stacked against the shed in the sun, so they were lain against the big green door, to dry. They used to be carried back carefully and lain on the back wall next to the smoking houses and were stacked there on a big wooden deck in order not to get wet when the floor was swilled. Everything was cleaned and checked over, the smoking houses were brushed out ready. It was always Alan's job to grease the machine and make sure all the parts were working, everybody breathed a sigh of relief when that was put back together and it worked.

At the end of each session of each day, the women would line up in the office and Dad would have a big ledger with all their names written down and would call their Christian names and they would all listen to each other's hours and if anyone made a mistake, they would shout out 'that's not right,' and Dad would correct it and he would write it down so they could all see him and then at the end of the season, he would total up and then they got their pay packets. This would keep them going all winter. It was very hard work; sometimes they had to wrap their fingers in rags, if they cut them. The kippers had to be allowed to cool before they were put in the boxes, they were hung insides together, so you had a pair, and packed like that.

People were often waiting for the kippers to be ready. Hawkers used to come and they would be waiting for their order, they went as far as Alnwick. We used to supply a fishmonger in Alnwick, - Downie in Narrowgate. The Tilley used to be packed with herring, kippers and crabs and taken into Alnwick. Jimmy Park used to sell them and Winnie Banks sold them latterly. When I was at college in Durham, there was a man used to sell 'Craster kippers' and I knew we didn't supply him, so I rang Dad and told him and he said for me to go in and tell the shopkeeper. So next time I went into town, I confronted the man and he had to take them out of the window.

The women would be standing round the sticks and they would be gossiping and chatting away and Dad would sometimes go past and squirt them with water, it was all good fun, there was a lovely communal atmosphere. At the beginning of the season they would be told how much an hour they would be paid. People used to wander in and look into the shed, they were allowed then, school trips used to come around and be taken into the smoking houses.

It was financially bad in the winter, the women weren't working and the boats couldn't go out in the bad weather, everyone was always keyed up ready for the season to start up again. You could get a dozen kippers for half a crown. People used to come in for bait for fishing and sometimes if we didn't have too many chores to do, Neil and I would set up two or three boxes on the counter and make a sign and sell the bait, it saved them going to the smelly gut-barrels and mooch around picking out the bits. One job I used to hate was putting the roe into a little dish, 'cause people used to like that.

Fresh salmon was very popular at first and then of course, the smoked salmon came later, in the 1970's. We used to get some salmon from Stephenson's at Boulmer. Garth Lowerson and Dad and sometimes myself used to go with the Tilley and used to stand and wait for the boats coming in.

Luke Robson in his herring yard.

Neil Robson

The fishermen used to always have their tea at 10 o'clock and if the boats weren't off - if there was a bad sea or there wasn't much doing, all the fishermen used to come along and Dennis Dawson used to come, and in the winter, when we were quiet, they used to discuss football and politics. It was really funny for a young lad to be sitting listening to them. You had about quarter of an hour for your tea and then an hour later they were saying, 'Oh, is that the time?' It was a more relaxed lifestyle in those days. The boats didn't go to sea, like Dougie does now. They pulled the boats up out of the sea. They didn't leave them in the harbour over the winter. If it was rough at all they didn't bother going to sea, the boats were smaller then.

I left school in 1970 so this would be in the 70's or 80's. The fishermen were making good money in those days that was when the nets came out for fishing for salmon, previous to that they used to fish with nylon nets and they only went out at night. I remember one exceptional season, Billie Smailes came in with 96 salmon about 5 o'clock and then Bartie came in and I think he had 150 odd and an hour later, the Silks came in and they had 250 salmon. That's the most salmon that's ever been landed in Craster in one day. In those days we used to weigh them all off and we had various people took various sizes, but we were here till about 1 o'clock in the morning weighing them off and icing them up and writing tickets for them. We used to go to North Shields with them early in the morning.

Herring was still being landed at North Shields then. That would be about 1972/3, 'cause there was a ban on the landing of herring on this coast. I think about 1977, they put a 10 year ban on the herring 'cause it had been so drastically over-fished. They were frightened to wipe the stocks out. We used to get the herring from Scotland. We would meet a wagon at Edinburgh. They used to come from Mallaig or Ullapool. They were the two main ports where they were landed. I used to go up at night with the wagon and meet them. My Uncle Ken used to say 'go and be there at 8 o'clock' and I used to get up for eight o'clock and sometimes I was waiting till 10 or 11 o'clock before the wagon got in, 'cause it was a hell of a road for a wagon to come down from Mallaig to Edinburgh and if there was an accident on the road, it used to get held up. There were no mobile phones that you could use to contact the driver to find out what time he was going to be there. Sometimes it was one or two o'clock in the morning before I got back. After that they started landing herring at Ayr and Tarbert. The Scottish boats used to fish at night so they landed early, didn't have to go far out to go to the grounds, so they used to be in Edinburgh early in the morning, so then I went early in the morning to fetch them.

Previous to that, North Shields was always the main port for the herring, and occasionally you would get them from Seahouses. There was a boat called 'The Paragon,' used to land them into Craster. If he didn't have a great deal, he used to ring up in the morning and let us know what he had. If he had more than we wanted, we used to take them to North Shields for him and sell them on the market there. He was one of the last driftnet fishing boats, the rest of the boats used to trawl or ring-net was the main way of catching them in Scotland and the driftnet were the better herring. That's why we preferred buying from him. Different boats had different ways. A lot of boats had their fish hold next to the engine room, and the herring used to heat up and the bellies would burst on them. We got to know which were the better boats, for landing the herring. At Seahouses they never used to box the herring. They landed them in bulk and put a basket down. They used to hold about 7 stone and we had to tip them into the boxes, whereas the boats that landed at North Shields, the majority of them boxed the herring and they were in better condition 'cause they weren't pressed down on each other.

'The Paragon' was from St Monans, which is in Fife. The skipper was called Alex Hut, and we used to buy herring if he landed at Seahouses or if he landed at North Shields we used to buy them from him and then we got to know him and he would ring up in the morning and say they were coming here. They used to do the Isle of Man fishing as well and then come around and do this, so they were at the herring most of the year. His son was about my age and he was at university, then he packed it in. He wanted to go to the fishing. I think it was '72 or '73 he was last here. I think the boat sank around the Isle of Man and we never heard from them since. I heard that the old man had died. It was funny 'cause they would come ashore and that was when the women used to work for us and the old cook took a fancy for Hilda Rogerson and she used to get all embarrassed, 'cause she was quite strait-laced. She used to say, 'He's coming up again, keep him away from me.' He was always asking her to go for a drink, but she never went to the pub or anything.

In the yard there were like the older women and the younger ones - with the older ones it always had to be done the same way. I used to make the tea for them when I was a kid, and they used to say 'Oh, go and put the kettle on.' They used to take turns buying their biscuits. They would buy them in the morning at Edward Grey's and in the afternoon, go over to Annie Jane's on the north side, so they were spreading it around. They would give me a shilling to go and get a packet of biscuits and if they were, say, 10d. I would keep the 2d, then next time I would get chocolate ones, that were a little bit more expensive, and they'd say, 'who's paying for these chocolate biscuits.' There was hell on, like. It was good fun.

You had the younger ones like Isabel Young, Sybil Dawson, Alice Shell, Vera Mitford, and Molly Simpson. Then you had the older ones, Belle Straughan, Annie Jane Norris from the north side, Bessie Archbold, Ethel Watson, old Mrs. Wilson. It was a right happy atmosphere. They didn't work every day, in those days. If there was bad weather, there was no herring, so they would get a day off, if there was a lot of herring they had to work a bit longer. They used to take their turns. The four used to come out to pack the kippers in the morning, starting off at 7 o'clock and then go home and have their breakfast, but we changed that and they used to come at 8 o'clock and work right through and the rest used to come in when the herring came in from North Shields. Ken used to go on a Monday to North Shields and me Dad used to go the rest of the week. He would ring up to say what time he would be back, 'cause some mornings the market opened at 8 o'clock, the auction, but some mornings if it was bad weather, or the boats were fishing further north or south, sometimes they wouldn't be in till 9 or 10 o'clock, or if the herring weren't of a particularly good standard and he knew that there were herring coming in later. The first ones went for a lot of money, so you would hold back and get them at a more reasonable price.

The haulage side of the business was always important, but it was just three months of the year in those days. We had fourteen lorries at that time, doing general haulage, and Willy had about twelve. Most people employed were from the village. The wagons used to come in about five o'clock or half-past with a broken spring or something else wrong and they had to be fixed for the next morning. My father, me and Uncle Ken used to do all that. You used to have to get them ready for the testing, washing them down and that.

Willie Mitford

There used to be a herring yard at Newton, my grandfather started there, he was a cooper and a curer. In fact my Uncle Luke and Jim were born at Newton. My mother was born here.

My grandfather came here to work and then he started up on his own. I can remember my mother saying, all the family worked for him and he always paid his women but if he had a bad year, he didn't pay his daughters. He used to move down to Yarmouth and Lowestoft, if the herring went south, they went with them. They had digs already booked for them, the family used to all go but then my mother had to stay at home to look after the younger ones. My mother once told me that if I was to look in the cemetery, the women had all died in their 50's. My grandmother had three children died, John was an infant, George and Willie were about 12 years old when they died, they were Luke's brothers.

The yard was all open when we worked there. It was very cold. There was a little door and they used to pack the kippers and the wagons used to stand alongside that little door on a Saturday, and go round Amble and all these places with the boxes of kippers and throw them through the door, they were all stone boxes then. I made the last wooden boxes when I was there.

They used to work the herring up here, before they went to Yarmouth and that and the women would be working in the dark and there were only flares, the only light they had, they were lit with paraffin, in the kipper yard and the women outside would have what we used to call 'a smokie,' it was just like a teapot with a big thick wick and they would fill that with paraffin, light it, either that or a candle in a kipper box. The women worked in twos, on piece work – my mother and my grandmother worked together. My mother used to gut, my grandmother used to pack the herring in the barrel – she was so small, she used to have to stand on a box to get down to the bottom. She had to go down and fit the herring in and then they had to work and put them on their backs and pack them all in until they came up to the top. Every layer was salted – they were just gutted. They were salted on the pier and then they came and tipped them on the 'farling,' which was the top end and they were salted again and salted all the time and then when they got them all done, the cooper put the lids on and then they were rolled around the village. The big day was when the inspector came and he used to ask for different boxes to be opened and if they got the crown brand, that they had passed, they got top price for them. After that they left on a boat from Berwick.

Herring inspectors are examining herrings in the barrels. Those that passed were given the crown brand, and top price.

One winter Ken decided he would do some bloaters – I used to go and help him at night. We used to steep them again to take a lot of the salt out of them, put them on the spit, hang them up and smoke them – now Yarmouth was a great place for that. They weren't as popular as kippers. We used to grill them on the fires.

The fishermen had a rod inside the door with salt herring on them. Everyone had a thing outside the door with their salt herring on them.

Winnie Hogg

When my mother worked at the herring, before the war, in the 1930's, she was a packer. There were two of them working together. One was gutting and my mother used to pack them into barrels. Sometimes they had a glut of herrings and they were there until midnight in the kipper yard. They worked by paraffin flares. When I was 7 or 8 I used to go along to old Lizzie's about 9 o'clock at night and get a can of tea off her mother and a can off my granny to take to my mother and go to the herring yard, so they had a break. They used to stop there until all the herring was finished.

I didn't realize until I was married how hard my mother worked. If we went into the kipper yard, her backside was in the barrel, sticking out of the barrel, 'cos she was the packer. They were on piecework. All these barrels were dotted around the village, especially around the pub. Then they went from there to Berwick, where they were put on a ship and apparently they were exported to some of the Scandinavian countries. That was in the summer. They had to work hard, to cover themselves for the winter, if the weather was bad, because they didn't get dole.

In the winter my mother baited lines. She was up at 5 o'clock in the morning scenning mussels and limpets. She would stop for a while and get us ready for school, and then she would do some chores. When the boats came in all the lines had to be baited with the limpets, ready for the next day. If they were snarled up, the lines, sometimes they were in a bait house, (which was at my granny's at that time,) until sometimes 12 o'clock at night. These lines had to be finished for the next day to go to sea.

When my mother was working till midnight, we actually lived with my granny. I don't know how much they got a barrel, but they wouldn't be paid much. There used to be a boat come in regularly from Eyemouth, called the Spes Bona. This boat was in nearly all the summer, loaded with herring at times, and it was lost with all hands in 1944. My father was very friendly with the skipper who was called William Patterson. We knew them very well, because they were always in, and they used to let us run around on the boat. We used to go and get cigarettes for the men from the shop. There were a lot of boats came in before the war, so they didn't have to seek the herring in wagons from other places. They really worked very hard. It was a cold nasty job. We used to get grass, which had to be put on the swills, where they laid the beads for the lines. My mother used to say, 'go and get some grass to put on there.'

Lena Shell

When I worked on the herring, there were seven on the bench and sometimes four on the tenter. We were paid 2 shillings an hour and when it finished it had gone up to £2 an hour. They could pay you what they liked. There was no minimum wage in them days. I started when the bairns were little, in the 1930's. There were about 12 ladies in the yard, some cleaning and some splitting and putting them in the tubs to be washed. I started splitting first and then I went on the tentering. They were handed into the shed to be hung up. Ken used to sit in the smokehouse, where the herrings hung. They were strung from side to side. The wood was just high enough so the herrings could hang.

The season started in May, sometimes April. The herring drifters were quite big, the 'Spes Bona' used to come in regularly. Billy Simpson used to run along the pier and along the back of the boat. There was no shop at that time to buy the kippers. You had to walk in the yard to get the kippers. The other fish used to come into Boulmer. Luke used to go there for it. The herring came into Craster. The boats used to come in and some used to lie off there and they used to go out to the bigger boats and fetch the herring in what you called 'crans,' the fish boxes. They used to lie off the harbour; they couldn't always get in because of the tide. There were also crabs and lobster.

The new gutting machine came much later, before I finished. Alice was on it – it must have been 50 or 60 years ago. The machine made a lot of difference because the fish went straight into the brine and onto the bench. They were fetched down to tubs and they were tentered. I have a photograph of Ken sitting in the smokehouse just watching the fire. The fish guts and things were dumped over the harbour wall. At the finish there was a wagon come in to collect it. It was a big industry here during the War.

The yard was all enlarged and a lot of alterations made. There was a place at the top for the sawdust to go and the shavings, then they fitted the bottom part with a long bench, so they could get more people cleaning. Sometimes there were two tubs, which had to be got ready to go into the smokehouse. At one time there were three smokehouses going, but as time went on you couldn't get the workers, so there were just the two smokehouses. Isabel Young worked for a little while, Alice and Sybil but they didn't work for long. Ken and Edith ran the restaurant.

Isobel Young

I went to work when our Neville was three months old. Me Mam used to look after him and I was there (from 1947) for 27 years. I saw a lot of changes. I was on the machine, it made a lot of difference, but there weren't as many people on the bench. There were only five of us women on the bench and the other women were tentering. We used to gut and split the herring. The machine did most of it. It was a happy place to work. We just worked from June until September - the herring were still coming into the harbour. The ladies tentering wrapped cloth round their thumbs. They used to get sore. It was very cold. We had plastic aprons, but we had to wrap ourselves up. When me granny used to go to the herring she used to wear long oilskins and she used to have a hot water bottle with her to keep warm. We also wore Wellingtons with socks inside.

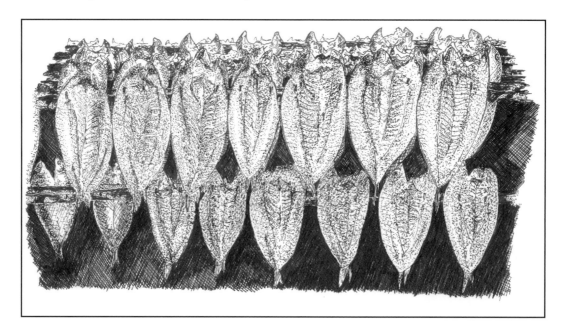

Vera Mitford

Our two were at school when I went to work at the Yard, about 1962 or 63. There were quite a few women worked there when I went, a lot of the older ones. Mrs. France, Mrs. Straughan, Mrs. Wilson, Annie Jane Norris, Bessie Morris, Eleanor Dawson - Ethel Watson was on the machine, then Alice and then Isabel. I started before the machine, we worked on the bench. I remember that bench was full when I first went in. It was Eleanor Dawson made room for me. They used to come and throw the herring right up to the bench, the little ones were at the top, the floor was on a slope. Willie's grandmother Robson, she was always at the bottom, 'cause she was tall. Ken was in charge. Garth Lowerson worked there. It was mostly women but some of the men helped to hang the tenterhooks. The men lifted the boxes and did the heavy lifting. Bill Seager was there at the same time as me. He was a cooper. He made the barrels. The barrels were for the crabs, covered with hessian, packed in sawdust and taken to Little Mill Station.

Everybody has a uniform now, but then we never even wore gloves, but we were issued with rubber gloves before the end. Our hands were yellow with packing the kippers, the oil made your hands lovely and soft. We had to wrap up warm. We kept all our old clothes for the herring. We had to stand on the wet concrete floors but the gossip was enjoyable, someone would tell stories. The young ones came, Nancy Grey, Sybil, Lila worked there.

Everybody let their money lie till the end of the season, every night you went over the office to give in your hours. We took turns to pack the kippers.

We always had a Herring Trip – It was just for the employees and their families. We would go to Harrogate, Edinburgh, go away early in the morning and back late at night. Ken used to organise it. Then the trips fizzled out and we went for dinner to the Saddle Grill at Alnmouth.

I've seen a lot of changes. You couldn't move for people coming into the Yard - schools, trips and they used to just walk about and watch us and talk to us. Now people are not allowed in for hygiene reasons. They were happy days, even in my grandmother and mother's day, when they used to work late into night, cleaning the herring, they were always singing. We really had good bosses. There was no television and very few cars, so we had to make our own entertainment. If we worked till late, and we were still there early in the morning, 'cause the boats were coming in all the time with the herring. Luke Robson would go to Eyemouth and hire a boat, he always got the 'Spes Bona.'

Garth Lowerson

I left school in 1962 when I was 15 and that's when I started working at Robson's. I was born and bred in Dunstan Square. I wanted to go on the farm the same as my father but there were no vacancies with Sutherlands. I tried to get in at Stamford but there was nothing there either.

My mother was down buying fish or kippers from Ken Robson and he said there was a job if I wanted it. There were no other young people working there. I was there for nine and a half years. Ken was like a second father to me. I did the gutting, tentering and packing the kippers. When there was a lot of herring being caught off Craster and the Farne Islands, the Craster fishermen decided to get nets and go fishing for herring, but there were so many fish that they had to be taken to North Shields. The season was from early May – June 'till September, when the herring became dry and however much heat you gave them you couldn't smoke them.

New faces came in all the time to buy kippers and I got to know a lot of people. There were two or three hawkers, McKays from Seahouses, Downies from Amble. There were people from Hexham and Corbridge came to buy. The Kippers were in wooden boxes at that time and they were posted out.

We all got our holidays in September, at the end of the season. We just worked the white fish during the winter. Ken bought them from various sources. The boats fished during the winter months and caught lobsters and crab in January. There were four boats fishing out of Craster then, Bartie Dawson, The Silks, Billie Smailes and Willie Archbold and Vincent Morris bought a boat. There were three men to a boat and then it went down to two.

The names I remember who worked in the yard with me, were, Alice Shell, Sybil Dawson, Mary Sheenan, Mrs. Wilson, Gracie Wilson, Doreen Simpson, Lucy Robson, Hilda Rogerson, Kathy Humble, Belle Straughan, Vera Mitford, Isabel Young, Bessie Archbold, Georgina Renwick, and Ethel Watson. Bill Seager, used to repair all the barrels and make boxes. Winnie Park, Sylvia Park, Joyce Shaw used to work in the shop. The time I was at Robson's, there were three lads started, Ian Baird, Alfie Shell and when I left Derek Greenley got my job. That was from 1962 until 1971. So many of them came and packed the kippers and then when the lorry arrived, the other girls would split the herring and tenter them and put them in the smokehouse.

I can remember that when the kippers were on, people were queuing out of the door from 1 o'clock. After lunch, the queues would be right out of the door, people from Newcastle and all over, especially on half-day closing in Newcastle.

Doris Clarke

I worked at the herrings, for my sins. I wasn't very good - gutting them. I couldn't keep a hold of the fish, they would go scooting along the bench and I think they thought I was a right one. They had their own knives. They used to hide them at night time. You never knew how much you were going to get. You didn't know how much the splitters got.

Did it depend on how many herrings you did? It would just depend on how long you had been there, I think. The likes of Annie Jane Norris and Belle Straughan and they all had a better wage. I mean I was just a rookie, but I worked there for about six weeks.

Willie Mitford

I work two days a week at the yard (now,) doing the post, putting stuff into envelopes. Sometimes I vacuum pack, if necessary. I went into the yard when I retired. Ken was ill at the time and I used to take him out in the car and that, until he died – I just carried on there, it was part of my life, being in the yard. My mother worked there. Vera says if I can get away into that yard, I'm happy.

Chapter 3   Shops, Trades and Taking in Visitors
'The shop was a meeting place – a social half hour in the day'

Betty and Edward Grey with their daughter Jane in the shop in the 1970s.

Joyce Shaw

When we came here in 1967, Annie Jane Nelson's shop was still here. There was Isabel's butchers shop down the street. Edward Grey had the shop. There was the Off Licence, belonged to Patience & Belle Mason.

Annie Jane Nelson's shop

Maggie Wilson

Mrs. Nelson's shop on the North Side was there before the war, she had a tearoom at one time and the Post Office for a short time. The Grey's had the Post Office at the West End for a time. Jamesie Smailes' wife, Annie and Ethel they served in the Post Office there, where Neil Robson's house is now. I think they packed up after the War. Annie Jane Nelson got it after that and she didn't have it very long.

Doris Clarke

Mrs Nelson sold lovely bacon and sweets, and probably cheese. Edward had the main grocery shop and post office. The post office used to be at the north side, next door to the rented one. That's why the telephone box is there, I think. When Edward took it over it was handy for here. The buses always stopped on the north side, they didn't come over here. They used to go down to the bottom of the bank and then back up, in front of Mrs Nelson's house. She was the parcel office as well. I think that all of the drivers used to be pleased of her cup of tea in the morning – and waiting for the first bus in the morning. She was very generous in that way.

Joyce Shaw

I can remember as a little girl, aged maybe about four and my father was doing something down at Annie Jane's shop and I was sitting on the little seat on the front, which is still there. I was sliding along the seat and I got the biggest spelk you've ever seen. I can remember that vividly and I had to run into Annie Jane's to get the spelk taken out. It was a grocer's shop and she was related to my granny, it was also a little tearoom.

Annie Jane was a fantastic woman – if someone came and sat on the seat beside the shop, she would think nothing about asking them if they wanted a cup of tea and a biscuit, total strangers. She was President of the W.I for years. Her daughter found her dead, sitting on the settee, with the Gazette in her hand. She was only in her 70's when she died.

Jimmy Shaw

That was our port of call on a Sunday morning, going over to Chapel, we used to call there and have a cup of tea.

Joyce Shaw

Annie Jane – was originally an Archbold but she married and became a Nelson. Her husband had been a fisherman but was crippled with arthritis and walked with a crutch. That's how she came to open the shop because she had to be the breadwinner.

Edward Grey's Shop

Joan Angus

In late December 1946, 1 left school, having reached the age of 14 years on December 15th. It was time for me to earn my living. No one asked me if I would like to continue my education, I was a girl - and in those days, we did as we were told. I had a job to go to in the village, a happy arrangement, since it did not involve travelling. Mr. Edward Grey needed an assistant in his shop and Post Office, since his wife Betty was about to have their second child. I worked in the shop for five years and enjoyed every minute. Edward sold everything from sewing needles to paraffin oil. I can't remember being asked for anything which Edward did not stock.

I started working in the shop for Edward just a couple of days after finishing school. Betty was due to have her second child. It was at Christmas time and everyone was posting their Christmas parcels and I was sticking Insurance Stamps on the parcels instead of postage stamps. We had to gently take them off. We had regular customers then, it was quite busy 'cause people didn't go to Alnwick for groceries - there wasn't a lot of transport. The Co-op van from Howick used to come and take your order and then deliver the following week. Edward sold everything. He had all sorts of medicinal cures as well - camphorated oil, Snowfire, Thermogene wool. There was a shop (Mrs. Nelson's) on the north side as well, not as big. We each had our own customers - people were loyal to their own shop. The Post Office was there in 1946, at Edward's. Mrs. Nelson had it for a little while, then Betty Grey took it on.

I would like to say that Edward Grey and Betty were a grand couple and Edward was an absolute gentleman – I haven't met such a nice man. He was also secretary for the Reading Room and if I had nothing to do, sometimes

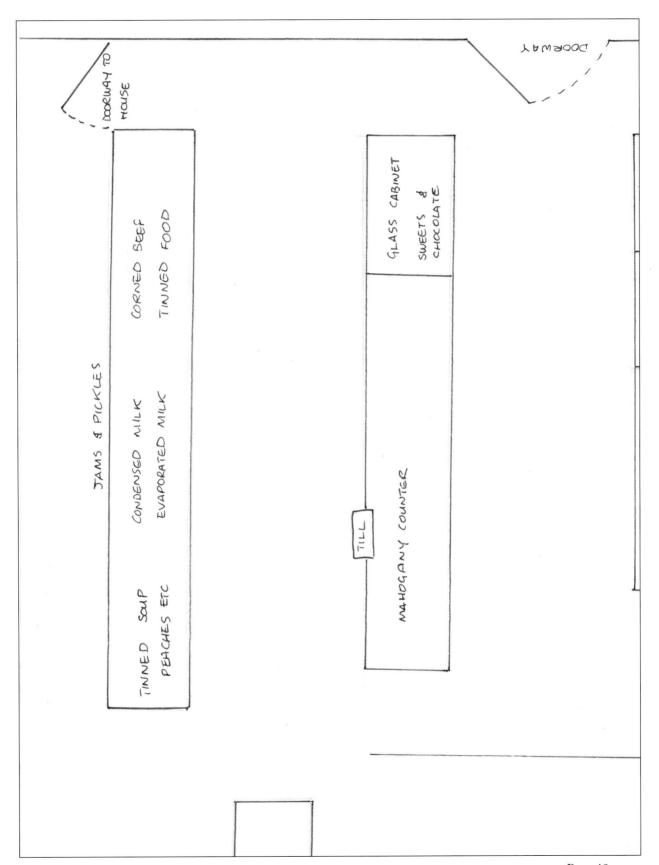

when he sent letters out when there was going to be a committee meeting, he used to get me to write his letters. Then I would get on the bike and deliver the letters. I used to deliver the papers as well, to the Towers, South Farm, Dunstan Hill, etc., on the bike. Willie Haddon had two little border terriers and I used to do the post when Eva was on holiday and you were alright if you didn't take your feet off the pedals of the bike but if you did the terriers would get your ankles. I was terrified, Willie Haddon used to laugh.

I worked for five years at the shop and it didn't change very much. We did the telegrams and they were delivered by bicycle to whoever and I can remember having to go to Cold Martin one Saturday afternoon and I once had to take an awful telegram to Howick to Mr. Moyer and his wife who had got word that their son had been killed on the 'Amethyst' in the Yangtse River and I was only 15 and I had to take the telegram to this elderly couple and I stayed with them while they opened it and saw that they were alright.

You also had a lot of characters - there were certain ladies I was frightened of, I won't mention their names, they were very dominant, you didn't argue with them. Things were rationed. You couldn't get coffee or tinned peaches and sweets were still rationed and these ladies would look at you as if you were telling fibs when you said you didn't have these things. Edward would come along and send me for my tea. Betty was a nurse, she was a very feisty Welsh lady and she was a good friend to me. She said what she meant. You had to say please and thank you when you came into the shop but her heart was in the right place.

There was still food rationing at this time and this lasted until 1952. Each person who was registered at the shop received – 2 ozs butter, 2 ozs lard (compound,) 4 ozs marg, ½ lb. sugar, 4 ozs bacon, 1 egg and about 3 ozs cheese per week and only ¾ lb tea and ¾ lb. sweets, and 1 lb. jam per month. If there was a child – children had green ration books – you were allowed 1 lb. oranges – when the oranges arrived, which wasn't very often. Bananas also, were scarce. There were no fridges or deep freezers or pre-packed food of any description. Bacon was hand sliced, the fats were put up in their tiny amounts, sugar weighed into blue bags, as were biscuits, which came in tins. We were, what I would call, proper shop assistants then.

Behind the counter were drawers full of Marrowfat peas, pearly barley, lentils, split peas, loose tea and in a wonderful old black tin, with a small top to keep the flavour in, ground coffee, which the fishermen had for their second breakfast. I can still smell that coffee when I think about it. In separate boxes behind the door, on the customer's side of the shop, there was Sloan's liniment, Thermogene wool, lint, bandages, Carter's Little Liver Pills, Beechams Pills, camphorated oil, Vick, Aspirin, Kaolin poultice, which came out of a blue tin, Snow Fire Ointment for chilblains, Vaseline and Zinc & Castor Oil ointment. We sold lyle stockings, silk stockings, special wool for socks, elastic, threads, linen thread, linen buttons for the men's long johns, needles, knitting needles, some sets of four needles made of steel and very fine, size 12 or 13, which were used for socks. There were Dolly Blues made by Reckitts, donkey stones for the steps, green soap, washing soda, Rinso and Oxydol - no biological powders then. We sold pots and pans, pan scrubbers, dishcloths, pegs and pails. We sold 4st. bags of flour and yeast, of course, which arrived in hessian bags from Mawson & Swan in Berwick. We sold cigarettes and baccy - 1/10d for 20. It would take all day to tell you what Edward sold but I must mention - Dainty Dinah toffees, Chocolate Satins, Black Bullets, Marzipan Teacakes, Fisherman's Friends and Lingo Fizz.

Carol Grey

(When I was a child) we sold all sorts at the shop. It stayed open till about 6 p.m. and on dark winter nights, the customers would have all day to shop, but they would come for 'six-penneth' of paraffin, in a pop bottle, at five to six. My dad (Edward Grey) had to get the torch out and go fiddling about in the garage, where there was a tank of paraffin. He had the patience of a saint. Someone once came in for ten shillings worth of liquorice laces. They were a penny each and all 120 had to be separated. He did it with good grace.

Before the shop was altered, you came in through the door on Church Street and you went down two steps into the Post Office. The shop was on the right hand side as you went in and the Post Office was on the left, and there was a window which faced east, and I can remember Barbara and I used to sit on the steps down into the Post Office, dad used to be doing the Post Office books and in those days he smoked and he would put the cigarette end on the lift up counter and Eddie would appear from nowhere, go underneath the counter, take the cigarette and disappear. Barbara and I used to watch this pantomime every so often, he would be looking for the cigarette and be sure he had one and it took him a long time to realise that it was Eddie who was taking it.

Eddie started smoking at Ned Dawson's, who had a little pipe and Ned used to put the cigarette in the end and Eddie used to smoke it. He smoked before he started school. You could set your clock by him. He never wore a watch but Mum used to say to him 'if you're that desperate for a cigarette, you come in at 6 o'clock and I'll give you one.' I remember one time she gave him a Capstan Full Strength and we all sat and watched him smoke it.

Going back to the Post Office, when the kippers came, well there would be hundreds of boxes, there were the quarter boxes and the big boxes and they all had to have stamps on. We had to lick the stamps on and wait for the postman to collect them about 6 o'clock.

Whenever Michael Robson went into the shop, Dad would say to him 'which team plays at Upton Park' (or whatever). Michael said that Dad knew where every football club in the country played, however obscure. Michael says that was one of his memories of my Dad was Dad and Dennis Dawson, on April Fool's Day, when the children came into the shop, Dad would say 'will you go to Dennis's and ask him for a rubber hammer?' So over they would walk to the Joiner's Shop and come back and say 'Dennis hasn't got a rubber hammer, but have you got a long stand?' and they were told to stand over there. Another one was asking for a tin of tartan paint.

You could buy everything at the shop, curtain wires, cough medicine, sticking plasters, bandages, it didn't matter what you wanted. When they were building the new shop, the Post Office was run out of the kitchen and the shop was run out of the garage. We used to play shops with real tins of beans etc., with real money and put it back in the till, but I used to like to go to Annie Jane's. I would take sixpence out of mam's purse.

Lizzie Sanderson went to Annie Jane's for bacon and she said 'I'll just have two slices and I'll get the rest at Edward's.'

Maggie Cullingworth liked bacon but she liked it cut on No. 1 which was paper thin and she used to get half a pound and her daughter was exactly the same. Maggie liked it just to shrivel up in the frying pan. Dad often used to give her a ham shank to make a pan of soup and every time she got one, you could go into the kitchen and there would be a shortbread sitting on the table, Maggie had made. Maggie lived next door to Doris Clarke and when she made shortbread for someone and if she made a mistake Doris used to get them. Auntie Eva used to make cakes for the chapel, she used to make pineapple cakes and things like that.

Scott's Butchers

Mike Robson

When you went up the Butcher Lane, there was Alfie (Shell) and Isabel (Scott) serving, and we used to go in, the bell would go and you shut the door, both of them at this time would be in the outhouse, so you would open it and shut it, the bell went again, we would do this several times. By this time Isabel would think there would be about four customers in. You would be standing on your own. She knew fine well what was happening. You would order some mince, and she would put the mince on the scales and she would take a bit off, then another bit off, it would take about a minute to get that exactly to the gram. Alfie Shell was a good man.

The day they killed the beasts was a Monday so you never went swimming down on the shoreline on a Monday because it was red with blood coming out of the sinks. All the herring guts and that used to go over the end of the pier in them days, barrel after barrel after barrel.

Off Licence

Adam Dawson

There was a small 'beer off,' not far from us on the North side, was run by Patience Mason, we used to call her Nanny Mason, and her husband. They were both Embleton folks, came from Embleton.

Marjorie Lumsden

As well as Annie Jane's shop there was another one on the North Side which was an Off Licence. A lot of men didn't want people to know they went to the pub, so they went there and sat in the back place. Old Geordie Dawson and Sep and them always sat in Mrs. Mason's back room. Geordie Dawson didn't go to the pub, but Sep did 'cos he drank rum. He used to complain about his stomach on a Sunday morning.

Milk Delivery

Marjorie Lumsden

Milk was delivered in bottles. Johnny Weatherson delivered in a can with a ladle. Violet delivered milk from the Scar (Howick Scar Farm). Her mother was a lovely woman. She walked across the Heugh morning and night with a milk-can and delivered to the village. Violet had a car. One of her sons, George Curry – he's dead now – he always carried the can to the top of the brae. It would be fields all the way to the shop then.

Violet Hall

We used to start from the Scar Farm at about half past eight in the morning with our bottles and crates. My mother, she was Catherine Margaret, used to have a can and she used to walk over the hill up there and actually she was expecting me when she was doing it. My brother used to help to carry the can to the top of the hill and then she used to go and deliver it. It was twice a day in those days.

Then we started with the bottles which was much easier – well I say that – but it was a lot of hard work, because when you got back home you had to wash all the bottles out and scald them and get them ready for the next day.

I can't say I enjoyed it. It was what I had to do, although you met people all the time and I suppose that passed the time a bit. You used to stop and have a chat with them. I suppose it took about two hours to get around. When you got back you had all the bottles to do and then your other jobs as well.

Craster and Dunstan was the farthest we went. There were other milkmen. There was Thompsons from Howick Seahouses and Johnny Weatherson, Ruth's father at Proctors Stead. Someone else did it for a while, and then Robbie took over.

You used to have the milk inspector maybe twice a year. We used to dread seeing him. He would test your milk and you'd be waiting to see what the reply was – to see if your milk was alright. I suppose it was to catch you out – to see if you were putting water in it.

If it was really bad weather my brother helped me out. Sometimes Billy helped when he was a boy. Billy will know what kind of car I had. (It was a Vauxhall Ten. The number plate was GR 8205. BC) I learned to drive in the war, when you didn't need to pass a test. I learned in the little field. They put posts in and I used to reverse back and go forwards. That's how I learned to drive. I used to tease them because my driving licence said I could drive a steam roller.

Travelling Shops

Doris Clarke

I always bought my meat at the butcher's, and the greengrocers would come – Bob Smith from Embleton. Then the store used to come – Howick store used to travel. Geoff used to work for them – he was on the bakery van. He came around two or three times a week. The store traveller used to come, once a fortnight, say you came on a Tuesday and they delivered on a Friday. That was the only way, if you didn't have any transport, 'cos you didn't bring things from Alnwick.

Jimmy Shaw

There were a lot of visiting traders, travelling shops and nurses coming to the village and some kept coming until recent times. I made this list from talking to people who remember the old ones

Grant the fruiterer	Weekly visit with van
Chapman	Draperies, paraffin, van
Nellie the sweep	Cottons, pins etc with pram
Miss Chicken	Draperies etc – came by bus, Traveller for John Archbold of Fenkle Street, Alnwick
Jimmy Young	known as 'The People's Provider,' sold groceries he came from Christon Bank
Co-op	Butcher and baker came weekly
Jaggers	Ice-cream, handcart
Billy Barber	Selling rabbits (father of Dolly Barber,

	Schoolteacher at Dunstan)
Drummond	bought rabbit skins
Taylor	9 am bus from Amble, collected shoes for repair, returned them next week
Hives	Sold china in kipper yard
Mountney	Sold flowers on the common at Dunstan every summer
Harry Dawson	Draper, came by car
Green	Scotch Draper, (now has shop in Alnwick)
Curry	Milk deliveries
Jonnie Weatherson	Milk deliveries
Bessie Durham	Milk deliveries
Willie Haddon	Milk deliveries
Thompson	Milk deliveries
Gerrard	Coal merchant
Arnott	Coal merchant
Charlie Smart	collecting dirty bottles
Rutherford	had buses that came to the village
Paitman	cobbler from Longhoughton, wife did upholstery
Short from Boulmer and Blyth	Nurses and midwives
Liz Walker, Craster (Billy Bunk's mother)	Nurses and midwives
Dorothy Curry (nee Rowell) Howick Scar	Nurses and midwives
Mary Paxton.	Nurses and midwives

There has never been a doctor based in the village and visits were made by Drs Waterson, Hall and Livingstone from Embleton and Laurie and Jackson from Alnwick.

The policeman for the village has always been based at Embleton.

A Fish Round

Winnie Banks

Before I started on the van and when I was off in the summer, I picked whelks off the rocks. We were penniless, as we had put everything into the house and Ian had put a down payment on the boat so we needed the money. There wasn't much down here so I went along to Beadnell and I would spend hours along there and used to get big sack loads and then Ian would come with the van and pick them up off the rocks. You had to pick at low tide. Ian and I used to pick in the winter and we sold them by the sackful at North Shields. They had to be certain size; the small ones were no good. You got a good price for them, as long as you didn't pick beside the sewage outfall – they were the biggest!

George Norris had seen me going up and down (to the harbour) to help Ian (husband) and he asked Ian if I didn't fancy having a fish round. I had said to Ian before I came up here 'mind, I'm not going to be a fishwife.' We already had a van but George did lend me his Mini van for the first week, 'cause Ian was using the van. George had a fish round for 40 years before I started, he came with me for the first week. He had run the round right down but the basics were there, he lent me his scales. He gave me all the profit for the first week. He sold the round to me for £50. The round covered from Embleton, Craster, Alnwick and I went as far as Felton, Boulmer and Lesbury and all the farms round about. I started doing six days a week.

I used to get the fish at Amble first of all as George used to get his there. Then I decided to try Seahouses but actually it wasn't as good so I went back to Amble, where the lads were brilliant, you always left with a smile on your face, they always had a joke, mind the language was awful, but it wasn't meant to be bad. They were very surprised that a woman was doing the fish round, when I first started they never swore at all and they called me Mrs. Banks, but they soon changed. I used to say they should have a swear box but they just laughed.

At first I just had cod and haddock as George had run the round right down. At first I used to sell frozen fish but I realised that wasn't the way to do it, you had to have good, fresh fish and you had to have variety. Gradually I built it up and then George Douglas, who ran Amble, knew that I wanted all the bits and pieces and he kept all that for me, whether or not it was 'cause I was a woman or not, I don't know. I went every morning to Amble, leaving here about quarter to seven in the morning. The fish had been landed the previous night and were kept on ice.

When Ian was fishing out of Craster, they were catching a lot of cod in the summer. I had to use his fish. George and them didn't mind because Ian used to take fish there. I've seen us filleting in the back lane at Craster. Derek Greenley from Embleton used to come and fillet for us, 'cause he worked for Kenneth. Sometimes there were boxes and I couldn't cope with them all. At first I used to be home for 2 – 3 o'clock in the afternoon but as the round got bigger I got later and later.

On a summer's day they would be filleting in the back and there were fish everywhere, even in the bath (the bathroom was downstairs) as we had nowhere to put it once it was filleted, so we would put it into boxes in the bath, you never got rid of the smell of fish. Auntie Eva lived next door and Mary Abbot was on the other side, they were good neighbours, the fish were never a problem to them, some people could have complained about the smell but no one ever did. Jimmy & Amy Bruce next door were fine. Winnie & Jimmy Park lived next door and Winnie was working at the Yard. We needed a bigger house. I sold kippers at the door on week-ends.

Most customers were lovely. A lot of people were older. They were the ones who bought fish. As the years went by the younger people didn't buy so much fish. I used to have a queue for fresh fish and used to make fish cakes galore, Elsie Browell used to help make them. We used to boil crabs outside the back door at Church Street all day and I used to pick stones of crab in that little kitchen and dress them as well. Sometimes it was 9 o'clock at night when I got finished. Of course I was younger then and it was our business and we were making a profit. There were days Ian couldn't go to sea but I was still working.

The first winter was hard, I can remember, it wasn't just my hands that were cold, it was my feet as well. I had next to nothing on, I don't know where I thought I was going. I had learnt my lesson by the second winter, I was like the Michelin man. I was warm and dry that was the main thing.

I had one or two customers who used to pinch off the van. I used to buy potatoes and they were in the front of the van and when I went to the front to get the potatoes, I had a tray of baked herring, you could see where the hand had been and I didn't realise at first but I had wrapped her fish up and I thought it had come undone and when I went to wrap it up and there was the herring stuffed inside. She had tried to put the herring in the bag.

I had different days for different areas, every week I had the same round. Customers knew which day I was due, I just blew the horn and they came out. I was reported once for being too noisy, somebody on night shift reported me blowing the horn – as the law stood nothing could be done about it but I said that I would have knocked on the doors in that street. The police couldn't tell me who had reported me but they told me which street, so I just knocked on the doors there.

I had up-market customers in Lesbury, they were all very nice. All my customers were very nice, I never had any bother, the children used to love to come to the van to see what there was. In fact, there's one girl in Alnwick, whose mother used be a customer, who recognised me as being the 'fish lady.' I used to get cups of tea now and then at the farms. I used to take things in for people, light their fires sometimes, post their letters. The Davison sisters Elizabeth and Mary, their mother from Chapel Lands, I used to have to go in there, make her cup of tea, get the plate, go and get the fish, go back and put the fish in the fridge for her. Sometimes I used to put her flask up.

They say it snows first at Shilbottle 'cause it's high. Newton on the Moor was always bad. I used to have to make my mind up first thing in the morning, 'cause once you'd bought the fish you had to do the round. I think I only missed one year, when we were snowed in for four days. If I broke down, I never had any bother, I would wave down the first car to come along. One year I had ten punctures in the year. Everywhere I went I was picking up nails etc.

I sold a lot of fish in the village. I could have been a millionaire if Ken Robson had let me. You could have sold every kipper you could get your hands on, at Clayport because then they were the lovely little fat herring and they were all landed here. I used to have to fight with him for boxes of kippers, he used to ration us as there were three or four vans used to go in there. I would ask for four or five boxes and I would think these aren't going to go very far, I could sell them on Clayport alone. If he was in a good mood, I might get six, he would say 'it's no good me giving them to you, I can sell them all here,' which was true enough. He was selling them to me at a cheaper rate. I used to go in on my hands and knees. In the summer, kippers were the most popular, otherwise it was cod and haddock.

I used to sell potatoes, eggs and vegetables, all the sea food, smoked salmon and smoked cod. Douglas's (from Amble) smoked cod were very good and I used to top up with Douglas's kippers, if I couldn't get enough from Craster. If Amble were good they were very good but if they had an off day, they weren't as good. I got the vegetables from Fieldhouse Farm, cauliflowers. I used to cut my own if they weren't ready for me. I used to get cabbages and broccoli from there as well. I used to get turnips and potatoes from Willy Haddon and then from

Ruby and Isabel when they had moved to Clayport. Isabel used to take orders from me for kippers, so I would put their kippers to one side before I got up there. When people got to know that, they were asking Isabel to take their order for kippers.

As the years went on and the kippers got bigger and younger girls started to take over the household, they wouldn't have the smell in the house. Gradually over the years you couldn't give kippers away. I worked 25 years on the round. George Norris was on the round for 40 years and his father before him. I knocked on doors and word got round quickly. There were two rounds as well as myself, one from Eyemouth and one from Seahouses. I used to do the hospitals and the school. I went to the Duke's School and into the kitchens at the hospital and all the girls bought their fish, and then the vans were stopped from going to the hospital. Most of them wanted dressed crab.

One thing I never forgot, it was a winter's morning, really icy, I was just going out of the village and I used to meet with Ruth Davison, when she was doing the milk, all over the place and we were always waving to each other. I was heading along past Scar Farm and the road was really icy and it was about 6.45 a.m. Ruth was coming from the other direction, I saw her and slowed down, she put her brakes on 'cause she saw me coming and she just came across the road and I thought she was going to hit me and it rolled over twice and the milk and crates were all over the road. I was sitting in my van thinking that she must be dead and when I got to the vehicle, she wasn't strapped in, she was just bruised, the van was upside down and she came out of the door and we both burst into tears. I put her in my van and took her home. When I came back Robbie was in the road sweeping all the broken glass etc.

One day when I came home and had just cleaned the van as I always did, I had just been to Christon Bank for the eggs, there were about 50 dozen eggs on the shelf at the back of the van. Dougie Hogg wanted some part for his boat, so they decided to take my van and off they went and on their way down Felton Bank, there's garages on the left hand side of the road and this woman was coming up the right hand side wanting to turn into the garage but she indicated to go one way and she went the other and she drove right across the road in front of them. Ian banged the brakes on and 50 dozen eggs came off the shelf and over the top of them and they were covered, they had to come straight home. They had to get washed and changed and I had to get a shovel and shovel the eggs out of the van. I think I saved about 20 dozen. The woman admitted liability but she wouldn't pay for the eggs or anything.

The Joiners' Shop

Willie Archbold

When anybody died in the Village, two or three of us kids, were curious and the Joiner, Mr. Jack Grey, used to make coffins and we used to peep in the door. They used to make the coffins in the Joiners' shop. There were three joiners, Mr. Grey and his son and there was two apprentices, there were four in there at one time, Dennis Dawson and Jackie Browell, they served their time in there. We liked to see what they were doing, we were curious. The Joiners' Shop dates back to about 1921.

Jimmy Shaw

Dennis Dawson's workshop was a regular meeting place for menfolk after calling at the shop for newspapers and fags.

Geordie Grey

After I left school, I helped my father in the Joiners' Shop, 'cause he was the joiner. The reason for that was that my older brother was a joiner but he was away in the Air Force, so I had to help in the family business. I wasn't cut out to be a joiner, I liked to follow the horses ploughing, and I wanted to be a farmer.

Jack Browell

I finished school, got a job in the Joiners' Shop and served my time with Jack Grey and Dennis. Jack Grey's son, John and myself worked in the Joiners' Shop. We made coffins - used to get the coffin sets and then John and his father went to measure the person up and came back and Dennis and I would make them. I enjoyed my time as a joiner, but was only getting 14/6d a week, from 7.30 a.m – 5 p.m. and Saturday morning.

Willie Mitford

They made the coffins in the Joiner's Shop. Geordie Grey's father was a good joiner and all the men he trained turned out to be good joiners. Ralph Dawson, the boat builder at Seahouses served his time there, old Adam Durham, he was a good joiner, and John Archbold. It was a very busy place in those days. Everybody used to end up there on a wet day. It would stop a lot of work 'cause you got on talking.

Garage

Joyce Shaw

On the North Side there used to be a petrol pump, where those gardens are now, opposite the new houses. There were sheds and opposite them there was a petrol pump and on it was a clock. I think you must have turned the clock if you wanted two gallons and then you would pump it for petrol, apparently it belonged to Old Rutherford, who had taxis down at the bottom.

Marjorie Lumsden

The buses didn't come down in the village and you had to walk, either from the pastures or from the pillars. They went down the hill and backed up and stopped. When Rutherford had buses, between Little Adam's house and the Stables, he had his buses in there and there were buses at Embleton.

Willie Mitford

I first delivered stone for the quarry and then started to drive for Willy Robson. The lorry was hired out to the council. I used to pick a gang up for the Council. After that I led out of the quarry, down to Newcastle, Durham, Middlesbrough, and places to council depots. I never did long distance – I was always home at night. Then we went on to agricultural lime, leading to the farms. We used to go to Ayr and Perth with lime and bring fertiliser back.

Cafes

Doris Clarke

To go back to when I worked at Willie Robson's, they built that little shop for sweets and ice cream, adjacent to the garage, where the Bark Pots is now. This day auntie was in the shop and I was in the office and she shouted for me to go in. There were 2 ladies who had missed the bus and they had a couple of hours to wait. They weren't young. She said was there any way of making a cup of tea for them. I had all the makings in the office, so I said just tea in a mug. So I made it and took it into them, and was stood talking to them, and that's how the Bark Pots was started.

They bought these wooden tables and benches to put outside and it was all right if it wasn't raining. If it was raining then I had to go over and open the big garage doors, but there was nobody to help really. I was in the office – then I had to make the tea. There was things to buy, but wrapped things, nothing cooked. When we did start selling teas, Nancy Grey used to make the scones, but it was just in the old garage. Peter Browell used to come and drape the roof with a herring net, and put some floats in. Then he got some old photographs enlarged, he had a wonderful selection. Michael used to have them around the new Bark Pots.

Mike Robson

There was the Choughs Tea Room and Shell Museum. Barbara (Dawson) used to ring across to the Bark Pots just before Easter and ask if we were open on Good Friday and we said it might be Saturday before we got open and she said 'well if you're not opening, I'm not, there'll be a lot of visitors here this weekend and I don't want them all.' They used to go into tea room and Barbara would say 'yes?' and they would sit down and she would say 'you can't sit at that table you must sit at this table.' They would get the menu and ask for two cups of coffee. 'Which cream cake would you like?' If they didn't want cake she would say 'you can't have a cup of coffee if you don't have a cake.' She dictated everything – where they sat and what they ate.

Christopher (Dawson, her brother) had the shell museum and he used go away in the wintertime and collect the shells, come back and make these little ornaments with them. He used to look out of the window and if a lot of people were coming into the café downstairs and nobody was coming up to his shell museum, he used to sneak downstairs and lock the door to the café, so everybody came in to look at his shells and then he would sneak back down again and open it. Barbara used to say 'we've had no customers today at all .' Christopher had them all up the stairs. In the springtime, he used to go away in the mornings to make his little ornaments and Mattie Stephenson worked for Tom Archbold, the joiner and they were coming along past the bushes at Howick and they saw Christopher's car parked and he was lying in a little sandy bay with no clothes on sunbathing. Mattie said that they got a spade out of the back of the van and cut a big clod of grass and threw it down on top of him and ran away.

Fred Stephenson

They were the first one's to have a café. Christopher used to go all over the world to get the shells. He had a brand new Mini traveller, a beautiful little car and he went away and he must have filled it with shells off the beach and they had flesh in and he brought it back and it was stinking. It was a right hot summer's day. It was health hazard. It was minging, mind. Old Percy Makepeace, he was a bit of a nosey devil. He always wanted to know the far end of this and that. He was retired, but he used to come into the garage. As I say, it was a right hot day and I says to Percy, 'jump in that car and put your foot on the brake.' I shut the door and he couldn't get out and it was stinking, like. That was a laugh.

National Trust

Doris Clarke

In my time I've worked with the National Trust, which was very interesting. That was in the quarry. Winnie got me the job, because she knew she would have to go into hospital. The Trust didn't want the responsibility of the toilets, so the council does that, and the information bureau is through the council. I wrote a couple of times for a job and we were there for the opening. It was opened for 3 or 4 months before it was officially opened. I enjoyed that very much. Avril Ions shared the work, three and a half days a week. I worked Saturday, Sunday and Monday and Friday afternoons. I got less work until I was only working Sunday's which was fine, good pay. Then I had that disc trouble in my back and I couldn't stand, so I had to come out. They've got computers now, which would be no good for me.

Taking in visitors

Joan Angus

There was no such thing as tourism in those days, there was no car park. They talked about taking in visitors, not bed and breakfast. Some of the residents of Craster had huts and they used to live in the huts and let their houses.

Winnie Hogg

Visitors came for a week or a fortnight and many came year after year. You got to know them. Now they come for the day in cars and you can walk through the village now and often you don't expect to see anybody you know.

Most people took visitors. My Aunt Bella took visitors, cos she wasn't married, and she took visitors all summer. She also went to the herring. When my grandmother was alive, she would go to the herring then, but afterwards when she had the visitors, she didn't go, and she had the same ones came every year. Some came from Yorkshire and they had a fortnight with my aunt every year. Then she had some people who used to cycle here from Newcastle, a husband and wife. They came originally when they were courting, and then when they got married they still came. They used to come to Craster years after, but then they came in a car.

Marjorie Lumsden

My father was on the dole, or whatever they called it then, in the 1930's when I was two, and for four years he never worked. Then he got a job in 1936, at Greenheads, the quarries. My mother had a lot of special visitors. There was one family, whose grandson is now retired to Lesbury - Atkinsons. Now they owned the Nielsen Andersen shipping line, and they used to come for six weeks when the school holidays were on, the grandmother, the mother, not the father 'cos he was at work, and the three children. They still come and see me, the children.

One night there was a dance in the Reading Room, which was a big do. I was only 13. Rosemary, the daughter and I were the same age. She asked her grandmother if she could go to the dance. My mother said you can both go if you come home by half past ten before the pub comes out. So we were allowed to go to the dance. There was a thunderstorm and all the electric was off in the village. We had a toilet on the north side, outside in the yard. So Rosemary and I sat in the toilet, from about half past eight, and cried because we couldn't go to the dance. There were no lights on and we couldn't go to the dance, and she still remembers that yet. The disappointment was awful. It was in the summer, but we still couldn't go.

Willie Mitford

Vera used to do bed and breakfast, we had a lot of nice people and made at lot of friends. We have a friend in Newcastle who is like part of the family now, she came and stayed when she was a toddler, her mother and father used to stay with my mother and they came for years and when my mother died they came to stay with us. There were two girls, one is dead now and we keep in touch with the other one. The same people came every year. In those days people used to stay for a week or a fortnight, it's not like now where they just come for one or two nights. They used to come by train in those days and get off at Little Mill. Some used to come by taxi from Newcastle.

Little Mill Station.

Doris Clarke

My mother and Granny Shell were cousins, and my father wouldn't go anywhere else for his holidays but Craster. We lived in Gateshead, actually before that we lived in Tyne Dock in South Shields, and my father used to send the case, advanced luggage, to Little Mill. Then we came up on the train perhaps a couple of days later, and the luggage had been delivered. We had to walk down from Little Mill. Who would collect the luggage? It was Lena Shell's nephew, who lived at Boulmer. He worked for the railway and he was the one, they called him Alec Rough, he used to drive a wagon and deliver all sorts. The case would be here when we arrived. We had to walk from Little Mill, about 3 miles, which was fine when it was a fine day.

Chapter 4   Quarrying and Pipe – making

Loading whinstone blocks onto lighters at the north pier.

Joan Angus

There were three quarries in close connection to the village. Two were sandstone and in the present car park was a Whinstone Quarry. The stone was crushed in a huge crusher, with great amounts of grey dust issuing forth when the crusher was used. Everything was covered in this grey material. The stone was then conveyed on a pulley system, to the South Pier bins, for export to London and other places. Huge blocks of Whinstone were also sent by large barge like boats from the North Pier. Whinstone sets for kerbs were also made by hand. My grandfather was a kerb dresser. The whinstone had to be hit in the correct place to split it. It is a very hard stone. The first quarrying recorded was 1772. Daniel Craster advertised in the London Courant for quarry workers for Craster Quarry. Craster Quarry was reopened about 1941, to provide stone for Airfield runways.

Jimmy Hall

Craster Quarry was closed before the war and it was opened again by a firm called Kings & Co. of Glasgow and then when Boulmer and Brunton aerodromes were built, they were fetching stone out of the quarry for the runways and they started blasting back again. In those days you could walk into the quarry and walk straight up to the top – there must have been 100,000 tons of dust. Dust was a waste commodity, you couldn't tar stone with dust on it, you had to get it clean to get the old gas tar off – that came from the making of coke in Newcastle. When I first went to the quarry they were using gas tar and then they started to get bitumen. You could sit in the clothes you're wearing now, it was ultra modern and it was 24 volts controlling 440 volt in the plant, so the whole panel was 24 volt. You just pressed buttons. In the old days, you pulled the tar, you tipped the tar in among the stone and all that sort of things, but then it became modern.

Quarrying Processes

Billy Lumsden

The quarry you know, my father in law told me that when he worked in that quarry up there, when they used to have the wire systems down to load the boats at the harbour, sometimes they would come at night and say we'll start at 7 in the morning, and if the boat was loaded by half past 10 they were finished.

The Whinstone Crusher.

Jimmy Hall

When I was 17, I started to drive for Robsons. During this time Craster Quarry was working. My father loaded the boats 'cause they came here from Beadnell because they weren't making money at the sea. They were catching 100 stone of crabs but they just couldn't sell them. That's one of the things that should have been kept – the engine and things that were in that quarry – where they went, I don't know. When it first started they had a big 2-cylinder diesel engine. They put a tar plant in after that, making tarmacadam and that was run with a diesel engine.

The quarry was quite interesting. They used to bring a ship in and it would go out on the same tide – they got about 450 tons. You couldn't see the North Side for all these chutes and the stone and the dust – it must have been terrible over there when it was windy. When the sea came in they had to have their bins full, for weight.

There must have been about 1000 tons sitting on that piece on the end of the pier. There were big wooden bins, which were taken down during the war for salvage – not knocked down, taken down piece by piece. When you were coming in from sea, you saw the bins long before you saw Craster.

Willie Mitford

The Quarry here was worked by McLaren then Crow Catchpole took it over and then it was closed and then Kings came in the wartime to get stone for the aerodromes, – they were a Scottish company. I went back to the quarry on piecework, breaking stone with the hammer, for l/6d. a ton. You had to break it up and fill a tub and take it down to the crusher – you worked in twos – I worked with Chris Breeze. Sometimes you filled lorries, which was easier than riding the tubs out and coming back again, that took time. We were making good money compared to what other men were making – if you made £12 a week in those days, you were making good money. I packed it in to start driving for £5.10s, but I wanted to get out on the road.

You had two hammers a 'slogger' and a 'mell.' The 'mell' had a round end and a sharp end, to cut a big stone. The 'slogger' had a sharp square and you cut sideways on – you had to know how to hit it. The stone had to be reduced to about nine inches to be able to get through the crusher. If you were cutting them for setts, they had to be cut specially by experienced 'knockers up.' Unbelievably in some parts of the quarry, the stone was harder than others – the south side of Howick quarry the stone was like cutting cheese, but it took a lot of breaking at the other side, coarser stone altogether. Whinstone is the toughest stone you can get.

One of the things in my lifetime, when I first went to the quarry, they had people that made setts, kerbs and things like that – you had to get big stone for that. They didn't have to have stone which had been burned by a very high explosive. The idea of doing that was – drill a hole, put gunpowder in, put a small shot in and what they used to call 'shake it.' When these shots were shook, then they would pour gunpowder down the back and drill the hole, that took quite a bit of doing, that was so they got stone that wasn't burnt.

Jimmy Hall

Later on the process of making kerbs out of concrete came, so what they wanted after that was a big hole which was four and a half inches, put a great load of gelignite down it and blow the whole lot straight over, 4,000 tons. All the stone – to start with – was hand drilled, a bloke melled it and knocked it up. He would knock up more than 20 ton a day. When I finished at the quarry there were no men there at all. We just blasted and used what we called 'plasters' – these were designed to fire to the hard, didn't blow away from the rock, blows towards it, and then after that there was demonstration blasting and I was at one of them and they called the bloke Hindley and I came in with a wagon and I had to take the explosive up for that bloke – the wagon body was half full of explosives. He wired this and explained to me that it was going to be one blast with a split second behind the other one, so it went in a shock right down the face and they got about 4,000 – 5,000 tons out at one time. What they did they blew the bottom out and the top dropped down the back.

Billy Lumsden

Luke Robson, Alan's father, had 2 wagons then, tipper wagons he used at the quarry, of course. I suppose there would be a lot of work for them when they made all these runways and suchlike along at Tughall and there was another one at Boulmer that they made. They were only for aircraft that were more or less in distress, somewhere for them to land if they were badly shot up.

Jimmy Hall

I went to the Northumberland Whinstone Co., from Robsons, in 1953, when the Quarry closed. It was very difficult to serve your time during the war – there was never any demarcation at the quarry, if there had been, we would never have got on in the future. I did everything there. I did the electrics there, everything from tar tanks, to putting new plant in and everything. It was all inspected. It stood me in good stead for the future. There was a different electrical system in the quarry.

I was driving a truck and one of the fitters hurt his hand and was off work and the gaffer asked if I would go to the garage for a little bit, so I did that, but someone else was driving my truck and I didn't like that 'cause they didn't clean it out. So I stayed in the garage – the old fellow came back, now he was a steam man so we were working on big diesels, it was very interesting. You see – if you are going to light a little fire to do something, a lot of people light a little fire and then they put coal on. Well you don't do that, you get all the coal and everything on there, because once you put coal on, you cool the fire down. That steams the boiler – you have all the vents set. I've never driven a wagon with a heater in.

Billy Lumsden

Basil Trail used to go around in a Rolls Royce, he lived over yon side. BT1 was the number. It was worth about £60,000, the number plate. He was sitting in the pub this Sunday. 'Oh yes' he said, 'hard work never killed anyone.' 'That's right Basil. The only people it's never killed are b****s like you, because you've never done it. I can tell you of half a dozen men who never retired, because they brayed their guts out in the quarry with a 14 pound hammer.' The next Sunday he says to me, 'I think I owe you an apology.' I said, 'no you don't owe me an apology at all. You see you've been brought up at the other end of the stick. You didn't know. The trouble with you fellows is you don't know you don't know.' I admired him after, mind, for saying that.

They are the same fellows who used to work all day in the quarry, when the war was on, then come home and work on the harvest field till dark at night. (They) used to break stone up with a hammer then, now they pick it up with a machine and feed it into the crusher. They've got secondary crushers now.

Jimmy Hall

There were a lot of people worked in the quarries in those days – there was Howick, Ratcheugh, Craster, Embleton. Embleton quarry had a railway that went to Christon Bank. The men used to go and work on the farms after they had been to work in the quarries. I knew a fellow, William Anderson; he used to come from the quarry every night and he worked for the fish merchant, Tom Grey. Jackie Grey was the joiner and undertaker. It was hard work in the quarries, breaking the stone. I've often said if these lot got time and went to Dartmoor, they would have laughed at that lot. They looked at the stone, it didn't matter how big it was, they could smash it up.

The workers started at half past seven in the morning, had a cup of tea at nine o'clock – a quarter of an hour – then twelve o'clock till half past for dinner, finished at 4.15p.m. All the stone men at this quarry were piece – workers. They worked singly, every man working for himself. When I went to the quarry in 1953, they were producing 300 tons a day and when I finished at the quarry, they had machines and that and were producing into the thousands. They had great big dumpers and that. Everything was weighed prior to that, even the tubs, everybody had a token with their number on and they put the token on the tub, or if there was an old truck leading it up, the drivers got the token when they came back so when it was weighed – they knew exactly whose tubs they were.

Willie Mitford

When I first started work, I worked for 4 pence an hour and when you got to fifteen it went up to five pence and it went up a penny an hour until you got to 21 and then you got a full wage, which for a labourer at the quarry, was about £2.10s. A man who broke stone would get about £3. I was working on piecework. If you didn't work hard you didn't make the money. It was a hard life, but you were fit. I always remember Jimmy Turnbull – he used to joke with me – he said that when I first came out of the Army, I had one hip pocket on one side and one on the other side and when I finished knocking up at the quarry, he said them two pockets were overlapping, as I'd lost such a lot of weight.

The Pipeworks

Eleanor Venus

We met in 1949 and were married in 1952 in Embleton Church. Ken travelled for a while 'cause he worked at the Ministry at Benton. He used to come for weekends when we were courting and he didn't want to stay in an inside job. He went to the Labour Exchange and all they could offer him was the Pipeworks at Littlehoughton and he worked there for 38 years. Trollope and Colls owned the Pipeworks then.

The first day at work he missed the bus home and he walked home and he wasn't used to wearing boots. He used to go down to the sea and put his hands and feet in. He worked from half past seven in the morning till four o'clock with just Sunday off.

Billy Lumsden

Angus Lowerson came (to Dunstan Square) in 1948; he's still there. He's 80 odd now. He went to work in the pipeworks. He says, 'I worked there 35 years and I hated every minute of it.' I wouldn't have liked to have spent my working life some place where I didn't want to be.

Ken Venus

The pipes were used mostly for drainage and sewerage. I was a charge-hand, then I was a crane driver for a while, then I was an inspector. Every pipe that went out had to be stamped. Mr. Pickup had been the manager and then Mr. Foot came – he was a Scotsman, he lived at Embleton. Ian Shiel took over after that, his father was the Coastguard. I was just a general dogs-body when I finished. I lost interest as I got older. They make pipes now for new estates. Most of the people that worked there lived in Alnwick. It wasn't a good job financially but it was regular work. We got sixpence an hour 'wet pay' 'cause you couldn't work properly when it snowed and the roads were blocked. You had to get the Snow Cat and clear them, rather than claim dole.

Marjorie Lumsden

Winnie left school at 14 and had a job the next week at the Pipeworks at Littlehoughton.

Ada Archbold

Our Winnie was working at the Pipe Works. She was younger than me and was getting twice as much money as I was, which I didn't like, so I said 'get me a job at the Pipe Works,' so she asked and she got me a job. Now what we had to do, was make reinforcements for railway sleepers and you had a frame and you had to set all these bars up – our Winnie was a link maker, she made them all twisted, all these links and we had to thread these links on these bars and then you had to get a pair of wire cutters, put the wire through, twist it round and cut it off. All these links, they used to call them banjos – we used to make about a dozen a day.

There was a railway siding for the Pipe Works, they had two parts. The main part, there was the quarry and then there was another part along at the Pipe Works. They had a little 2 ton crane and they had a big crane at our end and Bob Armstrong from Howick was in charge of that end and he used to call me for Saturday for overtime, but I used to only go in 'cause he used to let me drive the crane and it was on these lines. It was a small crane. I used to have my break with him and the fellows used to pull his leg, thinking he'd getten a young woman, 'cause I was only a teenager. I used to bike to Howick, leave the bike at his house, on a Saturday and get a lift with him.

Chapter 5   Farming

Willy Curry cutting corn with a binder at Howick Scar Farm in the 1930s.

Starting work on farms in the 1940 – 50s

Billy Lumsden (Dunstan Square)

I went to 9 different schools. Whereas the fishermen stayed put, farm people went from farm to farm, till we came here, and I said to my father, 'that's the finish, I've had enough of this.' (So you'd had that since you were a little boy? You'd moved about?) Aye, Aye. It used to bother me when I was a little lad. I used to think that if my father fell out with the farmer, then they would put us out of the house and then where would we go. You get these things into your head when you're a kid. That's why I thought, one day I would have my own house and nobody would be able to put me out. It was my mother that got all the work because some of the houses you went to were filthy. She had them all to clean out and paper, and before you knew where you were, my father was off to another farm. If somebody offered a pair of young horses or another shilling a week, he was away. Mind we had a good father and mother, we never could complain about that. When we came to Rennington, the windows had all been knocked out of the house. Old Jack Dunn, he was the joiner up there, and he had to go and get some board and board them up. The place was filthy. I said to my father, then, that's the finish. Then we came to Dunstan Square and we just stopped there and that's how we are here.

Eleanor Venus (Dunstan Square)

My mother was Emma Ord and she came here (Dunstan Square) in 1944 to do the dairy work. The farmer was Rowell. She did all the dairy work and made 38lbs of butter a month. We only had five cows, shorthorns. Mother milked them all by hand. My father was a cripple, he never worked. Mother had to do the dairy work to get the house they lived in and I worked on the land with a horse and cart – outside work, turnips and that. Then I went into the house and I worked in the house.

Geordie Grey (Craster Village and then West Farm)

After I left school, I helped my father in the Joiner's Shop, because he was the joiner. The reason for that was that my older brother was a joiner, but he was away in the Air Force, so I had to help in the family business. I wasn't cut out to be a joiner, I liked to follow the horses – ploughing – and I wanted to be a farmer.

I started farming when there was only horses, no tractors but during the war, we began to get tractors, supplied by the Ministry and then after the war, the tractors started to come along and it did make life easier. I enjoyed the horses when I was younger, it was more relaxed, there seemed more time to do things but then more machinery took over and there were fewer people on the farms but I would say I'm glad I farmed when I did but with regard to working, they have a doddle today, there's no heavy work like there used to be.

A lifetime in farming

Bill Curry (Howick Scar Farm)

Dad used to keep the little sheep for me, and I used to clip them by hand when I got back from school. I spent all my spare time at the farm. I cannot remember this, but they say when I was very little, about 4 years old, my mother lost me at Howick and couldn't find me. I'd walked all the way from Howick to the Scar; they could just see the little hat coming.

When I left Dunstan, I was 13. I had 2 years to do at Alnwick. We used to travel by bus, we had a pass. At night time there was a bus that used to leave at 10 to 4, and it came back to Little Houghton to the pipe works, 'cos there were a lot of men worked there, about 100 men worked at the pipe works and the quarry then. There was a bus that used to pick them up when they finished at 4, and I used to get the bus back to Little Houghton and run back home from there, so that I could get back to the farm. In the summer nights, it was a good run, about 2 miles. I would get back home about half past four. Sometimes I caught a man from the village with a little Austin 7. He would pick me up and bring me back. I got a quicker start then. I would be on my bike and along to the farm.

I would have something to eat, then I used to drive the horse and cart. I can remember dad drilling and ploughing with the horses. I used to like May time and the harvest time. We used to have a combine and tractor and I can remember when I was about 11 or 12 driving the tractor, cutting the corn. They opened the field out for me first, then I drove the tractor, and grandfather sat on the binder. My dad, Uncle George and Uncle Henry, would put the sheaves to stooking. We did a quick ten acre that day, it was all barley and it was all stooked by the time we had finished at night. It was 8 or 9 o'clock at night. We used to go round and round until we were in the middle where there would be hundreds of rabbits. The rabbits would be flying around, and we used to kill the rabbits, until we had a good heap of them. We always had a good dog for them too. We used to have rabbit pies. My dad would never eat a rabbit, he didn't like them. It was a tremendous life then. We used to stook the barley, and grandda used to do the stacking with my dad. I used to drive the tractor then as well, when we were picking them up. He would throw the stooks up on the trailer with a fork, someone would be loading them on the trailer. Usually, my Uncle Jim was on the trailer. We had a fellow who worked for the Ministry of Pensions in Newcastle, he used to come and stay at the house. He and my grandda were pals, he lived in Lemington, and he came every year for the harvest. He would give us a hand and sometimes drive the tractor. Now it is a doddle.

There wasn't the acreage of corn in them days; we maybe had three fields of corn, 30 acres or so. We used to grow 10 acres of turnips in those days. I never liked picking the tatties. I remember when I left school, the first tattie picking I went to, I got a right sick'ner the first day. I said to my grandda I'm not coming again. I'm going down to Dennis Dawson and get a job as a joiner. He says come here, and he gave me a half a crown, now come back tomorrow. I did go back. I've loved farming all my life. I like sheep.

In 1958 when I was 17, I went to Kirkley Hall [Agricultural College], I got a scholarship, and I went there for 9 months to learn how to farm. It broadened your outlook. We stayed there, only once a month were we allowed home. There were 23 lads and 6 lasses there. I still see the odd ones. I finished there, then came back and got a job in Thropton. I was only there a month. There was nothing wrong with the people, his wife was a nice woman, and I suppose he was quite canny. We had to go to thresh corn this day. Me and this fellow who worked for him, Jack Ainsley they called this bloke, he said, 'you go on the stack and throw the sheaves.' They had this stack, crikes you could have had a game of football on it, it was that big. There was me and the old boy went on the top of this stack, and of course when you're standing on the top it was easy to throw them on the thresher. We got down to what they call the easing; they build it square at the bottom and then taper it off at the top, so the water drains off. When we got to there he took a bad turn, and remember I was only 18 years old, and they left me to throw the rest of the sheaves onto this thresher. Well I was absolutely knackered, and by that time it was about 4 o'clock and we went in to have our tea. Then we went back to Thropton and had to feed the cattle in the dark. His son had never bothered his backside. I just got fed up with it. I was only there for a month or six weeks.

I came back home for a little. There was plenty of work, but there was no money. My grandda died when I was 16, and we'd moved from Howick to Scar (Farm) in 1957 – there was still my dad and his two brothers working on the farm. It was only a little farm, so I had to find another job.

There was one came up at Felton, and that was an experience and a half. I don't know how I stuck that. You got rice every day for one thing, for your pudding, every day. You talk about living rough, but that was something else. The kitchen table – on the end of the table was everything, from putting stuff on cows' udders, to sheep dip and disinfectant. God knows what else, and you had your meals at the other end. It was pretty rough. There wasn't a sink to wash yourself, just some bricks and stone trough and an old tap. It was pretty grim, but I stuck that for nearly two years. She used to get a thorn, you know a big tree, maybe six feet long, and used to stick it up the chimney. It was a big fireplace.

The milk used to be put in cans, and a wagon used to come every day for the cans, and there were these ten-gallon cans of milk with big handles on. Churns they used to call them, and you'd lift them up, they were a tremendous weight. The bloke on the wagon was far taller than I was and he was up a height and I was down below and I got all the weight. I used to dread it. There was no running water, and we had about 20 odd cows, and we had a pump on the back trailer and a tank on the trailer. We used to go to the well and pump it into the tank and bring it back. We used to do that at least twice a day – horrendous, absolutely horrendous. That was up to 1963.

There was a job came up at Manners, North Farm at Embleton. I applied for the job as a tractor man and got the job. That was grand that, 'cos I could travel every day. My Uncle George got me a car, a van, from the scrap man in Alnwick and he fitted it up – that's my Auntie Violet's husband. It cost £25 this van and I had it for quite a while. He maintained it and kept it running, and looked after it. I used to travel back and forward to North farm, come home for my dinner then back to the farm. We started at 7 o'clock in the morning, then back for dinner at 12. I remember after I'd been there for 6 months, I got a brand new Massey Ferguson tractor 65, and I can see it to this day. Its number was MNL 626. I also got a 4-furrow plough with it, and it was the only 4-furrow plough in the district. People used to come and watch it, and couldn't believe that a tractor could pull 4 furrows in those days. I had grand times on that tractor in those days.

(After further jobs at Preston Mains and Stannington)

In 1978, dad was going to retire, and I'd tried in all ways for him not to retire, and let me come back. He was going to pack it all in, 'cos the farming was getting a bit difficult. He said you're not coming back here to worry like what I have done. I spoke to George Strachan who knew dad, and he said 'you leave it with me and I'll talk to him.' He persuaded dad to carry on and take me back. He said, 'you'll never get another chance – it might not go right, but you've got to give it a go.' I'll never forget him for that. Then in 1977 – I used to go to test matches – I went to the test match in Headingley – red hot summer; Boycott scored his 100th test 100. When I came back from the match that weekend, father said 'I've had George Strachan on the phone; I've decided I'm not going to retire, I'm going to pack in. If you want to – you can come back home.'

Memories of farm work

Eleanor Venus

The stack yard (at Dunstan Square Farm) was filled with hen-houses, up this road were all hen-houses. The hens were free range and put in at night. We had turkeys and geese for Christmas. There were cows, sheep and poultry. Mrs. Rowell was a perfectionist. If she gave you a job you had to do it properly, and of course, at Christmas the poultry had to be dressed, for orders. The Turks Hotel at Rothbury used to buy the dressed poultry. I used to do that.

They made hay, grew barley, oats and turnips. I used to fill and empty eight loads of turnips a day, from the far tree, where the hollow wood is now, with the horse and cart. That was in the autumn and winter, the turnips were for feed. On a Saturday, we used to cut eighty swills to cover the weekend. A swill was a wicker basket.

We had holidays due and we had to finish singling the turnip fields before we could go anywhere. Singling was separating them with a Dutch hoe, push one forward and pull one back, so they've got more room to grow. If we went to the pictures, we always had to put the hens in when we got back, you were never free, there was always something waiting. The cows were milked by hand twice a day. After my mother died the cows were done away with. There was one cow, called Peggy, she was like an Ayrshire with big horns and she knew mother, she was down in this field and nearly put her horns through the porch window 'cause she saw mother in the porch.

Rosemary Gibbs

The Coxons – Jimmy's father and Freddie – they used to put Freddie in with the bull if they wanted the bull to go anywhere. He had such a good relationship with the bull. He had Downs' Syndrome, but he had a wonderful relationship with the animals. Uncle Shafto said that Freddie was playing in the field at the Bogie, with the bull. The bull was chasing him and then the bull would stop and Freddie would turn round and chase the bull, it was a game and if they ever wanted to move the bull, they would send Freddie to do it.

Fetching cattle from the mart

Geordie Grey

When we started in 1944 these were the only buildings that we had, what we called the byre-yard which consisted of a garage at the bottom, for the car and then there was two places there for stables, that was working stables for working horses and then there was just loose boxes, different people kept their horses there. Mr. Abbott the Fish Merchant kept a horse up there. We got the lot from Sir John Craster. We left that as a garage, kept that as a stable, 'cause we still had the horses and then we turned the next one into an 8-stall byre. That left one loose box at the top. At the top end was Scott the Butchers' killing shop, he used to keep the cattle till they were hungered a bit before they killed them. We both had the use of the yard.

The hunger house was at the top end beside the killing shop, where they fetched the cattle from Alnwick. In them days they had to walk them all the way, there were no wagons to fetch them and they kept them in there for at least 24 hours in what we called 'the hunger house.' They didn't get fed, maybe had a drink of water, because their stomachs had to be empty when we killed them. They would kill two or three a week and perhaps ten sheep. The houses were built in the 1980's. By that time I had got the tenancy of half the West Farm, so we shifted the animals up there. That sort of made this redundant. Anyways we were glad to get out, because we couldn't help sometimes making a mess, by fetching the cows to what we called 'the butcher yard' – hoyed them around the corner and into our own yard and shut them off there. You could never stop one or two of them making a mess on the road. Nowadays it wouldn't be allowed. In those days people looked for muck, as nearly everybody had a garden.

I can't remember when it was, but on the way from Alnwick to the killing shops, down through the village, a bullock escaped down to the harbour and swam into the sea and one of the cobles went out and lassoed it and Alf Shell, the butcher, he shot it in the sea, brought it ashore and bled it on the shore, the meat was saved.

The other thing was about the Irish Cattle that used to come to the Alnwick Mart. Again, there wasn't any wagons. My Uncle Tom had the place then and he used to go in with other farmers and would buy a wagon of cattle each and they were all to walk out to the farm. We walked them from Alnwick down here. I was only about 14 when they used to send me out onto the road. The worst was getting them over the railway line at Little Mill. I used to get a bit help there and I used to get a bit help when I come down nearer the farm. They were easy to drive 'cause, poor animals, they were hungry – they used to eat all the way on the grass side, there wasn't the traffic. You really had to drive them. They would never run away from you because they had been on the road and rail for about a week from Ireland. I've known at one time of 800 – 900 cattle in Alnwick Mart on a Friday and they would all get sold round this area, right along the coast here, there's some good feeding land down here and they weren't here very long before they were fat. Mind they were thin when they came – they turned around in no time.

When I started farming, I never had any Irish cattle, 'cause I went into milk cows. My Uncle Tom, he would buy a wagon which would be about 12 – 14 maybe, that was as many cattle as you could carry, 'cause we just had 40 acre. He used to summer those Irish cattle.

We couldn't live on 40 acres now, unless you were a market garden, but not ordinary farming. Now my two sons have the place and they have about 600 acres. That's what you need nowadays.

Seasonal farm workers

Billy Lumsden

When I was on the farm then, all the men who used to work in the quarry came to help us on the farm at night. I diven't knaa how they did it, 'cos it was heavy work then.

There was very little machinery in the quarries that particular time. They used to come to do seasonal work, at night. They used to help us at harvest time. I've seen them sit down to have their tea, and fall asleep, they were that tired. We used to get extra rations on the farm for the harvest, which only amounted to maybe, well me and my father worked up there, and you maybe got four ounces of margarine or another half a pound of sugar or something like that. Oh yes, cheese was the thing, you could get so many ounces of cheese. That was a week like, you knaa, when the war was on.

Teatime during haymaking at Howick Scar Farm in the 1930s

Geordie Grey

We used to get three or four women from the village and they would pull the bagies in the winter and before that was tattie picking time and we used to get the same women to pick the tatties and also a few school kids and we had some hilarious days. Other than that, the big day was the threshing day, when the threshing machine came in and each farm did two days threshing and that was really hard work. The corn, oats and barley were stacked and then threshed in the winter. It was all to cut with the binder, to stook, to lead, to stack and then it stood till winter when the threshing machine came.

We had no turkeys, but the women, I hope they don't mind me calling them the gang of women, used to go to the North Farm at Manners. He had a lot of turkeys and they used to pluck them by hand for Christmas. They had a good few days plucking turkeys.

Doris Clarke

I'll tell you a little anecdote about when I lived up at the square (1950s.) We lived there rent free, because if you took rent you had rental rights as a tenant, which we didn't. I was expected to work on the farm. Well, I had come straight from the office, and I hadn't a clue. Do you remember Nellie Butters, George Butters, his wife, and she was from Glasgow. She had a great sense of humour. You worked in pairs picking potatoes, tattie picking. This was on the farm at Dunstan.

The first morning I went out, I had my gloves on and my lipstick. What a laugh. It wasn't a very nice year to be picking tatties, that year, 'cos it had been very wet and they had gone boss – they were blue. It was awful 'cos they were all squashy. I was glad I had my gloves on. The second day, I couldn't get out of bed. I didn't know what had hit me. I couldn't move. It was very heavy work, and all stooping. I can remember the tractor coming from Long Bank Farm with all the ladies on the trailer. Well the same thing used to happen for the snowdrop pickers in the woods at Howick, and daffodils. They took them to the markets, but they had to be tied up in little bunches, and put into baskets. That was hard on the knees. Betty Williams and Doris used to go, and Sybil. That was seasonal work, with the potatoes at the back end.

Any amount of food in the war years

Billy Lumsden

There was any amount (of food in the war years.) On the farms you were allowed to keep two pigs, but you had to give in your bacon coupons, and you were allowed to keep two. Well we always had two. We used to kill them and salt them down. (How long did you keep the pigs before you killed them?) Normally they would be about 16 stones weight. You went by the weight of them. The sheds there, some people used to take them there to be salted, and they salted them in a sort of a barrel – put them in the brine – whereas, we didn't do that. My grandfather used to cure ours, and the sides of the bacon. He used to rub them with salt until they sweated. Then you laid them on straw, on about a foot of straw, so they could drain away. They lay there for about a fortnight. The hams and suchlike, well they used to have to get into the joint and put saltpetre and sugar. That used to cure them. By, it was lovely stuff, man. When you had it, it was about a quarter of an inch thick. There was none of this white froth floating around the pan then, like you get now. I don't know what they do with it.

We used to live like lords. There were about 6 houses up in the square, and for about a fortnight, we had spare ribs, and pig's cheek. We used everything. The only thing we didn't use was its squeal. My granny used to make the black pudding and whatnot. She bled the pig. You had to keep stirring it, like, to stop it clotting, and she used to put these little squares of fat in it, and mint or sometimes a little bit of sage. She made white pudding with the lungs. Everything was used, nothing was wasted. We used to come in for our dinner at 12 o'clock and, of course, we had the sheer legs set up ready to hoist it up on. Everybody had the boilers going in the wash houses, so you got any amount of water. The butcher used to come from Embleton, and the pig was killed, scalded, hung up and finished and we were back at work at 1 o'clock. Aye, everybody lived well on the pig, sausage and everything. Mind something I couldn't stick was pig's trotters. I could never fancy them. I like pig's cheek mind, cos we used to salt it the same way as we used to salt the bacon, but it was only in a few days.

Eleanor Venus

There was always a guffy sty, which was mine. I remember, Ken was off work, he had hurt his back. We used to give mother £5 a week board, and he was off three weeks and we had no money, so we sent the guffy away and we got £15 and gave it to mother for the board. The postman was Eva then, and we got the money from the Ministry of Agriculture then and she used to know what was in the envelope when she delivered it.

Joyce Shaw

My granny had hens and a pig, everybody used to have hens and a pig. One New Year my father, wasn't a boy at that time, he was a man, and he blackleaded somebody's pigs. I think it was for a dare. My granny had her last pig in 1943. My grandfather died in that year and she had no more after that, she was then 78 and she lived until she was 85.

Billy Lumsden

You know where I've got my allotment, up on what they used to call the tattie grounds. I just heard what they told me, that every house along the front had a strip of land which was eight drills wide, which was approximately 16 feet. It used to be marked with stones, and they used to whitewash them. Sometimes there used to be hell on, because some people used to shift the stones. They used to have deeds for that, I've got them, but they are at the solicitors, I've got my 'rocks' in a copy of the deeds as a north side owner, now (I'm sure he would let you have them to photocopy them.) Well he's got them, 'cos they are just a copy of the deeds. The squire at one time used to send the horses down to plough it for them, because they lived off that. They used to have potatoes and whatever they had. At that time there was no dole, and they lived on salt fish. They salted a lot of fish away, the herring and things like that, because if they couldn't get to the sea, well that was what they lived on. There was nothing easy.

Memories of Farm Dogs

Geordie Grey

To be farming with sheep and cattle, you've got to have a sheepdog. To my mind that's the only breed of dog there is – a collie dog. He's wise, he's very helpful and he's faithful. There's other dogs, but it never come across to me to have any other but the collie. One of the reasons I had him was, he used to work for us and help us, so you really need a collie dog. He was a great friend. We've had two or three in our time and it's grand to see a collie working the sheep. In my opinion, there is no doubt about it, they are the most intelligent dogs. They know what you are talking about. We never had trial dogs, we had working dogs. We only had one dog at a time, when one was getting older we used to get a young one to take over. A young dog never runs when the old one's there, the old one wouldn't allow it.

Eleanor Venus

We always had dogs – one called Rusty – a wonderful Lakeland Terrier. She use to go round the henhouses with me at night and she used to go round and round and if she went to the next one, you knew they were all in and if she didn't leave that henhouse, you knew there was still a hen out. She was a good ratter. We had calf pens and she was just a puppy, there was a rat's nest and she went in and a rat got her by the top lip and I didn't know what to do and she shook it and got it and there was never another one. We used to have the incubators up in the granary, for the young turkeys and we would go up at night and put the light on – the rats ran across the granary floor and Rusty would go up and she left dead ones all over. Once she had finished, she would go over them again until there was nothing left but the skin.

...and a horse

Eddie Grey

Geordie Grey's horse was called Dolly. I wasn't very old then. He used to take it up to the Turn Field or the Windmill Field and he used to bring her down and I used to ride on her back and she would come to the trough down by where Clippie had his hut. When she put her head down to drink, I thought I would slide down her neck into the trough. I wasn't very old then, about four or five. She could turn the tap on with her mouth for a drink. But she couldn't turn it off.

I can remember following Geordie with the plough and I used to pick all the worms up and put them in my pockets.

Carol Grey

Dolly was originally our grandfather's horse. He had two shire horses, Dolly and Bonny. He used to take them from the stable yard down to the tap trough, which had been installed near where the bus stop is now. As Eddie says, after they had been watered, granddad used to bring them to the kitchen window at the bottom house in Church Street. Barbara, Eddie and I used to stand on the kitchen window sill and feed the horses with apples before they were returned to the stable. I can still smell that horsey smell.

The farms surrounding the village are Dunstan Square, Proctor's Stead and Dunstan Hill to the north, Howick Scar Farm and Craster South Farm to the south, and Craster West Farm to the west.

Chapter 6   A Place to Live

Joan Angus (written notes)

Until the late 18th century, Craster village was still at the top of the hill, immediately north and east of Craster Tower. A map of 1723 shows an E – W road running straight down the bank next to the Tower, with 12 houses in 2 rows on each side of it, still to be seen in the pasture. The present road did not exist and there was nothing by the sea apart from the little cove where the fishing boats were beached.

The exact date of the exodus down to the haven is uncertain, probably about 1800. The haven was a natural harbour with two limestone islets (Muckle Carr and Little Carr) acting as breakwaters. By 1801 there were nineteen houses in 'Craster Seahouses,' as it was called until 1828. It had a population of 100.

The earliest cottages were along the North side, just above the shore, where the present gardens are now situated. Rateable value was one shilling and sixpence (1/6) in the pound. An old plan shows two cottages on West End and four on Dunstanburgh Road. The summer house on the South side is dated 1769, and was used as a picnic venue, and bathing cottage for the Craster family. I believe that this cottage is the oldest in Craster, albeit completely refurbished.

The village was naturally divided into the north and south side by a stream known as Craster Letch.

In 1906 the piers were built in memory of Captain Craster, killed on active service in India. As well as fishing,

Craster also developed a prosperous quarrying business, shipping stone by sea on lighters to be taken to London and Roker Pier. The stone was taken down from the quarry by an overhead rail system of wires and buckets, which were tipped into bins on top of the South Pier. These bins were taken down at the beginning of the Second World War, as they thought they could be used as landmarks for enemy planes.

South Side

Joan Angus

Other early buildings were – The Jolly Fisherman, Coquet View (1860,) the Old Square or Curtain, as it was called (1822,) Church Street, Coastguard Cottages (1870,) and the Reservoir (1820.) The gardens for the Old Square were situated where Robson's fish yard is today. There is in the middle of the present yard a well, completely covered up now. At this time, the most common family names were Archbold, Stanton, Smailes, Simpson and Grey. The old Square, built entirely in whinstone, was demolished in 1962 and rebuilt with modern houses. There were no flush toilets before that date in that area. Hence the chute below the shop.

Most of the houses just had one room, that's why babies had cradles, so the mother could rock the cradle with her foot, whilst baiting the lines. The women worked very hard and lived in a damp atmosphere all the time, their men came in wet and there was no means of drying, consequently the women didn't live very long. If they weren't working most of them were knitting. They knitted all their own gansies.

Jimmy Shaw (extract from house deeds)

There were formerly 14 houses in that part of 'The Curtain' which was on the site now occupied by seven houses on Whin Hill (no's 6, 8 ,10, 12, 14, 16and 16a.) In 1934, the tenants of those former houses in the 'The Curtain' were: 12 W Seager; 13 Mrs W Archbold; 14 Mrs J Robson; 15 T Straughan; 16 R & J Archbold; 17 J W Sheehan; 18 J Simpson; 19 Mrs W Grey; 20 A Straughan (snr); 21 Charles Vaughan; 22 J Carss; 23 T Grey; 24 Mrs Simpson; 25 Mrs J Hall.

Top right is 'Craster Curtain.' The huts in the foreground were known as the 'Black Huts.'

Adam Dawson

Now before my time, Craster had street lighting. There were cages on the corners of the buildings, where they used to put an oil-light in to show the fisherman the way down to the harbour in the wintertime. I didn't know that, but the relics were still there when I was going to school about 1910. They were like wooden cages with a light in, paraffin lights.

As time went on, we had a Dr. Jackson who came from Alnwick. Now Craster was in a bit of a state, and this doctor cleaned it up, starting with shells, mussel shells and everything, and he put Craster in a nice state. He cleaned it up, no pig sties, no pigs, no nothing, 'cos I mean then Craster was getting on its feet

The houses in Craster were all whinstone that was from the local quarry round about. There was no water in the houses, it came from a reservoir on top of a hill, there was a spring that used to fill this reservoir, but we used to be very, very careful with the water. We never used it for washing. Outside every house in Craster there was a barrel we used to have for washing the clothes and everything. We used to use rain water which was pure and clean. Everybody in Craster had a wash-house outside, there used to be a steel pot – they used to fill that with rain water. Now underneath that we used to use coal and sticks to make a fire to boil the water. That was how we used to wash our clothes.

To dry our clothes we used to hang them out in the gardens or on the bushes or anything. Everything was that clean; nothing was dirty. That was how we used to get them dry in the summertime. In the houses there were racks to dry the clothes in the wintertime, that's where we used to hang them up and the heat from the fires, coal fires used to dry the clothes.

Winnie Hogg

If it was a day when they weren't at the sea, my mother used to wash. Now that was another big job. We had a wash house. The night before they used to have a pot, which had to be lit early on to heat the water. From there the water was put into a big red barrel and then the clothes were put in and possed up and down. They were scrubbed, rinsed, put through a wringer, and put on the bushes, or a line up the top of the hills. At that particular time I put my thumb in the wringer, when I was small, and lost the end of my thumb and had to be stitched. My mother had to bake twice a week. All this was done with no electricity, no vacuum cleaners, no washing machine or anything like that which could help you. I never realized until I was married and had some of these chores to do, how hard my mother had worked.

At the Square the houses were in a square. The numbers were on the doors, the buckets over the 'shut.' The floors were cement. My Aunt Bella's toilet was so clean that you could eat your food out of it – she had all these things for pouring down, I think most people did. The upstairs had originally been lofts for the nets and everything, eventually they were made into two bedrooms – there was a ladder to get up. One of their walls was actually made of sailcloth. The floorboards were creaky. This was about 1927 – 28.

Gladys lived in Chapel Row and the man who owned the house wanted to sell it for £250 and her mother had four children and they couldn't afford to buy it. They moved into McLarens' house in the Square. It had two bedrooms, three rooms downstairs, kitchen, big sitting room and a parlour, which mother and father used as a bedroom. There were four daughters, so we shared bedrooms. There was an outside toilet, we had to carry buckets from the communal tap, did the washing in a poss-tub. We had a toilet on the hill and it blew away. There was no electricity at all and when my Dad got the electric in he said 'if I see any of it wasted, if you don't turn it off, we will get it took out.' We were that pleased that we had got these lights that we made sure we shut them off. We would go to peoples' houses and if they had the lights on, I would switch them off. If you wanted a good wash, you had to jump into the sea. My granny on the North Side had a flush toilet and we used to go there if we could manage it.

There were toilets over the hill, behind the kipper yards at the bottom sheds. One night it blew down in a gale, so we had to get Johnny Grey at the joiner's shop. He came up with Dennis to mend the toilet. As soon as he came in he said, 'Put the kettle on Winnie. I want a cup of tea first before we start on the toilet.' It was a box toilet; an outside closet. They were terrible. They were nearly all painted in what was called 'netty' pink. They all seemed to be that pink. Inside they were a deep pink and they smelled atrocious. They used to put down some sort of disinfectant, some sort of powder. They used to empty them at night. They used to put them down some sort of chute. We used to have a nail with newspaper on for toilet paper. It was the time when they published 'Lady Chatterley's Lover' and I was desperate to read it. My mother says you're not to read that mind. I was supposed to cut the paper up on a Sunday, and put them on the big needle thing. I was trying to keep this page with the story 'cos it was continued every week.

Doris Clarke

The bottom row was built in 1933 and that is Heugh Road. The Breezes' row was built in the 1920's, they are built of stone. That was the original row. We've got the board in our house that tells when they were built – it was on the inside of a cupboard door – it was a made by a foreman joiner.

Joan Angus

In 1947 there were:

> two grocery shops. E. A. Grey and G. W. Nelson;
> an off license (Forest);
> a butchers shop (Scotts);
> a hut that sold dressed crabs (Norris);
> a market garden (Baxter);
> two Herring Yards. T. S. Grey and L. Robson;
> two Sunday schools, C of E and Methodist;
> and at least 2 church services on Sundays.
> There were at least 6 cobles at this time and a taxi service to Little Mill Station and Alnwick. There were only 4 cars in the village at this date.

Adam Dawson

Now South Craster, it was owned by the Squire, all them houses there was owned by the Squire and they used to pay rent, the fishermen.

Winnie Hogg

I got married in 1949 and lived in the Square. We moved in with my mother. Later we moved into the house next door to this one and my mother lived in this one. The last man to leave the Square was Billy Simpson and, do you know what, he said, 'I'm not moving along to the old age pensioners' houses, I'll be carried out' and they found him dead in the house.

At the top of the Church Street are the Reading Room (right) and the Church of St Peter the Fisherman (left.)

North Side

Willie Archbold

I was born on the North Side, 3 West End, at my granny's, but when I was six months old, I come over to the South Side and I come over to the Square. We lived at No. 25 and faced the north, the Castle. It was right above the herring yards. There was five houses faced the north and two or three across the top and others down the side. I lived there from December 1935 till I came out in June, 1954 and when we came out there was no water in the house, we had earth closets. We put the electric light in ourselves, but the house next door never had electric in and it was still without electric till 1960 and he was found dead in the house. They called him Willy Simpson and I was an under-bearer for him. That was the last house that never had electric in.

There was a tap for seven houses and we had a barrel outside to catch the rainwater. There was a table alongside it and we used to wash with the rainwater. In the 1947 snow storm, the houses had slate roots with no felt underneath, it was a terrible storm that year and the snow came into the lofts and we had to go up and clear it out but that was an exceptional year, other years were OK.

Adam Dawson

All the houses on the North side, which was the posh area, were fishermen – they belonged to fishermen, and me granny's house, which is now called Coble Cottage, years ago cost a hundred pounds to build, which in them days was a lot of money – she was a Smailes, her name was Jane Smailes before she was married. Now me grandfather's name was Dawson, Edward Dawson, he lived till he was 84. Me granny lived until she was 88.

Billy Lumsden

The Sutherlands owned land in the village. The north side belonged to the Earl of Tankerville. Marjorie has got the Deeds – they were given to all the tenants. At first it was leasehold and he let the fishermen build 14 houses, but after they'd had a bad winter or something happened and they hadn't a lot of money, he gave them the freehold and he also gave them a third of an acre to go with the house, so that they could produce food to feed their families.

They had a thing called the 'north side owners,' which now I think is defunct, because all the records have been lost. If you had the land, you had half a vote, these north side owners. If you had a strip of land with your house, it was worth half a vote. I think all that has gone by the board now.

Joyce Shaw

The main influx of people into the village, prior to 1939, would be possibly, the coastguards. They came from places like, Plymouth and they would be here for a while and then gone. The other influence would be hiring's, the farm people, but there again they would probably only be coming in from a radius of 20 to 30 miles.

Moving in

Billy Lumsden

I wouldn't like to live any where else. It was a good place to bring a family up. I wouldn't like to live anywhere else. I've gotten on well there. This thing where they say you're an interloper, well I think it's just the way you think, because I've never felt an interloper. (Moved into the village in 1950)

Willie Mitford

I was born in Morpeth, I came to live in Craster when I was about 2-year old because my mother belonged to Craster, she was a Robson, my grandfather started the kipper business. My father was a Morpeth man. We came here during the Miners' strike (1926,) my father was a miner and we came here and he got a job in the quarry, with McLaren.

Early Deaths

Joyce Shaw

Apparently (many) people died of fever and it's in the Parish records. When I first read it I thought it was Scarlet Fever, but my granny said it was Enteric Fever, caused by the water and my aunt confirmed that and she said that the well was somewhere beside the kipper sheds, just below Michael Doherty's place. Apparently the water was infected because when they got piped water here, there was no more fever. The child mortality rate was high. You can see it in the family trees.

Marjorie Lumsden

Ada's granny lost two daughters within nine months and her husband within a year, with TB. He was 32 and her daughters were twelve and six.

Chapter 7   Childhood and schooldays

Schooldays

Joyce Shaw

I've heard from Eva Archbold – she went to Dunstan School – and she said they got
a visit from the vicar every week, but they also got visits from Mrs. Craster, that was
the Squire's mother and she would come and they all had to stand up and curtsey.

Billy Curry

I went to school in Howick until I was ten. I was born in 1941. I came to the school
in Dunstan after that. The teacher was Mr. Blackburn. The school in Howick was
just for until we were 10. I sat my 11 plus when I was ten, because of the way
my birthday was, you sat it the June or July if I remember rightly. Miss Wilson taught me at Howick. Then
Mrs. Taylor came after that. I failed my 11 plus, of course. We'd been at the farm along there, and we used to
bike from Howick to Dunstan. Then I used to go to the Scar for my dinner. I used to run the messages for Mr.
Blackburn. Old Mrs. Craster used to run the school and what she said was law. She was Rosemary Gibbs' granny.
She was always coming along to the school. Mr. Blackburn used to send her letters, and he used to say, 'Curry,
take that letter to Mrs. Craster and I'll let you away a bit quicker'. He used to let me go at 10 to 12, and she used
to live in the Bogie where Rosemary lives now. Then I would go to Scar and get my dinner and come back again.
My grandparents lived there, my granny died in 1948.

Adam Dawson

I was born 23rd December 1912. I went to Dunstan C of E school aged 5. It was the main school for all the
district – that was as for farmers all around about and the smaller places, smaller than Craster. Now we had a
good school – the teacher was called Mr Trevor. He wasn't the only teacher, there was other ones. There were
2 classrooms. We had some good scholars, we were very, very well educated indeed for our age, but we lost the
school master, he left. Now we had another one called Blackburn, Mr Blackburn, and he took ill one time, he
had to go to the hospital, and we got (what do you call those things Jean,) – relief teacher – got a relief teacher,
he was a young man. Well we took the school off him (laughter) – he had to go of course, 'cos we were a rum lot.
Now we got a woman teacher, she said she would buy us footballs, football shirts and everything, well that suited
us down to the ground. We got on very well with her till Mr Blackburn came back.

We used to walk to Dunstan. There was nothing else, so we used to walk it. Now on very bad days, we used to
get some very rough weather, our mother used to bring us our dinners up to school. We used to have all sorts
at school, we didn't miss nothing, we used to have May Day we used to dance around the May pole with all the
ribbons –we were all dressed up in whites and different sorts of ribbons on, it was lovely. There was a piece of
land outside our school, a good bit of land, and it was common land. Now the gypsies could come and stay on that
land for a few hours, but they had to go at a certain time, cos we used to use the common for football and May
poles all those sorts of sports.

I was a good artist when I was young, schooldays. Of course we used to have exhibitions in different places,
village places. There were flower shows, and the schools used to exhibit the drawings and paintings, and one
season I won the lot at Howick flower show. When I left school, the teacher said to me, don't bury your talent, but
I did. When my nephew went to school in them days, my paintings were still on the walls to show off.

If you were clever at school, you used to go to Duke's School in Alnwick, it was a high school, much higher, something like a grammar school in them days. Yes we had some clever lads and girls, and some went to Duke's school, and there was a Duchess school for the girls. The old Squire, I don't mean John, Sir John, I mean his father – he used to come to the school to see if everything was going alright.

I don't think life was that hard when I was young. We hadn't as many facilities as what you have today. When I went to school, you had to go to Dunstan to school and come back for your dinner and go back for 1 o'clock. There were no buses. You walked. Some were lucky and had a bike – that was a grand affair, if you had a bike. You were brought up that way and didn't know anything else.

I went to school in Dunstan – no canteens in those days. You had to walk up and down at lunch time. If the hounds were out, we used to go away with them and get into school late and we used to get the stick about six times on your backside, and if you laughed you maybe got another stick. We still thought a lot of the schoolteacher, he had quite a life with us all, 'cause he had ulcers and now that I have ulcers, I wonder what sort of life he had. He took about four classes. There were just two teachers and 60 or 70 going to school. There was the little room and then we went into the big room, where there about four different classes. We used to say we went to the High School 'cause it was up the hill. I was at school till I was fourteen.

Marjorie Clarke

I went to school at Dunstan and was taught by Mr. & Mrs. McDonald. There were approximately forty children at school at that time. I left in 1964 and went to the Convent in Alnwick.

I have many happy memories of Dunstan School, particularly in the summer, walking home along the cinder path and if we were let out early, if we were good, we were allowed to leave at half past three and we all used to run to try to catch the 3.30 bus, in which we got home much quicker than walking down the field and the road. We had lunch at the canteen, which were the cottages opposite the school, which is now the Cottage Inn. I can remember Mary Smail and also Bessie Morris cooked the meals, they were lovely meals. Most children stayed for lunch.

Miss Lauderdale with the children of Craster School in the year it closed (1984) : (from the left) David Hogg; Lisa Park; Sonia Grey; Mark Armstrong; Graham Archbold; Bridget Grey; Martin Archbold and Barry Armstrong.

Mary Smail

I was a school lady for 18 years, cooking. I liked that mind – with Bessie Morris. Paula was there. It's organised now, you had to get out at 60. I said to Miss Newbigin, 'I can't understand how they work longer at Newton School.' She said 'cos they can't get anybody. I think that's awful. They don't do what we had to do then. We had to peel potatoes. I had to walk to school, because the bus wasn't insured for me – the school bus. The children were in the warm bus, fetched them to the warm school. I had to walk home. George had the car then – sometimes he would come and pick me up.

Marjorie Clarke

On Friday there was a van used to pull up – Bob Smith's – and everyone always had 2d or 5d to buy various sweets. We would have lunch and then we would queue up. The 'in thing' was a pack of Gold Nuggets, which were chewing gum and were 6d, which was quite expensive.

We used to have Sports Day in the garden, parents weren't invited but we all used to do long and high jump, the one who jumped longest and highest was Dougie Hogg, no-one could ever beat him. This day took place on the lawn in front of the school. We used to play rounders on the common. Every year in February or March, we had permission to go into the woods and collect snowdrops.

I went to both the Church and Methodist Sunday School. I enjoyed them both and I used to love going on a Wednesday night, to Sunshine Corner – that was at the Chapel. That was great fun. Mrs. Hall used to make the orange juice and Mr. Kendrick ran it. It was always during the winter, to keep the children occupied, something to look forward to. We played wonderful games. It was so well organised, – really good fun. When we used to leave we used to play 'knocky nine doors' on the way home.

Dougie Hogg

Me and Dennis went to school together and we were always in trouble. I remember going up there, just before Guy Fawkes and we threw bangers at the teacher. We got into some trouble over that – got the cane in those days, got about six at that time. Me and him were always in trouble, like. When we were younger we used to play a lot in the quarry – there was a big pond there, and we used to get metal roofing sheets and gan down the crusher dust – dangerous but we never hurt ourselves badly.

We used to go along the Castle field and all over, build tree houses and things like that. The tree houses were handy because some mornings we didn't get to school and we'd hide in them. We really slipped up one day, me and my mate, Bob McLaren. We got up ready for the school, this was Seahouses school, and we went for the bus and then we run past the bus and hid up this tree house and we stopped there till about 3 o'clock in the afternoon, and had no trouble 'cause nobody had missed wer. We were sitting up in this tree-house, cooking something and this policeman come along, 'cause somebody had pinched some chain from the North Side, and we got into trouble then. Policeman said we'd better get away home – asked if we were off school. We said we were 'bad'. We got into trouble then, got a clip along the lug and put to bed. Dad wasn't ower bad.

Marjorie Lumsden

The hounds came out and whole school came out. Isabel Scott and Ella Seager, were the only two who didn't follow the hounds and when we came back, we were kept in. They chucked the fox's tail up in the air and I caught it.

We were used to getting the cane, but we never told our parents. We used to hide cigarettes in our knickers – the cigarettes that came ashore when the boats were torpedoed. We used to go to the quarry to smoke, several of the lads smoked. Once we went following the hounds, once we went seeking mushrooms and didn't come back. There was a lovely pond, which froze over and I remember you didn't go into school when that happened. The ice broke and several children fell in.

We walked to school and if one was late, everyone was late and you had to line up and get the stick. Mr. Blackburn was the teacher and had a quiz at night time and if you answered the questions right, you got out quick. Winnie, used to be good at that 'cause he used to read a story and it was a really interesting story, and when he went away he gave Tommy the books. Because everybody was listening, he would stop at an interesting bit and start again the following night. He would ask questions and say 'if you put your hand up then you could go.' One of the questions was what fruit began with 'N'. The answer was nectarine and we had never heard of that. Winnie was always reading books and papers. Mr. Blackburn was an excellent writer. Mrs. Blackburn was the treasurer of the W.I.

There were about 50 in the school and still just two teachers, Mr. Blackburn and Miss Barber. There were no school dinners –we came home every day, unless it was thick of snow and we would take sandwiches. We got horlicks in the winter and milk in the summer. There was a big stove and unless you were around it, you were frozen. You wore lots of jumpers and woollen stockings and things in the winter. We had wellingtons, mackintoshes and so'westers. We were never off school.

Joan Angus

During the war in Glasgow, I went to school in the morning and my sister, Jean went in the afternoon, in case all the family were lost if a bomb dropped. We were told that if the siren went we had to pick all our things up, you hadn't to run and you had to file out to the shelters. We came to Craster to my grandmother's in 1941 to get away from the bombing.

When Mrs. Coney – she was the schoolteacher – went on holiday, my mother and us three girls used to go and stay in the bungalow. My mother used to do their washing and I used to do the ironing. She was a proper school 'ma'm'. She wore long tweedy skirts, thick black stockings and flat shoes, a big woolly cardigan and her hair was parted down the middle and she had it pulled back in a bun and wore her glasses on the end of her nose. She used to eat those little square liquorice sweets and she used to hum. Both she and Mr. Blackburn used to cane or strap – she had a strap she called 'Mrs. Twankie' – the children, mostly the boys. Andrew Straughan – he didn't always go to school. They used to stop off in the lonnen, they had a little place where they used to bake potatoes.

Edna Simpson

When I went to Dunstan School, Mr. Blackburn and Miss Barber were the teachers. She lived down at the bottom of Dunstan. Her father was the rabbit catcher. There were just two classrooms and you were in the first one from when you started until about ten or eleven and then you went into the big room and finished your schooling. It was heated by a great big stove and on winter days we took our tea in a bottle and kept it hot on top of the stove.

Marjorie Lumsden

The Rochesters lived at The Bogie and on Friday afternoon, at school, about half an hour before we finished, Mr. Blackburn used to move everybody, 3 in a seat, to one end and it was called 'Tonight after I get my tea', and he'd call anyone out and you would get up and of course, you told a few lies. Tonight after I get my tea I will wash the dishes and get the coal and sticks in, just something to say but Willy Rochester got up this night and he said 'tonight after I get my tea, I'll go down the stack yard' and he stopped and Mr. Blackburn asked him what he would do when he got down the stack yard and he says 'I'll catch rats.' Mr. Blackburn asked what he did when he caught the rats and he said 'I chop their heeds off.'

Joyce Shaw

(After Dunstan School closed) the school in Craster was open 15 years. It was built in 1968 at a cost of £38,000. There were about twenty pupils latterly and there was debate on whether to keep Craster or Embleton school open. By comparison Craster was a new school and Embleton was a Victorian school, right on the road side. Craster had a huge playing field and a big school yard and was obviously very safe for children. The Church of England were more interested in selling the building, to make money, and the 'then' Vicar was more interested in keeping Embleton school open. At one of the meetings, Winnie and I decided to write to the Bishop and we said that if the school was to close would it be possible for the building to be turned into either sheltered accommodation for the elderly of the village, or into an old people's home, and I got a reply from the Bishop to say that the Church of England were very much in need of funds and that they would make more money by selling the building.

It was advertised at a price of £60,000. Nobody was interested at that time, so they rented it as an outward bound school. They were there a year or two and in the time they were there, I understand they never paid any rent, left a huge debt and the place was wrecked. It was in such a bad state of repair, it was knocked down and sold as a building site for four properties. There are currently three properties and I believe they were asking £60,000 per site.

Annie Jane (Nelson) was on the school committee and she was against the school being built there in the first place. She said it wasn't an appropriate place, as there were water problems. The school floor lifted twice. It turned out that there was a spring under the floor. It would have been better to spend the £38,000 to upgrade Dunstan School for the 14 years that Craster was open.

Nobody played around the doors in those days

Margaret Watson (nee Renwick) and Marion Gallon (nee Sanderson) playing in the harbour.

Willie Mitford

We used to play cowboys and Indians up the lonnen. In the summertime we all had boats and we used to go along the coast towards the Castle. We would spend all day sailing them in the pools. We were always in trouble because we didn't come back for our meals, nobody played around the doors in those days. We used to swim at the Hole in the Dyke over to Muckle Carr and along at the big hill towards the Castle. We never swam off the sand, we always swam from the rocks.

Edna Simpson

There were loads of places to play. We played rounders and cricket, everything, the girls and boys all joined in.

Marjorie Lumsden

I can remember playing on a see saw on the Heugh, when there were long planks, and we used to put them on a barrel. The Heugh was all rough grass, we used to play on it. We found lots of places to play, we were never off the rocks – they don't seem to play on the rocks like we used to – you don't get the weather that we used to. We used to go in swimming when it was raining, during the summer holidays. We used to play on the big hill, there was like a proper round swimming pool, when the tide went out, you could jump in. We didn't swim in the harbour.

When I was very young, my mother was working at the kipper yard, so you had to be there to come back for your meals. Winnie's mother bought her a watch for a birthday, so she knew when to come back in time for dinner, 'cause she wouldn't know where to look for the children.

Joan Angus

All summer we played on the rocks. Me and Jean had an imaginary game and we drew a house and we each had a little girl. Hers was called Norma and mine was called Thelma and we used to play this game all the time, without anything. We called it Nom Pel. It was a lovely long house with rooms going off. We used to do concerts on granny's staircase, get on the landing window and draw the curtains and we used to sing and then clap, just amuse ourselves. We played hopscotch on the pavement. We learned to swim in the harbour. We taught ourselves to dance when we became teenagers. The boys' club and girls' club were separate.

The days were always fine. We were out all day, just had to be in for our dinner. Our Jean used to look after Derek Watson and I looked after Beryl and we used to pretend they were our children and we used to make a picnic, just bread and jam, nothing fancy. My granny used to make toffee in the oven on a tray – sugar, vinegar and butter. It was brittle and hard. We used to put these two children in the pushchair and push them along the Long Heugh, and have this picnic. My grandmother used to bake, and make scones and things.

Marjorie Clarke

We also used to congregate on the other side of the Summer House in summer evenings, or we all met at the harbour wall. During the day we would meet at the white buildings which were the ruins of the quarry. That was the main meeting point. There were two buildings, one on one side of the path and one on the other which you had to climb up to and you could go inside to have a tunnel inside, but the larger one, which was on the other side of the burn, was much more dangerous to climb and not many tried that. We used to play in and around there and that was where everyone went, there were sometimes twenty children there. We played kick the can, which was the main game.

We spent hours there and of course, we used to be able to play in the quarry as well, because there was the quarry pond where we used to go to look for tadpoles, it was a natural habitat. There were never any accidents. We were all told not to climb up the quarry face. We just played around the quarry pond and there were old cars, which people had dumped and we played in and out of them.

Dougie Hogg often had hideouts along the Lonnen, because we were allowed to play in there as well. He had a massive tree house on the edge of the Pasture field. He had another one just behind where the Information Centre is now. It was built like a fort. He was marvellous at woodwork. I used to keep well away from there as there were always boys in there.

The other place we played was 'Swing Valley', the other little quarry. We used to spend hours there and the boys would shin up the trees and make swings, literally a long piece of rope with a knot at the end, sometimes tied with a stick pushed through – the idea was that you pulled it as far up the bank as you could, then straddled it and then let go. One or two swings would be made and someone would shout 'go' and someone else would grab it, swing round in front of you and straddle you and you would have two swinging. Gordon Angus fell from it and damaged his head, following which they were cut down and that was the end of it. I think he would be about 12 at the time. Children found their own entertainment.

Neil Robson

As a kid I spent a lot of my childhood around the yard, but also football was a great thing in the village, following the local team and also playing as youngsters, along in the square opposite South Acres. We used to play there and there wasn't a blade of grass left on that square. I remember one year we built some goalposts and the council made us take them down. Two old biddys lived in the houses and they complained and then there was a sign put up 'No Ball Games Allowed'

You would have a sandwich or something when you came home from school and then you were out playing football. There were the young ones and then the youths would come out at 5 o'clock when they came from work – I've seen maybe 30 people playing football out there at night. We would be there until dusk or you were shouted at to come in.

The harbour wall was another meeting place. As kids, you were never in the house. My mother was just on about it the other day – during the summer holidays we went out after breakfast and she never knew whether I would be in at 10 a.m. or 2 p.m. for lunch, you just went back when you were hungry. Nobody worried in those days.

Danger and adventure

Neil Robson

We used to build rafts and play in the harbour. I remember, one year there was a big log came ashore just below the playground and we all set too to hollow it out to make a dug out canoe. I got wrong off my Dad, 'cause we pinched some coke and tried to burn it out and everything. We spent weeks and weeks doing this and we got it into some sort of shape and we put an outrigger on and at high tide about 5 or 6 o'clock, half a dozen of us rowed it around to the harbour and in the morning it was gone – the fishermen had towed it out 'cos they knew someone would have been drowned. We were annoyed, like, Dougie and the lads, 'cos we'd spent ages doing it. It used to keep capsizing and we put this out-rigger on it, and it was gone in the morning.

Willie Mitford

They took the bins down during the war, they thought it was a guide for enemy planes, but in fact, they could be guided by the Castle. I think it was due to come down anyway, it was a wood construction. We used to climb up it when we were young. We used to get into trouble. I was always in trouble for something. We used to have a little boat, we called 'the punt 'which was my uncle's, who owned the kipper yard. He used it for ferrying the herring ashore when the drifters came and couldn't get into the harbour because they were too big. We used to play in that and I was always in trouble for being away in it. They didn't mind so much if we stayed in the harbour but if we went out, we got wrong. My father was against it ,'cause he didn't like the thing, he was never brought up at the sea. My mother didn't mind so much as she had been brought up at the sea. We used to go as far as the Castle and we would have to row back.

Ada Archbold

We used to play in the Castle, climb the walls, nobody looked after it when we were small, then they had a man from Embleton with one arm, he looked after it for a long time. It was probably dangerous now if you see a kiddie running along the wall of the harbour you would have a heart attack but you did it yourself and thought nothing of it. The same with the wood on the edge, we used to run along that, you're sure-footed when you're young and have no fear.

We used to go and skate. The girl who was the best skater in the district was Bella Mary's sister, Rachel. The water was just inside the Heugh, it really filled up. My father used to go mad when we went there in case the ice cracked. We used to take the brush up and brush the ice before skating.

Curiosity

Willie Mitford

When we were youngsters, we nearly all went up the butcher's shop, especially on killing day. They had a ring on the floor and the rope went through it, they went in and they threw the rope around the beast's neck and everybody pulled and pulled and they got the beast's head right down on the bottom, then they killed it. I first remember they used to stun it with a hammer and there was a spike in the other end and they put the spike into its brain. Later they got a humane killer where they put it against the head and it was like a stun gun. They did the same with the sheep. They used to put pegs through the sheep's throat at one time and bleed them. It was gory, but when you're a kid you don't mind, as you get older you can't stand it.

At one time, everybody went to the kipper yard, you cannot go in now like you used to, for Health & Safety reasons. At one time bus loads of school children used to come and be shown round the yard but now you can't do this. Nowadays children never get their hands dirty, we would be filthy and eating things with dirty hands and we had resistance, everything is too clean now.

Jobs and duties

Willie Archbold

My job, as soon as I come out of school and the other kids, we had to make a jug of tea and maybe a few biscuits and tek them over to the line hut 'cause it was away from our house, away on the North Side and they would get a mug of tea at the line cause they daren't go away for a full meal 'cause the lines had to be done, so they just had a quick bite and they would get their meal when they had finished. I used to have to empty the mussel shells into the harbour. The harbour was full of mussel shells. The boats used to crush them down and it made a grand place there. Of course now they're all washed away.

On 'blawin' days – that was a no sea day – rough weather, they would go to Budle Bay for mussels, with Kenneth's lorry. He would take them and leave them there and would go back for them to fetch the mussels home. I was off school seventeen times in 1947 going to there. You had no trouble getting time off school, as long as you took a note. I just had to help my father as he was getting a bit older. I liked it, but it was a cold job. There was a fisherman who played war with my father for me going there. He thought I was too young, but I was itching to go fishing and it didn't do me any harm.

I can mind one day in 1947, I came home and I was crying and Bartie Dawson telt my father off and said I shouldn't be here 'cos it was ower cold and I was ower young. But I went back 'cos I got off school all day. When we came back, we went on the top of an open lorry and we come back on all the mussels and we were on the top, no cover nor nothing – wintertime, there was snow. Every day when we come back we stopped at Bamburgh – I think they called it McDougal's and we used to stop there and get pies. I was kept off school quite a lot to help out and I liked it.

Joyce Shaw

My grandfather was a fisherman and I can remember my granny telling me – we used to play Ludo in the evenings and I used ask her things about what my dad did as a little boy – she said that when my grandfather was at the sea, (my dad) had to go away in the morning before he went to Dunstan school, with two zinc buckets and he used to have to go to the limpets, get the limpets off the rocks, they were for baiting the lines, and she told me that sometimes in the winter, he was so cold that he couldn't put the buckets down – the handles were fast to his fingers and she used to have to lift them –that was before he went to school.

Adam Dawson

Summer holiday we used to go and make Craster kipper boxes for pin money. We used to do OK. The wood used to come already cut and we just had to nail them up. There were large boxes, half boxes and quarter boxes, for the kippers to go in. That's how the kippers were sold, in these boxes. They had paper wrapped round inside, they were quite clean. They went to the markets to be sold, Newcastle, Alnwick and different markets.

Stories to share

Ada Archbold

I wanted a new bike and pestered my mother until 1 got one. It was £7. 1s with a pump. He charged me for the pump. I said to Edna to bike in to Alnwick and I would go on the bus, get the bike and we would ride back together, so my mother gave me the money. I went to the shop, pleased as punch, getting a new bike. Me and her sets off riding and gets down the Aln Bridge – we were seeing how far we could climb without getting off and I went smack into her back wheel and knocked two spokes out of the new bike. I didn't know what to do, so I told Edna to bike to Craster and I would go back to the shop to see if he would put the spokes in. He said 'that didn't last long'. He hadn't time to do it that day, he was busy and he said he would have it ready for Monday teatime. He said it would cost 2s to repair. I came back on the bus and I was thinking of an excuse to tell me mother, so I decided to say, it was in the shop window and there were other bikes behind it and he had no help and he couldn't get the bike out till Monday. I went back on the Monday and got it and she never knew.

Edwina Simpson

Mrs Richardson – through the field – Bella Mary, showed me a picture, 'cause it was her granny that lived in that house –that garden where that house is was like a field – there was no Joiners' Shop. My Dad told me that she was as deaf as a stone and he said that she had a muckle trumpet in her ear and he says that when they were kids they used to go to the house and would speak to her and she would hold the trumpet that they used to yell as hard as they could down the trumpet and she used the jump. Every New Years' day you got a penny and at Easter you got a hen's egg and nobody ever went twice, it was never abused.

Marjorie Lumsden

We looked through these papers and we used to look through the births, marriages and deaths and we knew a lad who come to Craster for his summer holidays, he was a lovely lad, Colin Nesbitt. He lived at Forest Hall and it was in the evening paper (his death, I think). He was a walking disaster, that lad. He died when he was 17 and 10 months. I had a photo of him. There were some Norwegian Scouts camping at Howick and they were in the harbour this day and the tide was right out and Colin was going up the ladder and there was a rung missing, down he came onto his back and I remember two of the scouts picked him up. Every time he got near water he was wet and one Saturday night, me mother wanted something from Howick store. We walked across long heugh – I went with her, and we walked right along and we got to Salter's Gate and here's the car parked and Alec and Ivy Nesbitt – she was sitting knitting and there were clothes all over and I asked where he was and he was in the car with nothing on except a clean pair of trunks. He'd fallen into the water at Salter's Gate. We reckoned he got TB from always being wet.

Ada Archbold

My mother bought me a mouthorgan when I was 13. I used to go to Christon Bank on the bike, for to learn and then I met this lad and I used to not bother going. My mother was paying the bill and I didn't turn up.

Joan Angus

My grandfather had a wireless which was operated by a very large battery accumulator, which was serviced by a garage. As children, we had to be quiet on a Saturday afternoon when the football match was on, if the battery was low. I am sure that is why I hate football.

I was christened in Craster church. It was a curate who christened me and mother took me to the church with my godparents and when asked what I was to be called, my mother said 'Jane' and the curate said 'divn't call her that' and my mother said 'I'll call her Joan then'. My granny was called Jane but the curate didn't like the name.

Memories of visiting Craster as a child

Joyce Shaw

I was born in 1928 and after that, we came to Craster every other weekend until he (my father) died in 1935, aged 39. So my memories (of Craster) way back, were the memories of a child. I always loved Craster and my mother told me that when it came time on a Sunday night to go back to Low Fell, I never wanted to go, I wanted to stop here. I never thought I would come here to live, not in a working life – in retirement perhaps. My grandmother lived until I was 21 and she died in 1950, so I came to Craster over all those years very regularly, including holidays. The War came in that time and of course you couldn't go away for holidays, so I always came here and spent nearly all my school holidays here.

When I was here – I loved going on the rocks and we went quite a lot to the Chanley Hole and the harbour. My granny would say to me, when I was 12, 13'ish, she would give me a basket and say 'hadaway and get some black sticks'. They were black because when they burnt the whin bushes on the hills, what was left were very brittle sticks which were marvellous for lighting the fire. As you can imagine, you got absolutely filthy and I really hated that job, but never mind I did it. The fisherman burnt the gorse bushes to clean them out, so that they didn't get too big.

Events

Adam Dawson

The weddings at Craster were in the chapel. Now when they came out, the custom was that the people at the end, all the relations, used to throw money away. We knew so we used to wait. There were sixpences and threepenny pieces and coppers. If you went down to that road to the Chapel you would find some now, buried in the soil.

Once a year, when it was nice weather, we used to go to Craster Towers. We used to have strawberries, tea and cakes. It was good. It was the old squire. Where they used to get the water from, there was a windmill in a field not far away from the Towers. It was pumped up, and we used to call it Windmill field, and it's still there. The day at the Towers was held on the lawns, and sometimes there used to be sports, running for the kiddies. It was good for us. Old Mrs. Craster was very nice, a very nice person indeed. She used to mix with us all the time.

Every New Year we used to go to Newcastle – we had a cousin who used to organise this trip. It was a very good trip. We use to go to Newcastle in a bus, go to the football match first, then go to a restaurant, Carricks, to have a good feed. After that we used to go to a pantomime. That was the day's outing. We used to get back about midnight.

Willie Mitford

Easter time we used to go round the farms collecting eggs and we had to be at the Tower at 11 o'clock and we went down and knocked at the door and Mrs Craster would come out and give us all a new penny – we used to stand for hours waiting for it. The Crasters saw to everything then, they owned the old houses. On rent day, when you went to pay the rent you got your dinner at the Towers. They always gave Christmas parties – everything that was on was given by the Crasters.

Chapter 8 Pastimes and social life

Jimmy Hall

The biggest change I find in this village is, if you go out, for instance to the harbour wall, you never see anyone, except a stranger. In those days, every night there were men on the harbour wall, arguing about football. Everybody had their dinner and walked down for a bit conversation. Everybody met at the harbour wall, it was the same at Beadnell Square and the kiln at Seahouses – there were always fishermen there.

Eddie Grey

It was good being a kid in Craster, where you knew everybody – not like now. There's a lot of nice people moved into Craster, but it's not the same. On a summer night down at the harbour wall, you couldn't get moved. It was a focal point, people just having a bit crack and that.

Eleanor Venus

If Nancy and I went to the pictures or anything, we were always in on the 8.15 p.m. bus. Never mind we went to the pictures, it was Susan Hayward and I always say it was the night we got our roots topped. We walked down the pastures and he said he (future husband, Ken) couldn't let me go on the 8.15pm – well the next one was 10 p.m. We enjoyed our walk and once again mother and Mrs. Lumsden were there to meet us. 'Get yourself over those fields as sharp as you like, your father's going stone mad'. I was 20 years old. We crossed Proctor Field and got home and I suppose my father was worried – he was upstairs.

Willie Mitford

I think we had a better social life than the youngsters have today, we used to cycle into Alnwick to the pictures. You either walked or cycled everywhere.

Doris Clarke

Mr & Mrs Browell were part–time coast guards. Jack was in the Royal Navy then and when he came home he used to bring Wally some tobacco from the ship, and he came over one time and says, 'are these any good for you?' He gave me a pair of bell bottom trousers, wonderful material, so warm. At the time, there was a sewing class up at Dunstan, and I made David a duffel coat. He was only about five or six. I bought the toggles and everything, and I was so proud of it. There was a sewing class and the lady used to work for Dodds in Alnwick. Mary Short served her time there. The material was excellent.

Dances

Marjorie Lumsden

It was a safe place to live, we used to go to dances at Embleton, Howick, Rennington. There were no houses here (at this end of the village,) just the Heugh, so there were loads of places to play. We played rounders and cricket, everything, the girls and boys all joined in.

Willie Mitford

As we got older we used to go to dances, it was the main entertainment you had. I used to go to about four or five dances a week, every village had a dance on a different night. We went to Rennington, Embleton, Seahouses, Alnmouth, Brunton Aerodrome when the RAF had it, Howick. Sometimes we had dances here. There was a big billiard table in the hall and we used to dance around it. I met my wife after I came out of the Army, in 1948 – 9, at Newton.

Bill Curry

I was pally with Eddie Williams and Adam Durham and we weren't made welcome in the pub at Craster, 'cos they wouldn't speak to us some of them old fishermen. I don't know if it was because we were young or what. It wasn't as big as it is now. We used to go to Embleton and Newton by the Sea, to the Joiners. I had a van, they didn't have a car, and we used to go across there. In those days you never bothered about drinking and driving. We went to the local dance at Embleton. The dances used to be good – Watty Frater and his Hawaiian Serenaders. They had them in the Creighton Hall. They used to come from Ayton, up in Berwickshire. He was just a little fellow. He had a Hawaiian guitar.

Billy Lumsden

You could go to 3 or 4 dances a week, if you were so inclined. I've seen us go to the pictures in Alnwick and walk out to Rennington, go to the dance, then walk home. Or Embleton – there used to be good dances in the Creighton Hall. You never saw anybody the worse the wear with drink or anything like that. The dance was the main thing, not going to the pub. Now they've got to go to the pub first, before they go anywhere else. I think that thing (TV) standing in the comer is to blame for a lot of that.

(So there would be a lot of people walking around the country lanes?) Wye aye. I've seen up to 20 of us walking along that road from Rennington. My boss, Mr Rowell at the farm, he asked my father to first foot him one New Year, and my father never went. He says to me will you be my first foot, and I said to him, what about my mates? He says fetch them all. I took about 14. We'd been to Embleton dance, and we'd stayed there until Auld Lang Syne, and then we came home. I took them up there and we ended up around the piano, singing like. We went every year after that.

They've married lasses from Rennington or Embleton, through the dances. At one time ye didn't get far. There was no cars nor owt. After the war there was the odd motorbike. Johnny Grey had his father's car, it was a little Austin 10. We were at Rennington dance, and I said how about a lift home. He said 'aye,' well there were about 10 of us and we used to drive along on the mudguard and keep hanging on to the little side lights. We all piled on, he started her up but she wouldn't move. She kept cutting out. He said we'll just have to leave it and come back in the morning. So we walked home, and we walked back on the Sunday, and you know the stay on an electric pole, the big steel stays, somebody had lifted it over and put the bumper bar around. It's a wonder we didn't pull the ruddy pole down. So we walked back home.

It was black dark, there were no street lights then. I once got fined for riding a bike without lights, coming from Rennington. I was coming along the top of Dunstan, it would be about half past 2 or 3 o'clock in the morning, and there was this car coming along with just little side lights on, and this voice said to me, 'look there's somebody lost', and I turned round and it was the police. He says, 'where have you been?' and I said 'I've been to Rennington dance'. He said you've no lights on, and I said, 'No. I haven't got any .' He said 'what's your name?', and I said 'well you know my name'. He said 'I'm asking you your name'. So that was it. We were working on the harvest at the time, when he came with the summons and gave it to my mother. I didn't see it. My mother says I've had a man here from Embleton, the police. You have to go to court for riding a bike without lights.

Maggie Wilson and Winnie Hogg

We used to enjoy the dances. We used to get the bus to Embleton or Howick dances, which were every Thursday night, they were excellent. A lot of convalescents from Howick Hall (wartime military hospital) used to be there. We had to walk back from the dances. The waltz was always the last dance and the partner you had for that was the one who walked you home, what a carry on you had getting the one you wanted! There were good dances at the Towers (Craster Tower,) they had one every Friday night. There was always a band. The soldiers got a band. Hilda Rogerson used to play on the piano, Dennis Dawson used to play the accordion. We used to go to Alnwick to the pictures, if we could slip away. We used to go on a Sunday. There were two cinemas, the Corn Exchange and the Playhouse.

Bill Curry

There were characters like Clive Douglas, always getting full of drink, singing 'Nobody's Child'. They'd come to the dances full of drink, in the village at Howick. There was always a play every year, and then they'd have a dance after, with a pooled supper. I remember Mrs. Carr Ellison, she was W. I. President in those days, they lived in the Rectory where Neil Robson lives now, and she used to talk Geordie. She had a very articulate voice, very posh, and then she would talk Geordie. She could do it very well. She was a nice woman, full of the joys of spring, always laughing and carrying on.

Fancy Dress Balls in the Village Hall

Joan Angus

My stepfather played the accordion very well, and they had a little band in the village. It was called B. Hughes and his band. My stepfather played the accordion. Vincent Morris was on the drums and Hilda Rogerson was on the piano. They played for socials, WI get togethers, and dances in the hall. He had the band for quite a long time. I was quite young at the time of the fancy dress balls, but we used to go to Mrs. Wilkinson on the end of the common at Dunstan and she had a kist of lovely things that you could get dressed up in. I can remember going as an Eastern princess with a long floaty affair, green I think, right down to my ankles. I think I had a flower crown on my head, and it was like an Eastern dance that they did. I can't remember if I won a prize. They had them often, and some people were extremely good about fancy dress. They were quite good of making up things, topical things of the day. Mrs. Humble was excellent; she used to get some rare ideas. Mrs. Humble was good at having parties, and all sorts of things. We used to have parties in each other's houses when we had a birthday, and she used to think up some super games.

Winnie Hogg

We had fancy dress balls. Billy and Laurence Humble went as —when was it they brought out the five shillings a week if you had a child? It would be in the 50's. Billy got an old pram – he was in the pram with a dummy and Laurence was wheeling the pram. I don't know what the motif was on the card, but it was to do with the five shillings that the government was giving people who had a child – family allowance – and they won 1st prize.

When Queen Elizabeth and Philip were married, Ada and Matt went dressed up as them. Mrs. Humble was a great one at fancy dress. She had some beautiful costumes and was very good. One year I went as King of the Road, I went as a tramp, and I got first prize – a clock. Another year I went in a box that my husband made, and I was pulling a ball behind me, I think I was a convict.

The children had a fancy dress Parade beforehand, and the adults had it later. Our Audrey once went as Mary Poppins and won 1st prize, and some people hadn't even heard of Mary Poppins. I had been away on holiday to the Lakes and had been to see the picture. Fortunately, there was some R.A.F. people judging, and they knew all about Mary Poppins, so she got 1st prize. I used to go every year.

Craster Feast

Eva Archbold from notes written in 1957

After weeks of spring cleaning, papering and painting, every woman was duty bound to be finished on the feast Saturday. In the kitchen the old black–leaded fireplace with the oven at one side and a huge boiler at the other, shone with its new coat of black lacquer, while under the bars where the ashes dropped, an extra dose of whitewash made it whiter than white. The ceiling, with its old oak beams, had been washed with great care in case you caught your hand on one of the big nails from which hung the home fed bacon. Two large hooks on which rested the telescopic spy–glass had also to be avoided. It was kept there in readiness to look for the cobles coming in, for in those days the womenfolk had to be on the shore to help haul up the boats at the capstan.

The closet beds with their straw mattresses and feather ticks were hauled out and thoroughly cleaned. The old grandfather clock would be ticking its approval of its new surround of wallpaper. Like the song, it had been nailed to the wall for 60 years and was a fixture. The steel fender, brasses and fire irons which had been in hiding for a few days, would emerge and be given another shine before being consigned to their final resting place. The new lino with the new progged and clicked mats which had been made during the winter, were laid and duly admired and an account given of the origin of the various materials used.

On one occasion the new lino was laid and the womenfolk were eyeing it with justifiable pride, when the son of the house appeared. He was just a 'bit callant', I was told. He was asked 'Tom, what do you think of the new lino?' with a hasty glance at the floor, he replied 'I would sooner have seen a new sail for the coble'. Needless to say this brought a storm of protest from the women, but as with all real fishermen, the boat came first, yes, friends, some of you may have guessed who this 'bit callant' was.

The Feast Saturday was a day of bustling activity. Howick Co–op wagon made a special journey the day before with last minute requirements, such as Feast hams, table baize, etc. The ham would be cooking and its appetizing smell greeted you everywhere. Feast loaves were in readiness also, for this was the time when your friends and relations paid you a visit. The cobblestones were weeded and the rainwater barrels and outhouses glistened in the sun with their new coats of tar. Everybody took care to have new clothes for the Feast. If you didn't the birds were supposed to show their disapproval in the usual way! The children showed their new outfits to their elders, who put pennies in the pockets. These pennies were spent at the shows and stalls which came for the weekend.

A report in Alnwick Guardian, 27th May, 1899, states that Broomhill Band was in attendance and that the races confined to fishermen, had lines as prizes. To mention a few names – Geo. Dawson, winner of 220 yds. handicap, received 2 lines and Thos. Smailes was second and received one line. In the boat race, James Sanderson's boat was first and received 6 lines and Thos. Smailes' boat was second and received 3 lines. All lines were worth 6d each.

Those mingled smells of newly cooked ham, feast loaves , freshly baked homemade bread, table baize, new lino, new paint and the scent of the nearby whin blooms, seem to linger in my nostrils and, were I able to make a modern fresh air spray from these, I would have no hesitation in calling it 'Craster Feast.'

Willie Mitford

All the villages had what they called a Feast, the children ran in races and there was a big greasy pole to climb, with a ham or something at the top and whoever got to the top got it. There used to be a few sideshows and they used to park alongside the wall beside the pub.

They used to have the Craster Feast once a year. They reckon they painted everything, if you stood still long enough, they would paint ye an all. I suppose they would come from Boulmer and Seahouses and all over, their friends like.

Neil Robson

There was a Craster Feast when I was a kid. The women used to play the men at football up at the Turn Field, and it was so funny watching them. They wore long dresses and wigs. There used to be parties in the village hall. I can remember there being a monkey with a magician once, and the monkey climbed the curtains and the bloke couldn't get it down. That's all I remember about the whole thing.

Adam Dawson

Now in the wintertime, we used to make our carpets, such as clippy rugs, and there was some beauties I can tell you. They never come out – we never used – them until Craster Feast. That was in May. Now in Craster village, when it was the feast, every house in Craster was painted. They were painted up ready for the feast and it was a feast I can tell you. There was ham; there was everything to eat, home-made.

For Craster Feast my mother used to make a spiced loaf. Now that was a fruit cake, a rice cake was a plain cake and scones, girdle scones. Craster feast always came on the Bank Holiday Monday in May. Every house in Craster was painted inside and outside, for the Craster Feast and the peg rugs used to come out that day. It was sparkling and clean. It looked gorgeous. Now my father used to buy a ham, a whole ham, and my mam used to boil it for the relations at Boulmer, 'cos they used to come on the Sunday.

Craster feast was a day of sports – that was on the Monday. Even the fishermen used to race their cobles and there was plenty of talent in Craster. They used to make small boats to sail in the harbour for racing. It was all racing, it was good. Also there was a pigeon race, I couldn't forget that. We also had a holiday, it was an annual holiday. We also had one on the Tuesday for the older men, they used to bring quoits. There was also a greasy pole, with a ham on top, and it was fun trying to get that ham off the top of the pole.

There used to be a colliery band come, and they used to play at night in the Reading Room, dances and all that. It used to be a sort of a carnival. It was great. The Jolly Fisherman was a very busy place indeed. We always had a good time. There were stalls, cups with fruit on and all sorts. It was a great day, Craster Feast. It was a great day and always has been. There was money and they gathered it through the year for the sports. The pigeon race you got money for that, there was money for the hundred yards. In fact I got 30 shillings, 'cos I came in second.

The Football Team: Craster Rovers

Billy Lumsden

There's always been a football team. When the war finished that was the best team they ever had. When all the lads came back from the war you know. They must have had a good team earlier when Adam Dawson played as well, 'cos he went to play for Chesterfield. That was before the war. They were kicked out the league, you know, for fighting. They were hoyed out the league like, in fact one of them was suspended sine die. They rescinded that later on. They used to play up at the Castle fields, at the top of there. Well you know it sloped towards the sea. A lot of the teams that came here reckoned it was a 2 goal start for the Craster team. They've still got their football team and they gan out the village for the lads. The lads come out of Alnwick. They enjoy it and they've got a grand pitch up there. Ally Grey let them have that. They got a grant, from Craster Parish Council of over £400 towards that club house, and Lord Howick gave that bit of land it stands on. They've been very fortunate in that respect like.

Adam Dawson

The sport in the village was football. Now we couldn't find a pitch as you know, and we eventually found a pitch. It was through the gate as you go to the Castle and the top fields were quite level. Now Craster is a very old football side, they had been playing for years and years, before we started. We had a good side in Craster. We used to play the North Northumberland League and there were some good teams in that league.

Even Alnwick had three teams in that league. There was Wooler, Amble and all districts around here. There was some good teams. Now we had a good side. There were 4 brothers of mine who played in the team. One season we won the North Northumberland League, the year we won was 1927 – 28. I was only 16 when I played in that team, but I was good. I was very good. (He left Craster to become a professional player at Chesterfield.) On the team was my brother Edward, he was the goalkeeper, there was Matt Stephenson fullback, and John Archbold, half backs were Billy Grey from Howick, Jack Carss from Craster and an Embleton boy called Varnum. Now on the wings were Riddell, me, my brother Ralph, Dickens inside left, and another Varnum, brother to the other Varnum, they were twins, and we won the league. If we were short of a player, sometimes Sir John Craster used to come and play for us.

When that (season) was all over, we were in the Reading Room and we were all presented with the medals and the cup from Sir John Craster. We used to play these Alnwick sides. They didn't like us, a village team, beating them and we used to have some rough games now and again, especially with the Alnwick Duke's School Old Boys. The trainer, his name was Archbold, the secretary, his name was Archbold. Our team was properly run, it was the best turned out side in the league, 'cos our mothers used to wash our shorts and shirts. They were spotless. We were red, our shirts were red and our shorts were white and we used to have red socks or stockings.

I was only young, only 16, and the secretary or trainer says to me, he threw the shirt at me, and said you're playing tomorrow at Bamburgh and that pitch was the cricket ground under the Castle at Bamburgh. We had a good game, a very good game indeed. I enjoyed that. Now my brother Ralph, centre forward, was a bit rough for the goalkeepers. If the goalkeeper got hold of the ball, he'd knock them into the net. That was his temperament. We played Alnwick United and their goalkeeper was deaf, stone deaf. As the game went on my brother says, 'you see that goalkeeper he's deaf, get into him, he can't see you'.

Our local rivals were Seahouses, a fishing village the same as us. There was some hard games there at Seahouses, the same when they came to us. We used to travel in a car, and the car was a Rolls Royce, belonging to an Embleton proprietor, he used to run the football teams around to where they used to play.

Neil Robson

The Craster football team used to get big crowds watching them, even at the old pitch which was on top of the Castle field. There would be 50 or 60 people watching and they would get a bus to go to away games. I think I was fourteen when I first started playing. I went to Swarland, it was a night game and we went for a half past six kick off, they were struggling for a team and I had to play. There were three fathers and three sons playing then, there was Michael and Willy (Robson,) Dad and me, Les Turnbull from Embleton and his son, Michael. I think we won as well.

I remember my Dad telling a story, they were playing Seahouses and someone tackled a Seahouses player and broke his leg, not intentionally, and they had to escape in the cars afterwards. They used to bring the boats over from Seahouses when they were playing Craster. They reckon there were once about 300 watching a Seahouses game at Craster. My Uncle Willy was a character on the pitch. He was a hard man, and they reckon he scored as many goals with his hands as what he did with his head. I remember him scoring a goal one day when he was on the line, he was leaning against the post and he flipped it in. Him and my father kept the football team going for years.

We never had any changing rooms or training facilities. A few of the lads used to go for a run, now and again, but we were young lads, we were reasonably fit anyhow. Willy used to run the mini bus. He was always late 'cause he had work to do at the garage before he could come. The bus was as slow as a snail. If you were playing Berwick or somewhere like that we would say we would leave at one o'clock for a three o'clock kick–off and we'd still be waiting at two o'clock and he would come strolling out eating a sandwich. You'd get to about Belford and he would shout 'we're going to be late, you'd better get changed' and everybody's scrambling about in the bus, trying to get changed.

I remember once we were playing this team called Pirate. They were a pub team from Berwick and they were a good team, some right hard men amongst them and we were about five minutes late for the kick off and the referee was getting all impatient, and we all dived off the bus all ready and in about two seconds we were ready to play. We beat them up there and in the return game they were a bit nervous, 'cause they were top of the league. Dougie Hogg was a hell of a bloke at centre half. I mean, he was rough as hell and there was this bloke called Jimmy the Brick and he nudged Dougie as he was going to head the ball, elbowed him, and Dougie ran about 50 yards and kicked this bloke up the backside, full bore, and flattened him. That was the end of him, we never saw much of him after that.

Craster Rovers team for the final of the Northumberland Minor Cup (1950:) left to right) back row – Bob McLaren, Alan Robson, Paddy Raeburn, Tommy Thompson, Alan Beveridge, Adam McLaren – front row – Dennis Dawson, George Williams, Willy Robson, Peter Cain, Bartie Dawson

Minutes of the Committee Meeting held on 4ᵗʰ April 1950
Committee Meeting held in the Reading Room. Members present: Messrs Scott, Mitford, Beveridge, Sheehan, Simpson, Shell, Raeburn, Archbold, Forster, Charlton R. The minutes of the previous meeting were read and adopted. A team was selected to play King's College at Portland Park, Ashington in the final of the NFA Minor Cup. Team as follows: Thompson T, McLaren R, McLaren A, Robson A, Raeburn L, Beveridge A, Dawson D, Williams G, Robson W, Cain P, Dawson E. Team will leave Craster at 1.30pm. Teas will be ordered at the Grand Hotel Ashington for 5.30pm. All players plus three reserves, Secretary, Chairman and trainer and 3 committee members will receive complimentary for the game.

Extract from the Berwick Advertiser
...many soccer fans in the area can recall some of the powerful Craster teams of the past, and remember how difficult it was to cope with their sloping pitch.

But it was not ground advantage but strength and skill which took Craster through to the cup final. In the quarter final against Spittal, the teams drew 2 – 2 at Craster, but then the Rovers went up to Billendean and gained a tremendous 4 – 2 victory. Craster then went on to reach the final, only to lose 3 – 2 to King's College on an Easter Monday in April 1950.

Paddy Raeburn congratulates the cup winning captain of Kings College, as Stan Seymour looks on

Bill Curry

I was only nine years old when that team got to the final. Bus loads went. The village was empty when we went to Portland Park in Ashington for the final. I cried when we lost.

Joan Angus

I am not a great advocate of football for several different reasons, but we all used to go to the important games. I remember going to a cup game at Seahouses, between Craster and Seahouses, which were great rivals to start with. Somebody kicked Adam McLaren and his mother, old Esther went onto the field with her brolly, threatening the man who had kicked 'wor Adam'. She threatened what she was going to do with this brolly if he did it again. I don't know if anybody can remember that, but I can remember vividly, in my capacity of being able to laugh. I saw the funny side of that. It would never happen today. It wouldn't be allowed. Can you imagine anybody going on the field with a brolly in a threatening manner.

Fred Stephenson

That incident with the brolly started the week before down at Craster. We were playing Seahouses at Craster and Bobby McLaren was a very hard tackler and he hit Carl Dawson with a heavy tackle and Carl had to go off with concussion, so the next week they were at Seahouses and Carl stood and niggled at Bobby the whole of the game. Bobby said, 'keep a hold of him after the game' and they had a right free for all, there was a ring of people standing and of course, Esther always had the brolly and she used to shout at Bobby. Bobby McLaren played right back, he was a very hard tackler, but I wouldn't call him a dirty tackler. He used to dive to head the ball from about two foot off the ground. This was in the late 1940's 1950's. We had a very good team then, but there were a lot of good teams at that time, Craster, Seahouses, Belford, Spittal.

Winnie Hogg

We went in a bus, to see the football. About two bus loads went out of Craster, to a cup game to Seahouses. I went with my dad and Tommy, who I was courting at the time. It was a freezing cold day, so we ended up in The Ship – in the back room, and the two of them had a glass of whisky and my dad got me a glass of lemonade. It was freezing cold.

When we got to the football match, we used to stand beside Esther, who was Maggie's mother, and old Addison, who was her aunt, and they used to shout at the players. However, Adam McLaren, Maggie's brother and Bob McLaren played as backs, and she shouted, 'I'll take your B legs out of you' and she shouted that they were going to have a battle on the side of the field. I can remember that, it was really funny. The women went regularly. They didn't follow them so much in the bus, but they went when they used to play in Craster. There was quite a big crowd, 'cos they had a good football team. They had most of the men who had come back from the war. Adam McLaren was an excellent footballer – Adam McLaren and Bob McLaren, there's Alan Robson and Paddy Raeburn, Alan Beveridge, Bartie, Thompson the goalie, and Geordie Williams, Dennis, Sybil's husband, Willie Robson.

Fred Stephenson

There was a Scotsman lived at Embleton, he was a policeman and his nickname was John Barleycorn. His real name was John Purvis. He used to come to every game at Craster to keep an eye on everything and of course, in those days, they used to sell cloakroom tickets, for a raffle to pay for the referee. They were illegal and Billy Lumsden went around one day and he said to Mr. Purvis, 'would you like some tickets Mr. Purvis?' and he said 'would you like six months behind the bars?'

The Pub

Joan Angus

There was, before 1824, a small school in Butcher Lane in the house now occupied by Miss Isobel Scott. This house was also at some time used as a pub, run by a Ralph Archbold (1788 – 1846,) who was known as Ralph the Britton and who was often in the hands of the press gang. Most of the men had two occupations. Ralph 'mine host' was also a fisherman who had the Steamship called Zetter. Ralph's wife Eliza kept the pub going for another year after his death. In 1847, the Pub was transferred from Butcher Lane to Charles Archbold's house (the present 'Jolly Fisherman'.) The new publican, Charles was also a fisherman, and evidently a 'jolly one', hence the pub's name. The pub was used, at that time, for the needs of shipwrecked sailors. After Charles died in 1855, his wife kept it going until 1859, when a Robert Grey took over. He was followed by his son Harry, who also ran the shop in Church Street. The next 'mine hosts' were George Fortune, Peter Ormston, Walter Proudlock (1940 – 63,) George Renwick, Harry Wood, Mr and Mrs Albert George and now Mr and Mrs Billy Silk.

Leek Club

Alan Dixon

Craster Leek Club started on 21st November 1966 and it covered Craster, Embleton, Howick and Newton by the Sea. The first show was in October 1967 and the total prize money then was £241/ 10s / 10d. At that time the annual fees were £3 and pensioners paid 15 shillings. The first Chairman was Billy Lumsden and he remained in office until 1991. Paddy Raeburn was secretary for the first two years and then George Butters was secretary until he died in 1983. I took it on in 1985 and I am still doing the job now.

The first committee was Peter Angus, Eric Archbold, Jean Breeze, Jack Browell, George Butters, Adam Durham (snr,) Lilla Foster, Syd Wilson, Harry Wood. The biggest membership was 45 in the late 1970's. It is now down to 24 members, but it is still one of the strongest leek clubs in the area. Billy Lumsden has won the George Butters Memorial Cup eleven times since it was presented in 1983, and he won the 'best in show' a few times before that, as well.

Billy Lumsden checks his leek bed. He has won the George Butters memorial Cup eleven times since it was first presented in 1983.

Pigeon Club

Eddie Williams

The Pigeon Club used to have about 27 members at one time. There were the Durham brothers, Adam's father and his Uncles Bob and George, Tommy Simpson, Willie Harle, Freddie Watson, George Butters and Sid Wilson (Colin's still going.) There was Dennis Dawson on the north–side. My dad had them with his brother Geordie and when he died, about twenty year ago, I ended up with them. Clippie had a bungalow with half for making and mending nets and pots and the other half was for the pigeons. Then they moved on top of the quarry.

They used to ring them where they first had the shop down at the kipper yard and Willy Robson used to take them to Little Mill Station.

Geordie Curry was in for a few years up at the Scar. There were the Silks. Stephenson from Boulmer, Henry Longstaff from Newton. It was Craster and District – well it still is. Carol Grey is the secretary. Her father was in it. It's down to about eight members now.

Carol Grey

The Pigeon Club has been in existence since about 1947, although I think some flew in Alnwick before a club was formed here. My father used to tell his two favourite stories; one about Bill Archbold (Clippie) and one about George Butters.

He said that George Butters, who had a droll sense of humour, came into the shop one Friday morning after the Racing Pigeon Weekly magazine had arrived. Dad said to George that there was a grand scraper advertised in the Racing Pigeon, but that it was a bit expensive – about £4 – a lot of money. Dad said he just hesitated a second or two, then replied, 'it doesn't gan itsel does't? '

The other was during a Channel race. The birds must not have been home on the Saturday, which meant a very early rise on Sunday. Bill and dad were waiting for the early arrivals and dad said he would go and make a cup of tea. He went up to the house and had just put the kettle on when there was a rattle at the door and Bill put his head in and said, 'Have you got a blue hen away?' Dad said, 'Yes'. 'She's hyem then', said Bill.

There's many a good laugh to be had when we are ringing the pigeons ready for racing. Another funny story I remember was when we were talking about everyone having their turn for racing well and winning. We were striking the clocks and Willie Harle said, 'everyone has to swallow the bitter pill'. Benny Williams (Eddie's father) was standing next to Willie and he said, ' hm them uns of Horton's (who was always winning) must be sugar

Carol Grey has been secretary of the Pigeon Club for about

15 years

coated.'

Reading Room/Memorial Hall

Joan Angus

The Memorial Hall Foundation was laid in 1887 and the Hall was inaugurated in 1889. At this date the Hall was called 'The Reading Room'. It was used by men to go into and read their papers and to play billiards. The billiard table was huge and when dances were held, the dancers danced around the table. The table eventually was removed up to the Towers, but what happened to it I have no knowledge of.

Doris Clarke

They were places for men to meet. When we first came here there was a club for the men, it was Reading Room, not Memorial Hall. Was that part of the Memorial Room? No it was the Reading Room. A lot of people still call it the Reading Room. They paid into a club, and if they were sick, they got a little bit back.

Jimmy Hall

There was a billiard table in the Reading Room, it was kept control of, they didn't run riot. You listened and you watched shots. That was every night. It was taken out to make room for dances. Lots of dances in those days, there was quite a lot to do.

Alison Newbigin

In the 1960s there was a notice in the local shop saying the Village Hall would have to be taken over by the parish if no-one would come on the committee – which was nil with no cash. Doris Clarke and I came on – Doris as secretary and I was treasurer – and we stayed on for years.

In the early years it was called the Reading Room, where people could come and read the newspapers. There was no door into the kitchen. You had to climb the steps onto the stage and go down the back stairs. There was a hole in the kitchen wall adjacent to the hall, it came out near the radiator. Everything had to be passed through the hole into the hall, or carried over the stage.

My brother planned the present door and steps into the kitchen and put the metal beam in the kitchen to support the ceiling and stage above. We got grants from the County Education and Alnwick Council, but you had to pay the bills before getting any money.

There was no central heating in the early days. There was a coal fire on the stage and a coal fire boiler in the kitchen. Coal was kept in the two outhouses outside the front door. Also there was a huge billiard table which went to Craster Tower for the soldiers. After the First World War, the hall was called Craster Memorial Hall. The Crasters had given the hall to the village in the 1880's and they are still the trustees.

Doris Clarke

I can remember being on the Hall committee as well. There was a notice up in the shop, that if people didn't come to this meeting, it was going to be closed. Eva was desperate to get rid of the job, and so Alison and I went to the meeting, and we ended up by her taking the treasurer's job and me taking secretary's job. I did that for about 30 years. If you don't get interested in the village, you only get out what you put in. At the end of the war, nothing had been done. There were no improvements. Nothing had been done to that hall, purely because of apathy. There was a committee, but they didn't look forward. Like a house you have to do jobs every year. Allison and I put a lot of work into the hall. I took over the Sunday School when Alice Durham wasn't well, and Mary Smail's daughter, Eileen, she used to do it. Jean Breeze and I did it for a long time.

Adam Dawson

At a Christmas there was a party in the Reading Room with books as prizes, and everyone had a present off the Xmas tree.

Scouts, Guides, Girls Club and Youth Clubs

Craster Guide and Scout Group in the 1970's

Doris Clarke

I joined the Guides in 1940. We used to go to Curry's hut at the Guides along there. It was a shed – it's just for storage now, down on the farm. We used to walk over this back way. I remember who ran the guides, she was called Miss Barbara Nichol.

I can remember coming to services in the village, the Sunday school being involved. You used to go to the Tower and pick the snowdrops for Mothering Sunday. There were Scouts here, and they were just ticking over, with the two Greenley boys, and their father who used to take them to Seahouses and the girls used to say there was nothing for girls. So when she got to about 12 years old, I said to Pauline, we'll see what interest there is. So we had a meeting and there was about 14 turned up. So we started the Guides here.

One of the years there was the tidiest village competition. Everything was grand except one of the judges said that the church ground had let them down, because it was so high in weeds and grass. This was in the 70's. Willie Mitford by this time had taken over the scouts and Mr. Alton took the cubs. Mr. Alton was the Chapel Minister, he was younger and dedicated to the Scout movement. The guides, scouts and cubs, decided to do the Church garden. The boys were doing the hard work and the girls were doing the weeding. We got everything done, put grass seed down, raked and made borders for people (I remember Bessie Morris put those first roses in by the doorway.) Then you could buy a rose and dedicate it in the bottom strip. It was just a wilderness.

That was one of the things that came out of the guides —plus the fact that we used to go camping. We went to various places. Not too far. We went to Budle. We took the leaders on camping training to Chillingham Farm. She was the commissioner and she was very keen. That was wonderful. They had a pig farm and they were all different ages and sizes. The little ones got out one morning. Somebody must have left a gate open and they ran around all over the place. The tents went down, the kids were screaming, the piggies were screaming.

We went up to Ford Castle, 'cos the scouts had a camping ground up there. The last one was Scremerston, and there wasn't enough to make a camp, so I cancelled and that was when the guides closed. When you got girls who were indifferent, there was no point in doing it. Pauline, Audrey, June and Kay Charlton all the ones who had been keen, were 17 and they weren't interested any more.

Joan Angus

There was a tragedy with the scouts that happened on the 6th August 1931, the year before I was born. The scouts went off to camp with Percy Adams, who had founded the first Embleton Group, on moving to the area two years previously. I believe he was the curate.

They were camping at Norham on the River Tweed and arrived on the 3rd August. On the Thursday following at 12 o'clock, Albert Butters was playing around the edge of the river, with all the other scouts. He being the adventurous type, he waded deeper, although he couldn't swim. Desmond, who was looking on, heard a scream as Albert got into difficulties and watched frantically as William Butters who could not swim, ran into the water to aid him. He grasped hold of him to hold him up and at this point Percy Adams, who was in a boat nearby, had seen the commotion, and he dived overboard to swim to them, but on reaching them he too was pulled under by a strong current.

One of the seven remaining scouts ran to the 18th, 19th and 24th Midlothian Girl Guides which was about 200 yards away to obtain help, whilst the other 6 stood on the bank, powerless to help. When the Guides arrived, Miss Stewart, the leader, organized two girls who were strong swimmers to swim into the area, and look to see if they could find them. They couldn't find the boys or Percy Adams. Eventually the police arrived and at that point Miss Stewart sent the guides back to their camp and she took charge of the 7 remaining scouts, and drove them back to Craster.

The police dragged the river for hours in the vicinity of the accident. They thought they'd been caught in a salmon hole, but three fishermen who were about 200 yards upstream spotted the boys lying face downwards. The fishermen, Mr. Shepherd, Mr. Muckle and Mr. William Muckle whistled to the police.

When they lifted the boys out, they were holding each other's hands. They then took them to the church at Ladykirk. It was awful. Back at Craster a phone call came to Mr. Luke Robson asking him to convey the message of the tragedy to the family. He walked up to the quarry in Craster where George Butters senior and other male seniors of the family looked toward him. George was allowed to return home and break the terrible news to his wife. My grandmother was overcome with grief, and Jock Butters, the eldest boy in the family, had to go and identify the bodies. He became very ill after that and was off work for a whole year because of it. It would be called stress now. There wasn't such a word in 1931. Desmond was also there and it must have been horrific for him too.

William Butters was awarded the Scouts Medal for Valour, and Baden–Powell sent a letter to his mother, conveying how sad they all were about it. They are both buried at Embleton in the churchyard at Spittalford. It was a huge, huge funeral. It must have been really terrible for the family. My granny didn't talk about it, but we asked her one day and she said, 'the awful thing about it was, they came into the house and put their scout hats and their staves onto the table'. After that she didn't talk about it, but she was terrified after that about water, and warned us girls who lived with her for three years, to watch the tide coming round Muckle Carr, 'cos it came in like galloping horses.'

The story that came out when Tricia did a project for her school English class that my grandmother had said that her husband had said, strangely enough, on the Monday that the boys had gone to camp, that he had dreamt that he was walking through Longhoughton village, the place of his childhood, when he saw a policeman walking towards him. The policeman said, 'Oh you're just the man I want. I want you for a funeral on Sunday.' It was that Sunday that the boys were buried. It was a huge funeral, by the way, tremendously big. The procession went from Embleton Church to Spittalford. People walked then. It was half a mile long.

Girls' Club

Eleanor Venus

I used to go to the Girls' Club when it was at the Tower, in Nissen huts in the Tower grounds. I remember we used to have a rota for making the drinking chocolate, it was the cheapest you could get and if ever you were the hostess, you made it extra strong. It used to make me come out in big lumps because it was such cheap chocolate. We had some good nights. We used to have speakers and demonstrators. It was organised by Lady Craster. Miss Kell, the sewing teacher from Seahouses used to come, she was very good. I can remember one night, we had a PT night and I went to do a handstand and Edna Simpson was supposed to catch my legs and I fell and was knocked out for quite a while.

When I got married there was a lovely spread in one of the dining rooms in the Tower and we had a lovely night. The Girl's Club was very popular. There was a Club in the summerhouse, beside the pub. It was on two floors.

Joan Angus

We went to the Girl's Club every week, and for a while I was the secretary. When I left to get married, I got a lovely letter from Lady Craster wishing me good luck. We had some lovely nights at Craster Tower. We were taught how to sew and do craft work. We once had a dinner for our parents, and Lady Craster had it in her kitchen, inside the Towers, and we had soup, then pheasant and then sweets afterwards. We invited our parents to join us and we had helped to do the cooking, so I remember the Girl's Club with very happy memories.

It was somewhere to go, because in those days there were no facilities for young people, in the village. Most of the girls went; from about 13 till you got married. It might have been earlier than that, I can't rightly remember. There was no youth clubs then, none at all. The Girls Club and Boys Clubs were segregated, unless we had a social, and then they got together. I remember I was terrible about being able to keep my laugh in when you weren't supposed to laugh, and Billy Lumsden used to make me laugh. I used to laugh out loud, and then I got into trouble.

Marjorie Lumsden

The girls club was run at the Towers. There were a lot of girls in it and some married women in as well during the war. You had to be left school before you joined. Mrs. Craster ran it, and Mrs. Learner, during the war, she was evacuated here. Her husband was in the R.A.F., and she ran it. We had all sorts of things, keep fit, how to make buttons. The highlight for me was when they were affiliated to some girls club, you could go on a holiday, and I went twice to Whitley Bay. I was about 15 and we went to Rockcliffe House, right on the front. We had a great holiday there. The following year there was 4 of us went, we paid 25 shilling a week, and that was for full board. The first year we went it was when the Hoppings were on the Moor. We got the earliest bus, we couldn't get in till 4 o'clock, but we went to the Hoppings and spent a good bit of our money, before we ever got to Whitley Bay. It was a great place Whitley Bay then, they used to come from Scotland every year.

Boys Club

Billy Lumsden

We had a boys club, and you know that little house outside the pub there, there's a little cottage there on the right hand side, well the council let us have that. It was a condemned property then, but a fellow called Joe Young used to be the boys club leader, and he was a master at the Duke's school, and he was also on the council at Alnwick and he let us have it for a boys club. There was also a girls club, which was run up at the Towers, and Lady Craster was in that. We had scouts, a scout troop and we used to go away for camping weekends and for a week and all, down to Leyburn in Yorkshire. There seemed to be quite a lot going on, but of course mind, there is a youth club now. I don't know how often they meet, and Alan Punton is in charge of that now.

When we had the boys club, we used to sometimes go to Newcastle for weekends, to Grainger Park Boys school. You could take boxing, drama, orienteering or anything like that. It was really good. The lads were interested. We used to have concerts. We used to have them on 2 nights here and then the big night of all was when we went to Boulmer. I suppose there was no televisions.

W.I.

Doris Clarke

When I came to live here I joined the W.I. and I've been a member since. I didn't join when the kids were too little, but then Wally used to like to go for a pint, and when I went out he would be waiting with his coat on, for me coming home, so he could have the hour down the pub. I used to love dancing. Wally had two left feet. Mrs Brewer who used to live at Seahouses and Rachel Thompson came to start a class, Scottish Dancing Class, through the Education. I said to Wally that I was going to join. If it hadn't been for her getting me interested in Scottish Country Dancing. I went with Allison, she couldn't remember the dances and I couldn't drive, so we helped each other. Once Mrs Brewer was finished here, we used to go to different places. 30 years we went dancing. The W.I. really has been a backbone, cos I didn't join anything else. It has done a lot in the village.

Mary Smail

I was in the W.I. I was at the end of the teapot always. I was asked if I missed the W.I. and I said I miss the teapot. I enjoyed it.

Chapter 9   Lifeboat and Coastguards

Jimmy Shaw

During my 25 years as a founder member of the Lifeboat Committee and treasurer of both the committee and the ladies Lifeboat Guild, Craster village raised over £60,000 of which, roughly, £40,000 was donated to central lifeboat funds at Poole, whilst £22,000 was put aside towards building a new boat house. Poole commented that Craster was one of only three lifeboat stations to be self-supporting and, in addition, able to send money to central funds. The ladies put a great deal of hard work into organizing the annual Harbour Fete and were handsomely supported by the entire populace.

Willie Mitford

When I was a youngster the wreck came ashore at the Hole in the Dyke, called the 'Hara Fagra' it was loaded with pit props. The next one I can remember was on the sands at Newton and there was one at the Cushat, just below the Castle, it was like a trawler. My uncle, Luke Robson, had sets of clothing to clothe anyone who came ashore from the wrecks. It was the Shipwrecked Mariners' Association. He was their agent here and after that he would take them to Alnwick and maybe fit them out with clothes.

The Lifeboat

Keith Williams

Now from a personal point of view those were my first ever services. They were on the 1st May, 1982, which was also my 21st Birthday. We got a framed letter of appreciation, and you thought 'no big deal' because we actually exercise in worse conditions than there were that day. However, the rescue that sticks in my mind was the one that came in eight days later. We didn't have two in one day - we had two simultaneously. Initially we were

---

Lifeboat Section Secretary's Report 31st January, 1983,

Mr. J. Browell thanked the Ladies' Guild, for their wonderful effort on Fete Day and also the crew of the Coastguards and two crew members, Mr. N. Robson and Mr. K. Williams have both received framed letters of thanks from the Chairman of the R.N.L.I., the Duke of Atholl, for two services carried out on the 1st May 1982.

---

called to a small rowing boat with three adults in, which was being blown out to sea off Football Hole. We went across there, threw them a line, with the intention of towing them back into Newton Haven. Because the boat is quite conspicuous on the sea and it was a calmish day with a bit of a swell, another boat came in on the south side of Newton Point, basically to see what we were doing, caught a wave broadside and went upside down, throwing approximately (can't quite remember) three adults and four children into the sea, with no life jackets. We then found ourselves in the situation where we had to cut the first casualty free, promising to come back later, whizzing round the point and fishing everybody out of the water, back to shore and then returned to get the rowing boat. I suppose because children were involved the rescue sticks more in your mind as being a rescue worth doing. On that shout was myself, David Clarke and possibly one other crew member.

In my opinion the village is dying, with so many holiday homes and that coupled with the advent of the motor car has lead to an off licence closing down, a shop closing down, three mobile shops a week no longer come into the village. All these small things have slowly been eroded, but the one thing that has been constant is 'the boat'. On Fete Day, the thing that never ceases to amaze me, is that people turn out and help, who you would never feel would be interested in the boat, but they turn out to help on the day, to raise the money to keep the boat here.

This summer we have had ten callouts, in total, which is great for this boat. Not wanting to take anything from the boat as it is today, I must say that the heyday for it was probably the early 1980's, late 1981 up to 1983 – 84 and the reason for that was that the fishing was so good off here. You could look out of the Station on any Saturday or Sunday and you would see more than fifty small boats out there, fishing for cod, they were even trailing boats up from Lancashire and even further south. The place was crammed out with boats. This was pre-mobile phone and people not so switched on about sea safety, so inevitably we had a lot more calls then, or so it seems.

Martin Browell

I'm currently one of five helmsmen. The designation of the crew has changed over the past few years and we have five helmsmen and the rest are designated crew. That broke the mould as my family have always been Coastguards, my father ran the Station here and my own brother Peter, was a Coastguard. I signed up and had my medical and then I moved back from Luton and have been here for the past ten years and have been involved on a regular basis ever since, to the point where I am now – Training Co-ordinator – which is a new role introduced to combat this new litigious society. In the early days everybody was taught by the previous crew. I was taught by Gary Jobling and David Clarke. Nowadays it's all written down in books, so that's my role. Totally, off the top of my head, in ten years I've probably rescued 30 people, windsurfers blown off shore, boats breaking down, etc.

I'm really proud of what I do and the one time that I felt really important was the time when a small rowing dinghy was blown off Embleton bay, in a very strong westerly wind, father and four young children aboard. To bring those children back in safely and to see the look on the mother's face gives you an immense feeling of satisfaction, which can't be put into words. The children thought it was a great adventure, but mother wasn't too happy. One of the things about the Station to me, is the fact that I have actually turned jobs down to stay local and be part of it. In the grand scheme of things that may sound stupid, but that's a conscious decision I made at the time. I was offered a job in Glasgow and I didn't take it and one of the reasons for staying is the Lifeboat. It is the focal point of the community.

Keith Williams

Since 1969 – 70, the Boathouse has been hired out to various organisations within the village, to hold a Tea Day, to enable them to raise money for their particular organisation. Without the Boathouse, they would be unable to raise money, which is vital money for these organisations. The bigger picture is we help the Church and the Church helps us, who helps the Youth Club and so on, which makes the Lifeboat the focal point of the community.

Martin Browell

When the maroon went off, the village ran to the harbour, en masse. The harbour wall was thick with people, some to help launch the boat. Those people stood there from when the boat went out until it came back in again. Even when I started, all the people would be there waiting for the return of the boat – you felt like heroes. The village men used to grab the trailer and push it, which was quite a spectacle and, in hindsight, very dangerous.

In the early eighties we used to go to sea in thigh high boots with a thin yellow jacket and leggings, offering no warmth or protection at all and certainly if you went over the side you were in big trouble. Now we have dry suits which have made it much more versatile. It's not encouraged, but in the right circumstances we can now enter the water to assist a casualty. We also have our Huggie Bears, with thermal protection. The boat used to be launched by pointing in the right direction and letting it go and tentatively hanging on. There was quite a bit of skill involved in negotiating the breakwater down there. If you made a mistake the boat would have been lost on the breakwater and of course, from a health & safety point of view that couldn't be allowed to continue, so we have now progressed from using a winch which was purpose made from a starter motor and now we have the quad bike which is a great advantage. It has had no problems in launching the boat, recovering it is a little bit tricky, so we are now progressing to a tractor.

Iain Parker

One Sunday, Neil Finlay and I were pushing the boat down when the tide was out and that was really hard work, pushing on the sand.

Martin Browell

Craster has one of the fastest response times in the country. The time me and Punter went out in the summer, the crew timed it and it was six minutes, from the pagers going off to out of the harbour.

Keith Williams

One of the things that the R.N.L.I. really frowns upon is if a lifeboat, particularly a 'D' Class boat, goes upside down and if that ever happens you have to have an extremely good reason as to why this has happened, and the one good reason that they will not entertain is that it was a freak wave. That can be a bit of a problem when that is exactly what has happened.

One day, a nice bright, sunny day, Martin and myself were out on exercise. There were only the two of us available, so you are limited as to what you can do as far as an exercise is concerned, however, we took the boat along to the north end of Embleton Bay in a particular area called Jenny Bell's Carr. I happened to point out that there looked like a new big beach hut which had been built, so we decided to sit there with the engine idling and admiring this beach hut, but we came to the conclusion that it had just been creosoted. So we sat there for a good ten minutes which was plenty of time for any sea to have run underneath the boat. If you can sit there without any great concern for ten minutes, you know the sea is calm. Also, unbeknown to us the microphone button was stuck in so we had the whole Channel Zero in the area blanked out and anybody on that Coastguard channel could hear the conversation Martin and I were having about this beach hut.

Anyway the next thing was we decided to go. Had we not decided to go and had just sat there, we would probably have been OK. What happened was, Martin put it into gear, just started to bring the boat around, perfectly-timed to catch a wave on the rear quarter, which must have been bigger than any wave that had come under in the last ten minutes. Next thing we know, we were in the water. Now you are trained for this, but when it actually happens and you didn't see it coming, the shock took our breath away. It was still flat calm, so you are puzzled as to what has happened.

Of course, you do what you're supposed to do, which is get all the crew together, get onto the upturned hull of the boat and then you rig the painter line, which we have quite nicely braided. You rig it through the first handle, and put it through the third one and then you effectively make yourselves a loop to hang onto so you can stand on the upturned sponson and right the boat, just like righting a sailing dinghy. Now whenever you practice this there are three crew, on this occasion there were only two. We had a lot of trouble getting the boat over, by which time we were totally exhausted and we were getting in a surf line so we swam the boat ashore upside down and grabbed a couple of people off the beach to turn it right way up. We told them to go to the nearest pub and dial 999 and tell the Coastguard, as our radio had broken. We told them to say we were OK. The last thing we wanted was Seahouses Lifeboat coming down to rescue us. What we planned to do was to say we were upside down – we were on the beach, could the local auxiliary coastguard bring our trailer over and recover us on the trailer.

We then decided we would save face if we could get the engine started. There are instructions on a procedure to get the engine started if it's been turned upside down. We got the engine started and decided to go home, but we couldn't tell anyone we were going home, because we didn't have a radio. We didn't know what to do, as if we went home and the auxiliary came looking for us, we wouldn't be there and there would be all hell let loose with Maydays going out. We got the boat back to the harbour at 3.10 p.m. in the afternoon and by just after 5 o'clock that afternoon, a brand new engine was delivered and a fully serviceable radio fitted and an Inspector arrived, from the Middlesbrough area. He came to make a report as to what had happened and before he started he said, 'Right lads, now I want you to tell me in your own words what happened, but before you go any further, there is no such thing as a freak wave.'

Martin Browell

I felt that if there were any recriminations from this, I was going to pack in. There was nothing said. We both got a letter from the Director of Operations, sorry to hear that it happened, take care, learn from mistakes and keep up the good work.

Iain Parker

I've been a crewman for about 12 years. I joined because a few mates of mine were on and said it was a good crack and it was all good fun. My first rescue was on an absolutely horrible day. We couldn't get out between Little Carr and Muckle Carr. We had to go out to the north between Little Carr and the coast. I was the last one to get on to the boat and I just got my dry suit zipped up and I was buckling my lifejacket on and we came out of the harbour mouth. Andrew Browell was on the radio and Peter Angus was on the helm. Andrew was on the radio and bouncing up and down with the waves and he hit his nose on the anchor box and it was bleeding. We carried on – it was a windsurfer in Newton Haven and it must have been a Force 8 or 9. It took a while but eventually we got towards Newton Haven. There is a clear water entrance in, but we were going so far along and we thought we were in the area, but because of the weather we couldn't see where we were. We turned into Newton Haven, but we turned into the rocks, as we got in, we were just sitting on a wave going in, which was easy enough. The Coastguard shouted and said that the windsurfer had managed to get back to shore. Without even thinking about it, Peter just turned the boat round and we were looking upwards as the wave was about 12 feet above us. We went through two or three like that.

Mike Robson

There was once a call-out to say there was a boat in Football Hole. Its engine had failed. We went around, got the boat, took a line to tow him around into Newton Haven and the lad sat back and opened his cans of beer, while we were pulling him out. As we were pulling him around the headland, this speed boat came up, too close to the rocks, caught the rocks and tipped over. We were under a great deal of pressure that day, and when we saw the boat tip on the rocks, we cut the rope of the boat we were towing. We said to him, 'get back and get your oars and we'll come back and seek you in half an hour' and went to rescue the people who had got onto the rocks. Thereafter we went back for him.

The worst rescue that I went on was a one day we were playing football on the south side here and the rockets went off when we were on the pitch. The first one went off and we didn't think anything of it. The second went off and we knew that we had to go. There was David Clarke and I went running down to the lifeboat. We had our football strips on. There was a strong westerly wind blowing that day and we got word that there was a boat in difficulty at Newton.

We kept to the shore along to the castle and when we got to Embleton Bay there was a bit of a sea. The helicopter came over the top of us and he got to the boat before us and he winched the lad off the boat. We were getting close to the boat and the winch man came down from the helicopter. We must have been a mile and a half, two mile off, not the best of weather. He said to us, 'the bloke we picked up wants his boat saved. Can you get to the boat and bring it back?' He said, 'I know it's a poor sea, just take it on and cut the rope after you have steamed for a couple of minutes, and you've made the attempt'. So David says, 'I'll tell you what it is. We'll get something for this. We'll get the boat back to Craster and we'll get something for bringing it in.' I think it took us about ten minutes to get to the boat, and it must have been at least an hour to get back. We had the lifeboat oilskins on. They weren't as good as they are these days. The water had got everywhere. It was through the football strips. It was about March time. There were two people in the harbour who helped – well they rushed us out and I'm sure David got a bath on the north side 'cause both of us were suffering from hypothermia.

We got this boat back to the harbour and that night we heard that these two lads came down to Newton, had gone to the pub and had a good few drinks and then decided to go and test their engine. When they did this, the engine spluttered a bit, then the wind caught the boat and blew one of them away out and the other one ran and rang the Coastguards to get the Lifeboat and the helicopter to rescue his pal. They came back that night, collected their boat and I don't think we got a 'thank you' for going out for that rescue. We certainly got a chill. That was one of the worst ones I was on. It was February or March time, in the '70's.'

Coast Guards

Les Crate

My family has been associated with H.M. Coastguards since 1868, when a Mr. Carss arrived at Newton by the Sea as a full-time coastguard. Most of the local Coastguard Stations, including Craster were formed in the mid 1800's. They were run on military lines and attached to the Royal Navy. Their duties, apart from dealing with shipwrecks, were policing of the coastline for ships attempting to land smuggled goods. About the 1920's full-time coastguards were replaced by part-time or auxiliary coastguards, who were mainly fishermen or had a close association with the sea. They were responsible for dealing with the many shipwrecks which occurred along the rocky, treacherous Northumberland coast, rescuing the crew by firing rocket lines to the stricken vessels, which were used to attach breeches buoys to the ships and the crew would then be pulled ashore and saved.

During the two big wars – the first and second world wars – the auxiliary coastguards were drafted back into the Navy and used on a full-time basis to patrol the beaches. They were armed. They had rifles and machine guns and were responsible for keeping the public off the beaches and again it was run on military lines.

After the wars everything went back to normal and the local coastguard at Craster continued as a rescue team with the rockets and breeches buoys and they used to transport themselves to the rescues by horse and cart and later on by tractor and trailer. I myself joined the Coastguards in 1961 as an auxiliary and it was then run by a Mr. George Browell. Our main tasks then, apart from if there was somebody lost along the coast and we did a beach search, was sitting in a lookout at Cullernose Point, during rough or foggy weather, looking for ships in distress. Fortunately there were not very many, I think two or three in the 1950's. During my time in the Coastguards along there, we never ever saw a shipwreck. We did rescue one or two people off the cliffs, having seen them from the cliffs, when we were sitting there. By this time Craster had an inshore rescue boat which was a big help. We changed then from the old telephone system to radios.

When Mr. George Browell retired, his son also George but known as Peter by most locals, took over. His son Peter also joined the coastguard, but later joined the lifeboat crew with his brother Martin. Things progressed slowly until about the 1970's, when we became mobile, got Land Rovers and 4-wheel drive vehicles. Our job changed then. They did away with the breeches buoy and we were given cliff rescue gear and we formed a cliff rescue team and a beach search team, which was different from the old days because there was more technology involved. Fortunately, again we didn't do much cliff rescuing, but we were trained to do it. We had one or two people with broken legs on the beaches and we managed to get them into hospital. By then we were working the helicopters, the Sea Kings, which was brilliant. By being mobile our area extended from Amble up to Holy Island. We had one or two nasty incidents. One Christmas, a man was fishing off Cullernose Point and was washed into the sea and drowned. That spoiled Christmas a little bit. Two days after that rescue Peter Browell died, which was a very sad time for us all. I then took over running it for a while. There were one or two rescues, but nothing really dramatic. We had a couple of crashed aeroplanes off the coast and went looking for and found bits off Dunstanburgh Castle. One of my jobs for a couple of weeks was transporting bits of crashed aeroplane from Dunstanburgh Castle to R.A.F. Boulmer.

In 1986, there was a particularly nasty incident happened. One of our local fishermen, Harry Armstrong, went away fishing in his small salmon boat, up to Goswick Sands and unfortunately, the boat tipped in the surf and Harry was drowned and we spent two not very nice days up there, looking for him. We found him dead in some salmon nets. That was a local tragedy. It was a nasty rescue as there were thunderstorms and we had to keep coming off the beach and we knew after a while we wouldn't find Harry alive. His mate from Embleton was alright, one got ashore and one didn't. One of the first things I remember, on the Sunday night before he went to sea on the Monday, he bought a battery from me to start his boat up and that was the first thing I found when I went on the beach.

Once we were on patrol at Seahouses and somebody said there was a little dog in the water and they couldn't get it out, it was behind the breakwater. We discussed what we were going to do, whether to jump in the sea, which was pretty rough and it looked cold but there were two little kids crying in case they had lost their dog. We didn't have a lot of time, but then the helicopter came overhead and we radioed to them and although one of their policies is not to rescue animals, they must have been in a good mood that day and the winch man came down, hooked the little dog out of the water and I took it back to the children and obviously they were thrilled. There were all sorts of small rescues, like kids lost in the dunes. One little lad had been lost for three hours and we found him sleeping in the dunes at Bamburgh Castle.

There were about twelve of us in the team, there was a Team Leader, a Deputy Team Leader, we all had our jobs to do and when you went on a rescue, we were all pretty well trained, you knew exactly where you were going and what you had to do and you just got on with it and did it and went back to pub at night and talked about what had gone on. There was a good social side to it and there were medal presentation nights which were famous and lasted a fair few hours. I was in 25 years and got a long service medal, which was very nice but the memories are better than any medal! I was proud to be in Craster Coastguards.

Chapter 10   Church and Chapel

Doris Clarke

We went to chapel twice a day and the church twice a day on Sunday, everybody went. We used to go to the Chapel Sunday school and the Church Sunday school, then we would go to the Chapel in the evening and the Church in the afternoon.

The whole idea of coming to live in a village - if you don't join in with anything, it means you are not mixing in at all. So first of all when I lived with Granny Shell and then with Lena, they were both church women. It was just a natural thing to get up and go to church with Lena. I had already been confirmed in Gateshead. The Church played a greater part in people's lives then.

Craster Church was built in memory of T. W. Craster. It was at first meant to be a Sunday school, but became a Chapel of Ease to the Parish Church in Embleton. It seats 130 worshippers.

The Sunday school used to have the treasure hunts up at the Towers, and they would have an afternoon up there. They could pick flowers with permission. I remember taking part in a concert up at the Hall, and Mrs. Craster (Rosemary's grandmother) wanting to know who the child was singing something to do with 'daddy being in the army .'

Billy Lumsden

Things have changed quite a lot in that time, when we were youths, nearly everybody went to chapel or church then, and the chapel used to be packed. They used to hold these things called soirees, they had a supper and everybody was invited, sort of thing. The place used to be packed, but it's all changed now.

My father-in-law told me once, there was a fellow called Nightingale came here to preach, and he was one of these hell and damnation sort of preachers, and he got them all to throw away their pipes and baccy. They were hoying them on the rocks on their way from the chapel, and he says they were all going back with a candle and a jam jar looking for them at 12 o'clock at night.

Fred Stephenson

Some of these fellows were quite good singers, like Pittas Bob and Dodie Archbold and they were great Chapel men. I used to go to the Chapel every Sunday and if anybody sang above Pittas Bob he used to put his head back and almost shouted, he didn't like anyone beating him.

Even the ministers that used to come to the Chapel were characters. Many of them were lay readers. There was one called Dick Young. He was an undertaker at Seahouses, and he used to come and preach from the pulpit. He hated drink and he used to get up and shout 'BEER IS BEST … left alone.' We used to laugh.

Carol Grey

Pittas Bob used to suck black bullets and pass them along the rows of the Chapel. I can still hear him sucking them.

Adam Dawson

All of the fishermen were Methodist of course – very religious indeed. In me granny's house, before the chapel was built, they used to have the meetings there. The Craster people built the Chapel with their own money. It was properly built by skilled men. It was heated by pipes from a boiler which used coal or wood. There were a lot of Archbolds in Craster, but the Chapel was started in me granny's house – Dawson. The old religious fishermen used to preach in the Chapel, used to give a service, there was Stanton, there was some Smailes and there were some Archbolds and Scott the butcher. The fishermen and Scott the butcher were very, very religious and they used to preach themselves, give the services. The parson came from Seahouses; the real Methodist parson came every Sunday. We used to have a Sunday school, and all the children used to go to Sunday school and the local teacher was Bob Taylor. He used to preach.

Joyce Shaw

The village was very strong Methodist, but the children had to go to the C. of E. school. I've heard my mother say that my father, when he went, had to go to the Methodist Sunday school, which was in the morning, and Church Sunday school in the afternoon and you had to go. Even Winnie and Marjorie went to two Sunday schools.

Craster Church

Rosemary Gibbs

Craster Church was built in memory of my great-great grandfather Thomas Wood Craster, who was the eldest son of John Wood of Beadnell Hall. Thomas's mother and grandmother had both been Crasters. Thomas inherited the estate from his uncle Shafto Craster who died in 1836. Thomas changed his surname to Craster by Royal Licence. Thomas Wood Craster died in 1867 and the church was probably built a little later, about 1870, as a Sunday School Hall; it then became a Mission Church serving the local community and also the large number of fishermen who every summer followed the herring shoals around the coast. Embleton Holy Trinity Church remained the parish church for weddings baptisms and funerals until 1978 when the Craster church was dedicated to St. Peter the Fisherman. After that baptisms and funerals were allowed to take place in the church.

Many of the church fittings were given in memory of the Craster family and latterly members of the congregation. The east window in the church was given by Amy Craster in memory of her father, John, who died in 1895. The glass is a copy of part of a window designed by Joshua Reynolds d 179? for the chapel of New College Oxford. It is thought that Amy Craster may have chosen this window as she was a friend of Caroline Rooke, who lived at 'Paradise' in Embleton. Caroline's father, George Rooke, was vicar of Embleton from 1830 to 1874 and her grandmother Lady Rooke (nee Harriet Sophia Burrand) was one of the ladies chosen by Sir Joshua to model 'justice' in the complete window in New College. Our window was re-leaded twenty years ago.

The wooden pews were given in memory of Thomas's widow Charlotte Pulleine Craster (nee Roddam). The reading desk, designed and made by Robert (Mousie) Thompson in Yorkshire, was given by family and friends in memory of my grandmother Hilda Craster who played the organ for forty-seven years. She was a daughter of Canon Osborn, who came from Malvern to the parish of Embleton. Hilda married Thomas William Craster in 1897. The church silver was given in memory of my uncle Shafto Craster, who played the organ for many years, and also in memory of my mother Phyllis Carr-Ellison, who was Shafto's twin sister.

Our organ was presented by Jimmy Bruce in memory of his wife Amy (nee Robson) who died in 1986, and the font was given in memory of Tom MacDonald who was the schoolmaster in Dunstan and then Craster from 1955 – 1972. It was presented to the church by his family in 1995.

Canon Parke worshipped in our church after he had retired and left money for a beautiful stone cross to be erected on the roof of the church.

The latest addition to the church, 1998, is the beautiful window designed by Leonard Evetts in memory of my mother Phyllis and her brother Shafto Craster.

The Chapel

In 1869, (Matthew) Stephenson, the story goes, was fishing out of the Tyne – the Craster fishermen of the day operating at times beyond home waters – when, a singer himself, the Sankey hymns sung by men of the herring fleet- favourites, one may be sure, like 'The ninety and nine', 'When the mists have rolled away,' 'Faith is the victory' - so impressed him that on his return home he taught the hymns to his children, then to neighbouring children, so that before long his house had become a Sunday afternoon regular meeting place for children and parents alike.
Extract from '100 Years On: Craster Methodist Church 1880 – 1980' p 7

Great reformation here' wrote diarist (William Gibb) Dawson on March 13th, 1870, the emphasis on revivalism and converts, on changing attitudes and habits, among them an upsurge in teetotalism. That reformation, that revivalism, went on in Craster throughout the '70's, and made telling impact on village life. An annual Whit Monday revivalist rally with tea on the grass at Dunstanburgh Castle – the special day in the year on which best china tea sets were produced by the ladies and transported thither in clothes baskets – coincided with the Craster Feast, traditionally held over Whit weekend.
Extract from '100 Years On: Craster Methodist Church 1880 – 1980' p 8

Entries of another diarist, fish curer Joseph Henderson Archbold 1879 – 1880
December 7 – Revival going on, several young people brought in. John Stanton, Robert Stewart, young John Smailes, Thomas Smailes, our Charles and Joseph, with some more.
December 11 – Great revival still going on – 15 or 16 brought in tonight.
December 12 – The revivalists round the place every night and doing great work for the Lord.
Christmas Day – We had a grand soiree down in the shade ('shade' or shed, implying herring shed). Several young men told of their conversion and experience.)
1880
January 22 – We have had a meeting about building a meeting house on the North Side. Ralph Archbold has agreed to give as much ground as will do to build it on.
March 27- We had meeting tonight about a chapel and got grant to build.
June 19 – subscription books out for erection of chapel.

> *June 21 – Our Joseph brought in first load of lime for builders*
> *June 27 - Masons commenced work*
> *July 12 – Chapel foundation stone laid. My name, with names of 11 more chapel trustees, put in a bottle, which placed in foundation stone.*
> *Extract from '100 Years On: Craster Methodist Church 1880 – 1980' p 10*

> *The first roll of 12 trustees: William Henderson Archbold; Matthew Stephenson; Joseph Henderson Archbold; Ralph Archbold; John Smailes; Robert Archbold; Charles Archbold; Ralph Simpson; Charles Archbold (William's son); Hugh Archbold; Thomas Smailes; John Taylor Stanton.*
> *The predominantly Methodist families Archbold, Stephenson, Smailes, Simpson, Stanton, – not forgetting Dawson, Taylor, Grey, Scott, and their various branches; old family names as synonymous with Craster as its famous kipper!*
> *Extract from '100 Years On: Craster Methodist Church 1880 – 1980' p11–12*

(The Craster Methodist Church built that year (1880) at a cost of £474 from Whinstone quarried locally, and first opened for public worship at a thanksgiving service held on Christmas Day morning)

The late Eva Archbold, for 65 years a chapel member, recalls her early memories in a diary note:

> *Among my earliest memories of the chapel are that of Jim Stephenson keeping an ever watchful eye on the big hanging oil lamps. The wicks had to be dead straight, and if a tail dared show itself, instantly out would come Jim's step ladder so that he could reach the lamp to re-trim it.*
>
> *Highlights for us children were the Christmas party and the Sunday School Anniversary. We said our pieces and sang our hymns, then as we grew older, after having first attended Sunday school, we went on to morning service in the chapel.*
>
> *I so well remember coming down Chapel Row and smelling the Sunday joints being roasted. Annie Scott, the butcher's daughter, would say, 'You cannot beat Scott's roast beef'. Sometimes we were given a slice of bread dipped in the roasting tin, and didn't we enjoy it!*
>
> *On Sunday afternoons we used to walk up to Dunstan to go to the C of E Sunday school, and in the evenings it was back to the chapel. How thrilled I was to join the choir and, at the age of fourteen, to become a chapel member.*
>
> *At Whitsuntide there was always a fruit and vegetable stall in aid of chapel funds at Piddah's Corner, now Dunstanburgh Road.*
>
> *Craster had no reliable street lighting in those days, and the moons phases decided the dates of any special services planned for the dark nights. Flash lights were in their infancy, and to light our way in the dark we usually made do with a candle in a jam jar.*

Ref: '100 Years On: Craster Methodist Church 1880 –1980' including diary extracts from: William Gibb Dawson 1870; Joseph Henry Archbold 1979 – 80; and Eva Archbold 1950's.

Chapter 11　　　　　**Wartime**

SISTERS IN ARMS
WINNIE AND ADA

Winnie Hogg (nee Archbold) and Ada Archbold in 1945

The First World War

Willie Archbold

My uncle couldn't get into the Navy in the First War and he volunteered for the Royal Artillery and he was at the Somme in the thickest of the fighting and there was news coming here to my mother about people getting killed and injured and everything, all round about at the farms and houses and it was terrible. There was 60,000 slaughtered in one day, British and Germans. Him and another lad from here, he came out of that Hell and then went down on his doorstep, it must have been his time.

Joyce Shaw

In the First World War, my dad's eldest brother, who was James Edward Archbold, he was a school teacher, he was in the Durham Light Infantry, because he was at St. Bede's College, Durham when war was declared, so he went into the D.L.I. He was taken prisoner at Passchendaele. They first of all got word that he was missing in the

July and they never got word that he was a prisoner until the January and he spent his prison time in the Salt Mines in Poland. He didn't get home until 1919.

My mother and father actually met here during the First War. My mother was here on holiday on the 4th August, 1914, the day war was declared and they met here at the end of the first War.

Adam Dawson

We had the home guards. They saw a man loitering about near the Dunstanburgh Castle, so one of the home guards – of course he had a rifle – went and said, 'Come on, I'm going to take you in. You're a spy.' When they got him to Craster he was one of the Craster folk – Charlie Varnum. He wasn't a Craster man, he came from Leicester, so he didn't talk Craster twang. Dode Simpson brought him in, all the way with a gun at his back and it was Charlie Varnum.

Second World War

Joining up

Willie Mitford

I went to the Army in 1943. I didn't need to go into the army. I could have been exempt 'cause they were bringing men out of the Army to work in the quarry to get the stone for the aerodromes. I went in February, 1943, to Clitheroe in Lancashire, then I went to Chester to train to be in the Engineers and from there I went to Aldershot, from there to the Isle of Wight, then to Felixtowe, to Scarborough and trained for the Normandy landings. The Normandy landings were pretty rough. It was no picnic. There was a lot of fighting before we got through by Caen and we were kind of stuck for a long time because the British were up against the Panzers. The Americans moved, but they weren't having the heaviest fighting, the Panzers were against the British and Canadians at Caen and that held us up. We got to Falaise Gap and cut a lot of the Germans off and once we got to that, we went straight through, no stopping until we got to Paris.

Dennis Williams

My uncle, Geordie Williams, joined up in June 1939. He was drafted into the Green Howards, and then he was posted to Norway. I heard that they didn't expect a hard time, but they hadn't reckoned on the German Storm Troopers being there. They were ambushed and my grandmother got a letter from the War Office on April 28th 1940 to say that he was missing in action. The lieutenant in charge of the advanced party also wrote to her on May 9th to say that his platoon had gone to cover the retirement of another regiment when they were attacked. The letter said they had gone out 'cheerfully to do their job thoroughly and nobly.'

Anyway, back here in Craster, there was relief on May 21st 1940, when they heard from the War Office that he was 'reported interned in Sweden'. It said, 'he is described as being in good condition except for his feet'. After that they got a letter from the Red Cross to say they couldn't get any letters or parcels to him. It was August when they heard again from the Red Cross that some soldiers and sailors might be exchanged and he might be returning to England. They found out later he had escaped through a forest when the platoon had scattered and he had made his way, on foot, into Sweden. He got back home on a fishing boat. I still have a newspaper article about it. Some people said he should have stayed in Sweden, because he was posted to the jungle in Burma after that. He was awarded the Burma Star.

He worked in the quarry with my dad, Benny, who was in the R.A.F. They both played football for Craster Rovers.

Ada Archbold

I joined the A.T.S. in 1943, stationed in Bristol a lot of the time as a Radar Operator, had the time of my life, I wouldn't have missed it for the world. I was driving one day, it was when the Italians had surrendered and these Italians came to work with the Army and they sent one on the wagon with me and he used to sit on the tailboard and I used to tell him he would fall off. We went to the ration stores in Liverpool and a Corporal came with us, he was in charge. We got the rations, come back and I backed up to this Nissen hut where they were putting them in. We left the Italian and went into the N.A.A.F.I., give him about an hour to get it off-loaded and come back, go on another job, maybe to the brewery, Bents or Ind Coopes breweries in Liverpool, for the beer for the Officers' Mess. Anyway, this day when I got back, I backed up, just give him room for the tailboard to drop, got straight out, never looked, straight into the N.A.A.F.I.. I was the first one out and I said to Joe, the Corporal, it's time we went and when I got back, I always made sure he'd put the tailboard up again. All the rations were still in and I thought he'd fallen off the back of the lorry. I'd warned him about sitting on the back. I says to Joe that the rations were still there and he wasn't. I thought I would have to report him missing and we set to off-loading the rations.

I was worried sick. It come to dinnertime and he hadn't turned up and I said we'd have to report him missing and the Corporal said 'Oh, he'll turn up'. I went for my dinner and I couldn't eat it when the door opened – I thought it was a policeman coming to say that they'd found a body in the road. After dinner I said I'm definitely going to report him missing. I set off for the guardroom. I had to go around two bends and here he's coming, all smiles. We called him Sammy, he was little, a real Italian and he said he had heard me say in the morning that I was going to stop for a packet of cigarettes and I stopped for a policeman on point duty, just near Aintree, there was a shop nearby and he thought I'd stopped to go to the shop and he jumped out and when the policeman waved me on, I went away and left him. He could speak good English. He found his way to the station, then he had to get a train to Ormskirk, then he had to get a train to the camp and that's what took him so long.

Jimmy Hall

I went into the army in early 1944. When I joined it was the push before the Rhine, in Belgium, I was in the 52nd Lowland Division, H.L.I. When the war finished in Germany, I was in Bremerhaven and then we went across to Brussels and stayed there for a bit and then they decided they were going to do an assault on Japan, so everybody from the 56 Group, they made new regiments and they made a new division. So I went into the First H.L.I., came home on leave then went back to Calais. We were watching Ivy Benson's Band, actually, and she came and said they had just dropped the H bomb, the war's over.

We had this trouble in the Middle East with the Jews and the Arabs, so I was sent to Cairo in what I was standing up in. I had no gear, nothing. Went to Tel Al Kabir, picked up vehicles and we were on the golf course in Jerusalem. I could never get into Military Transport at all. I tried all ways. I was a Corporal Section Commander then and there was a notice come up on detail that they were stuck for drivers, so I applied for it. When I got into driving, I had the best job in the army. I was driving the Quartermaster, so I got new boots and any manner of things. When he retired I took him to Port Said. When he left I drove big vehicles and I was MT Sergeant within six months.

Willie Mitford

I had just come home from the Far East, I went there when the Germans were finished. I was put on what they called 'the Burma posting'. The Japanese were still on and we went out to India and were preparing to invade Singapore. When they dropped the atom bomb, the Japs packed in and we went over and took over from them in Singapore.

Wartime in the Village

Marjorie Lumsden

Winnie and I got machine gunned during the war. My mother said if you go to Howick stores on a Thursday you might get a chocolate cake, which was as hard as flint, mind, but there was chocolate on the top. So we went to Howick store, Winnie & I, on our bikes, and on the way back, on the hill besides Curry's farm, Winnie said to me, 'there's an aeroplane that's low, very low.' The noise was different. She pulled me down behind the wall and we heard this machine gun going – we definitely heard the machine gun and the plane went out to sea, very low. It was like a drone. It had a totally different drone. We never thought any more about it till years later.

Doris Clarke

We were living in Gateshead at the time, when the war was threatened, and we were evacuated, through the school, before the war started. We already had gas masks given, and had been shown how they worked. (Did you feel scared as a child?) No it was great, it was exciting - we were going away. We were shown how to put the gas masks on, and we also had a pannier bag – it had two pouches joined together with a strap. The name was embroidered. We made them ourselves. This was how much preparation went in before the war. We went to Gateshead East station, which wasn't used as a passenger station then, and by the time the train pulled out, we had eaten all of our bait. However, we were sent to Stokesley in Yorkshire, and nobody wanted us, because me two other cousins were there and an aunt, and my mother said if nobody would take the four we were to come home. We were issued with brown paper carrier bags with iron rations in, like tins of milk, tins of meat, different tins.

So in the Market Place in Stokesley at 5 o'clock in the afternoon, nobody wanted four. However there was this butcher, his mother and daughter (the wife had died,) so there were three generations, living in the house. They had an upper storey which we used. This was what was called the 'phoney' war, because nothing happened, and we came home after five weeks.

When we got home, there were no schools opened, because they had all closed down, when the kids were sent away. We went to someone's front room, for about 10 or 12 weeks with this lady, I don't even know if she was a teacher. There were about 10 or 12 of us. Then my mother decided to send us to Craster. It was done through the government. There was six shillings a week paid to my Auntie Mary, just me - my other cousins didn't come, and once we got home from the school evacuation we split up. We were all only children. I came up here in 1940, and I had to register at the school.

That was an eye opener, Dunstan school. Auntie Mary said, 'you can get those petticoats off for a start'. I had two petticoats on, one flannelette, one liberty bodice and a silky petticoat on the top and long stockings, which hitched onto these rubber buttons on my liberty bodice. She said you can get them off for a start, so I did, and went into knee socks, which if you fell down you didn't put the knees out. (Did the village accept you?)

Yes. We used to walk up to school, so if one was late, then everybody was late, and you got the cane off Mr. Blackburn who was the teacher. Mrs. Coney used to be in the girls at the other end. Miss. Barber was there for a while, but Mrs. Coney was the teacher. The girls used to go into her end for sewing and she taught the young ones. I enjoyed it. I just remember the nice things. I don't think you remember the rotten things. Being away from home didn't seem to affect me. My mother used to come up once a month to see me.

What I can remember mainly was, when I came, I didn't like vegetables. I didn't like this and I didn't that, but when I got here, I had to eat them. There was a garden full of vegetables and they were nice and fresh. I do remember, Ralphy Shell was still at home, Jean's husband was in the army and she used to sleep here. Ralphy used to be a good shot with the sling and many's the rabbit that was caught. I used to be fascinated to watch them skinning it, because when you live in the town they were already skinned. I was fascinated to watch Auntie Mary break the legs over the end of the bench, cut the head off, and pull the skin back. It was a lovely dinner, gorgeous with all the fresh vegetables. That was one thing that stays in my mind. My mother used to come up once a month, and there was a shilling a week pocket money. We used to sneak on the rocks. That was the little sketch we did. We used to get under the wire and play down on the rocks.

Geordie Grey

I started farming when there were only horses, no tractors, but during the war, we began to get tractors, supplied by the Ministry and then after the war, the tractors started to come along and it did make life easier.

Jimmy Hall

Craster Quarry was closed before the war and it was opened again by a firm called Kings & Co., of Glasgow and then when Boulmer and Brunton aerodromes were built, they were fetching stone out of the quarry for the runways and they started blasting back again.

Marjorie Lumsden

When the soldiers were at the Towers we used to have excellent dances there. I had a partner who could jitterbug like nobody's business. Nowadays, they want something different on every time they go out. I went out in the same dress every time.

Willie Mitford

The Germans dropped bombs at Howick, right on the corner beside the Hall. One was dropped in the woods there. We used to sit out on the harbour wall and listen to the planes. If they dropped anything it was just as they were going out, to get back as soon as they could.

There was a radar station on the top of the Heugh and then they put the Italian prisoners of war up there. They were working on the farms. The huts were so far down the hillside, there's a little brick building which I think has been a cess pool.

A government department came to Craster and demanded all the fishing boats to be requisitioned for war work, but in the end it fell through. During the last war the local fishermen went to sea just the same, but they had to look out for mines. It was a dangerous job. There was plenty of fish and they made lots of money during the war. There were quite a lot of Craster men in the forces during the war, and there were two killed. They were George Robert Archbold and the other was Charles Smailes Caisley. During the last war there were home guards, and they used to go along the coast during the night, to the Castle and back to guard the coast. In the last war there were soldiers, which made up a little army to guard Craster and the coast. They were Home Guards.

Violet Hall

We used to go to dances in the Hall in the wartime. That's when they had a great big billiard table in the middle of the room. You used to have to dance around it. Eventually it went to Craster Tower.

The troops, the Home Guard, the Reading Room committee, and the billiard table 1941–1945

Reading Room Minutes

June 20ᵗʰ 1941
Mrs Craster also wished to know if the billiards table could be moved so that the troops might have dances, but the committee were unanimous that the table should remain untouched

Feb 9ᵗʰ 1942
The subject of the soldiers using the room for dancing was then raised and Mr Harbottle moved the following resolution – that the soldiers have the use of the room on specified nights at the usual dancing charges; that they must use the floor as it is at present for space, and that A.R.P. material on the stage must be carefully moved and replaced. This was seconded and carried.

Complaints that the Home Guard were using the room more often than they should and being careless with the lights, were raised and it was agreed that the secretary should find out what period of time the 2/6d rental covered.

23ʳᵈ Feb 1942
A letter from Maj. Carr-Ellison re the use of the room for the Home Guard was read and discussed. It was agreed to leave the matter over pro tem.

The hiring of the room by the soldiers for dancing was mentioned and it was agreed that the Reading Room should pay the caretaker.

19ᵗʰ Mar 1942
The question of the troops hiring the room every Monday night for whist drives was raised. Considering the number of times a week the room is let, and in fairness to subscribing members, it was agreed that there was no evening available for such whist drives, and that a letter to that effect be sent to Lieut. Young.

7ᵗʰ July 1942
The unruly conduct of people near the room, when dancing was in progress was then discussed and it was agreed to display a notice in future warning people against drunken behaviour in or near the room.

It was thought that the hirer should be held responsible for the behaviour of those who attend.

8ᵗʰ Oct 1942
A letter from the Home Guard was then read. The writer stated that the men would not be able to drill efficiently in the room this winter, owing to the billiards table and asked that it might be removed. It was carried unanimously that the table be left where it is. It was then agreed to adjourn the meeting pending enquiries.

15ᵗʰ Oct 1942
Correspondence regarding the billiards table was read, and the committee re-affirmed its decision of the last meeting to let the table remain in the room. It was agreed that the secretary should acquaint Mr. Sinclair of this verbally, as Major Carr-Ellison had written to him and not to this committee.

A third key of the Reading Room, in the possession of Mr. A Straughan – Home Guard - was commented on, and it was agreed that a note should be sent to him, asking for its return to Mr. Rutherford.

26th Nov 1942

The minutes of the last meeting – and before being signed, the matter of the key was raised. After a letter from Maj. Carr-Ellison had been read in which he said that the Home Guard must have the key during the National Emergency, it was agreed to let the matter drop for the time being.

It was then mentioned that the Adj. 2nd Batt. Home Guard – Alnwick Castle – had made certain proposals regarding the billiards table. These were i) to take down the table ii) to store it iii) to replace it at the expense of the military authorities. After discussion it was agreed that the table should remain untouched.

28th May 1943

Regarding the moving of the billiards table; it was proposed by Mr Rutherford, seconded by Mr. J Grey that the table should remain in the room. This was carried.

26th Nov 1943

It was then agreed that a letter be sent to the Home Guard to state that i) they must find their own fuel and ii) to draw attention to the indentations on the floor.

22nd June 1944

As the room has been occasionally left in an untidy state by the Home Guard, it was proposed that a letter be sent to Mr. Sinclair requesting him to look into the matter.

Regarding the new billiards room, Mr. Young said that the Boys' Clubs Association might be able to help. The committee agreed that Mr. Young should get information.

9th May 1945

Mr. T S Grey then introduced the matter of moving the billiards table, and after discussion the voting was as follows: For moving it – Mr. Charlton, Mr Straughan, Mr. Young- Against moving it – Mr. J Grey, Mr. Rutherford. These two men then resigned from the committee.

The table is to be stored at the Towers

Food & rationing

Ada Archbold

I went to Alnwick on my bike, got a pound of butter, two blocks, my bag was full. I was pedalling up through Denwick and the butter dropped out the bag and the wheel went over it and I chucked it over the hedge and the next week butter was rationed.

Winnie Hogg

One day in the war Lord Hah Hah [Lord Haw Haw] was on the wireless saying that people in England were starving 'cos they had little food, and I mind my dad going right up to the wireless with a bacon sandwich and saying, 'smell that – that's home cured bacon, that!'

Willie Archbold

My mother still made cakes, but from about 1940 – the baker came round with bread. Sunday dinner used to be a rare thing, lovely roasts, but during the War, the fishermen, or anybody that lived in the village would catch a rabbit up there and Mr. Rowell didn't say nowt, as long as you didn't pull the dykes down,(the dry stone wall at the back of the hills) because when he first come there, my father was up there (on the hills at the back of the Chapel) and got a rabbit, and Mr. Rowell said he could take a rabbit any time you like as long as you divn't get into the dykes 'cause if you pull the dykes down, I'll chase the lot of you.' It was about 1953 when the myxomatosis came and the rabbits kept us alive during the War, 'cause the meat was on ration. My father caught loads of rabbits, he had a little bit net and if there were footprints in the snow, he would put the net around the other side and kick the side of the hole with his foot and then he had it.

During the War we used to have two pigs, most of the fishermen had pigs during the war. We kept them over by the North Hills.

Joyce Shaw

During the 2nd World War the people of Craster didn't go short of food. They were much better off than people in the town, because they had hens and most families had a pig, which was a bacon pig. When they killed a pig there was black and white pudding and all sorts and you shared with your neighbours 'cause there were no freezers, therefore everything had to be eaten, it was no good keeping anything. The fishermen did get an extra ration.

Billy Lumsden

The war was on and there was any amount of fish and stuff then – any amount. On the farms you were allowed to keep two pigs, but you had to give in your bacon coupons, and you were allowed to keep two (pigs.)

Winnie Hogg

One year, just after the war, when everything was still rationed, we kept pigs up there at the top of the tattie grounds. This particular time my mother, father and brother had gone on holiday, they never had much holiday, but they had gone to Yorkshire to do some fishing with people they knew, and I was left in charge of my grandmother. We had a dog at that time called Lassie; she would put her paws up to the window and bark like mad.

My grandmother and me were having our tea. It went away and came back again and did the same. I went out to the top of the hill where we lived at the time. It ran down and looked over to the hills and started to bark, and lo and behold the pig had got out. I was in charge of the feeding time 'cos my dad was away. I wasn't really bothered about it, but it was ready to kill, and there it was running around on top of the crags. I thought my dad will come back and kill me, so I went and got some of the fisherman. I went and got a bucket with some of the potato and things which was boiling the meal, and Tom Grey said, 'is that all you're feeding it with?' I said 'yes', and he said, 'well that's not very much'. So it must have been starving of hunger. It had jumped right over the top of the sty, but they chased it and got it back in the sty. Otherwise we might have lost it on top of the crags. I was going out with Tommy and he got some wood and nailed it right over the top of the sty, so it couldn't get out. It got some good feeds after that.

Mines and shipwrecks

Jimmy Hall

In 1942 there were two big mines come in, took the windows out of all the houses.

Doris Clarke

We used to sneak on the rocks. We used to get under the wire and play down on the rocks. I remember the mines coming in adrift, there were two of them. They bobbed about off there, it was 1940 – 41. I watched one of them and it went off as I watched it. It hit Muckle Carr and exploded. The second one -the tide must have been coming in, and the coast guards were keeping a watch on it, and we were evacuated out of those houses. I went to stay with Mrs. Straughan, you know Mamie Straughan's mother. They lived next door to where Joyce Archbold lived, where John had the joiner's shop. So we slept there for one night, and it did go off during the night. There were no windows left. There was shrapnel stuck in the garden. This house that I'm living in now has got signs of mine damage. You can see the lines have been filled in. It's not a very good job.

Gladys Simpson

In 1940 – 41 the mine went off and when the second one went off we went to Grace Ellis's house. I was going to the pictures that night on the bus and they were all leaning again that wall. It bobbed and bobbed and everyone was waiting for it. When we came back, Edward Grey's shop window was out. I was kneeling on the seat watching it go off and it hit Muckle Carr. There was pieces of shrapnel stuck in the walls at Mrs. Grey's. Doris says our houses have the cracks yet on the outside, we've had them filled in but they appear in other places.

There was a convoy hit off there and when the tide was coming in all these tins of pencils and boxes of cigarettes come in. My Uncle Bob came from Seahouses to go to sea with me dad, he got that house next to Lizzy Grey, in the corner and me Uncle Bob must have getten some and put them in the loft and I forget who moved into the house after them but they said they went up to the loft and found tins of cigarettes. All the fishermen had them in. Clippie had them, Isabel used to get them and we smoked full strength Capstan on the way to school and in the quarry. Winnie used to hide them in her knickers. We got five woodbines and went the back of the summerhouse and didn't Georgina look through the window. We'd been to the shop and got some old newspapers and we were lighting the cigarettes with the newspaper.

Joyce Shaw

When the War came, we couldn't go onto the rocks because there was barbed wire all the way along the banks, there were little gaps when we used to go, but you weren't really supposed to. There were mines washed up and one weekend when we were here, a mine went off (a sea mine.) It blew my granny's small bedroom window clean out and others on Chapel Row.

Willie Mitford

The houses were all evacuated along the bottom. We lived nearest in the house Edith Robson lives in now, when the mine went up. It shattered the windows of several houses, that was in 1941. They knew it would go off at a certain time, when the tide brought it onto the rocks and once it hit the rocks it would blow up, it was coming in between the Carrs.

Geordie Grey

The thing I remember most about here was during the war, was when the mines came ashore. We had a big one just below this house, what we're sitting in and the police and everyone came and evacuated us to the other side of the village and about one o'clock in the morning this mine went up. It had been dropped in the sea and had floated in and when it touched the rocks, it blew up. So I can always remember my father coming back here and all the windows were out, the ceilings were down, the plaster was off, all these houses along the bottom end. That's one of my vivid memories. I was at school then and I can remember taking bits of shrapnel. I was at Alnwick School then, and I would give bits to my best friends. There was one piece found up beside the Towers. We could see the mine sitting on the rocks but it didn't come in until the tide turned.

Geordie Grey

There was also a sea mine that came in about six o'clock at night. It came over the top of Muckle Carr, never went off, floated in onto the shore and it just settled there. The police and coastguards got us all evacuated and about one o'clock in the morning, when the tide came in, it moved it again, touched one of the tentacles on it and it blew up but we were all evacuated.

Adam Dawson

During the war there was a ship left Tyneside, Newcastle, and she was a general cargo ship, she was full of cigarettes, clothes, everything. Now she was blown up not far away from the outside of Craster, and cigarettes were washed ashore by the thousand. I got some. My father sent me a box of cigarettes, and everybody else in the village had cigarettes and all sorts of stuff. I was probably still in my mother's arms, but I can remember going behind the castle, Dunstanburgh Castle, 'cos there was a submarine came ashore there. All the crew – it was rough weather – were lost. They were foreign. When I grew up, I was working in Embleton in my trade, and somebody came to me and said, 'do you know those men that were lost'. Well, I could tell them. Do you see that castle there? Well that's where they were lost, and they are buried in Embleton cemetery. They had come all the way from Sweden or somewhere, they used to fight for us during the war – they were all lost. They are all buried in the cemetery at Embleton. This was the First World War.

Now in the Second World War, there were the mines. They used to wash ashore, in an easterly gale, and they used to go off. My father and his brother had a coble, they used to go fishing, and there was a mine came ashore on the rocks and some men came to Craster and asked the fishermen if they would go and catch it. They all refused, but my father and Sep said they would go and fetch it. They went not far away and fetched this mine into Craster. This ministry man went with them to fetch it off. My uncle said 'what about us sat here?' This officer said, 'you know nothing about it. Just go up'. Anyway they brought it ashore, they towed it into Craster harbour. Everybody in Craster was gone. When they got the mine in, the man just turned it over, screwed something off and got all the powder out and set it afire.

Willie Mitford

There was a boat blew up during the war, it was beside the Farne Islands and all the cigarettes, Chinese money, tennis balls, pencils and things came into the harbour. At Newton where these come up, they buried them in the gardens, some had them hidden in the dungeons at the Castle. We went and collected tins but when you opened them up, the tobacco was alright but the papers were wet so you had to rescue the tobacco and roll them again. It kept us going for a while.

Prisoners of War

Eleanor Venus

When I worked out on the land, the prisoners of war used to be along the top and they had Nissen huts there, they helped on the farm. They used to help on threshing days, one was called Franz, he was a nasty piece of work, he couldn't stand the English. I had a collie dog and I was on the top of the thresher and I had my coat just lying down and he went to pick the coat up and the dog went for him and he ended up in hospital having his nose cauterised. There were some nice ones, one of them wanted to marry me and take me to Germany

There were Germans first and then the Italians and they were on top of the crag and I used to go along the bottom with the horse and cart with turnips on and they all used to come and wave. They filled their mattresses with chaff. George Renwick used to be the guard and he was supposed to guard them but he was courting and he would go off and leave them with the guns and he would say 'Don't do nowt silly while I'm away'.

Edna Simpson

When the prisoners of war were here they used to come from the radio location when the water was outside our house and there's still the cement thing there where the tap was. I think the first prisoners were the Italians and then the Germans were the second lot of prisoners. They were below the west end of the Heugh. They had a proper irrigation system and it was lovely, it was terraced, they came down twice a day for water at that tap. The Italians made a lot of things to sell, rings, cigarette cases, toothbrush handles.

I eventually went to Belford Station and I finished my time there and the Italian prisoners of war were stationed near Belford and they came down to work at the station. There was a huge wagon at the Station, it was a storeroom for flour and we used to pack it into this place and then they would come and put it into small sacks. It took two prisoners to one sack. They brought their packed lunch and their tea in bottles and we used to fill the fire buckets with hot water for them to put their bottles in to keep warm. They also worked at the farms.

When they lived at the Heugh, they were self-sufficient, but there were British servicemen there. Geordie Renwick was a guard. He was courting Ena, he used to give his gun to the prisoner while he went courting.

Joyce Shaw

There used to be a prisoner of war camp along the back of the hills, they were Italians and they didn't come into the village at that time but they used to come down between Chapel Row. When the Italians went away, we walked round the Nissen huts 'cause they had pictures round the walls. They worked on the farms.

Billy Lumsden

I came to work on the farm at Dunstan Square in 1943, and I came to live in the village after I got married in 1950. When I first came to Dunstan Square there was a prisoner of war camp up on the hills there, the Italians were there first, then the Germans came. Before that, before they had them there at the prisoner of war camp, it used to be a Radar station and there was a big mast there which they took down later on. In fact the concrete block house – where they had the big engines that drove it, which was Rolls Royce - is still there. They took so much of the hill away and they had 4 nissen huts set back into the hill, stretched right down. I remember once the P.O.W.'s thought they would put P.O.W. right along the hills in whitewash stone. After they got them finished we had to bury them all 'cos you see them for miles away.

We didn't have any at Dunstan Square, the land army. 'Cos we used to get-the prisoners you see – the Italians or the Germans. When they closed this one here, the German prisoners were at Embleton. That's when I learned to drive a car. The boss was away with his brother and Mrs Rowell says to me, you have to take the prisoners home. There were four of them and it was just a little Ford car like. Well I drove a tractor from when I was a kid, but when it came to getting the car out of the garage, I kept bumping it. I got them in and got them to Embleton and one of them could speak relatively good English, he says 'thank you very much, but tomorrow night we will walk.' We ended up pushing it out of the garage.

(So they mixed in then, these prisoners?) Aye, one, I never knew his surname, but we called him Franz, he only had half a heel on his right foot, and I asked him one day how it happened. He had been in Russia and he had climbed out of this ditch and there was a machine gun dead in front of him, and it fired. He threw himself back and as he went up it took his heel off. He was dead lucky like. He said if they'd been there another month they would never had gotten back, they got a real hammering like.

They were good workers, different to the Italians. If it rained the Italians used to pack it in. I lent this lad Franz an old bike, and because we were all out at weekends, of course they couldn't go to dances like, they went around the countryside. He arrived back one night and said they were moving to Wooler, and then back home. The war was finished by then and he brought the bike back and it was like brand new. I said to him you'll have to go and see the boss mind, when you come back, cos he'd worked for us for about 3 years, and I took him up to the farmhouse like and the boss said he would run him home in the car. I didn't see him after that. By he made a rare job of the bike mind. We got on all right with them, they were good workers ye knaa, the Germans.

During the war, Craster had some prisoners of war, and they were Italians, and they were stationed just behind the cliffs at Craster, in wooden sheds. There wasn't many, but they were good artists. Some of the paintings were in this shed. They also made a road up to it. They were loose, they could have escaped at anytime, but they didn't. They used to do a lot of work for the village folk, 'cos they couldn't go anywhere, they did a lot of gardening and lots of work. Of course the village folk used to look after them well.

Costs of war

Willie Mitford

There are a lot of names on the memorial in the Chapel and the Church of the men of Craster who lost their lives in the Wars. All the men that were at the Coastguards up here were all killed in the War.

Roll of Honour

1914 - 1918

Harold J Fern	Robert Smailes
John Harvey	Jesse Budgen
Robert Woodcock	Luke R Smailes
William Carss	Alexander Mason
Daniel Carss	William Bradwell
John W Smailes	John Archbold
Arthur Denmead	Edward Simpson
Llewellyn Denmead	

1945-1945

Alexander Anderson

Stephen Sinclair

Charles Smailes Caisley

Frank Taylor Watson

George Robert Archbold (missing)

There were a lot of young men in the village who lost their lives, in both Wars. Take for instance, George Robert Archbold, who was an only son, his plane went down near to the end of the war. On the memorial in the Chapel it's got 'missing'. His mother would never say that he had been killed.

Aftermath

Joyce Shaw

In the war, men went away and met women when they were away and brought them back. In the last War, a lot of men went away and also women. Most of those people brought back wives and husbands from Scotland, Wales, Ireland, most of these peoples' descendants are still in the village now and that brought in new blood. Before that, they might meet someone from Embleton, Beadnell or Boulmer but not a lot farther away. The War was a good thing in a way because it brought much new blood to lots of little villages.

Winnie Hogg

(After the war, I thought) I might re-join the Army – I had got used to being in the A.T.S. and quite liked the life. Life was a bit quiet from what I'd been used to. I had made a lot of friends. For a lot of people coming from close-knit communities it was like the world was opening. There were a lot of people signed on when the War was over. You got all your food and clothing and the money you got was just spending money. You got free passes and everything was taken care of.

Chapter 12   Some Village Characters: 'they are the people you miss'

Winnie Hogg

Villages were very close-knit before the War. People had to have nicknames in the village at that time because there were so many members of the same family, fathers and sons with the same Christian names. My father was called Scottie Archbold, George Archbold was called Cuddie and William Archbold was called Clippie. In the Smailes, there was Pittas Bob and Fire. Little Adam was the harbour man. You wouldn't have been able to differentiate, without the nicknames – there was Raffa Archbold. There was so much inter-marrying between the families at that time. People then started to move away and others came in.

Joyce Shaw

My great grandfather and great, great grandfather were both called Akins. My grandfather was Little Akins. At one time there were twenty-three John Archbolds, and they all had a by-name, to distinguish one from another. I know some of the by-names – Beachy Bob, Jack Shil, (Shilbottle Jack,) Crappy, he was a right bad-tempered man, then there was Foxy, Pittas Bob, Derby Jenny, Clippie (Bill Archbold,) Sailor Bill (the man who built the 5 houses in Chapel Row,) Aad Scottie, and Dode, These names were still used when we came here in 1967.

List of by-names from Eva Archbold's diary (1957)

Shimar	Sanderson, North side, father of Mary Ann, Lizzie, etc.
Tucker	Thos. W. Archbold, my father, son of John (Crappy.)
Tart	Jack Stanton, South side, father of Rachel, Maggie Jane Seager etc.
Robin	Robert Archbold, father of Roger, etc.
Toodle	Thos. Smailes, brother of 'Beech.'
Camel	Wm. Dawson (Church Street,) married Nance Simpson, father of Chas
Solomon	James Archbold, (Church Street) married his cousin Jane Archbold, father of Sam, Raffa, Jane, etc.
Little Akins	Joe (Tate) Archbold's father.
Old Akins	James Archbold father of 'Little Akins', possibly from Acton, where the family once lived.
Cast	James Archbold, North side, married Mary Gibb, father of Wm. Reid Archbold.
Clippie	Wm. Gibb Archbold married Liz Bell, father of Eric etc.

Jack Bowling	Jack Archbold, Tom Bowling – Tom Archbold, brothers of Mary Jane who married Jos. Carss.
Farmer	Geo Simpson, built 7, Church Street, uncle of Nance Dawson.
Billy the Trumpeter	Wm. Dawson, built 5 Church Street, father of Camel.
Scotty	Adam Archbold, married Jeannie Stephenson - son of Piemy, father of Ada and Winnie.
Crappy	John Archbold, my grandfather.
Hinchie	Jack Archbold, married Ellen Smailes and built house at North side
Foxy	Ralph Archbold, Annie Jane Nelson's father.
Fire	Thomas Grey. Esther McLaren's father and brother to Bob Grey, who had the Pub.
Piemy	William Archbold, father of Adam and brother to Foxy.
Shilbottle Jack	Jack Shil - John Archbold, he lived at Shilbottle when young. He was Crappy's cousin.
Beech	Robert Smailes, married Peggy Stanton, built house on Garden Terrace, (West End.)
Pidah	Jack Smailes, Fire's brother.
Winker	Wm. Stephenson, belonging Boulmer, married Bella Archbold nee Smailes,
Hemp	Wm. Dawson, son of Edward, father of Robert John - North Craster.
Dice	John Smailes, father to Pidah.

Ada Archbold

Lots of people had nicknames. Mary McLaren's father, she was Smailes, and Fire was her father. When our grandmother used to reminisce and she would be telling the tale and she used to say 'can you mind' – 'can you mind old Shil and old Ha' and old this that and another and we hadn't a clue and I remember one story in particular, either Shil or Ha was the perpetrator of sticking the Christmas tree – after Christmas – they used to make the heap for the potatoes and they stuck it in the heap for a joke. That was at the Square – one of the houses that faced over the North side. Shil collected wood, what sort of wood, I don't know. They called one of my grandfathers, Winker. He used play marbles and used to wink. They called my grandfather on the other side, Pimie.

Marjorie Lumsden

There was Pittas Bob, old Jennie Renton was married to Pittas. His surname was Smailes. She was an old tartar her. One night we were waiting for the bus with my Aunt Eleanor and we were shouting and she was in bed and she was going to throw the pot out of the window at us.

These bye names, they all had them. Because they were all called after their grandparents and their great grandparents and they all had the same name.

Characters

Little Adam

Marjorie Lumsden

I don't think my grandfather would have been to Alnwick. It was a day's journey to get there, unless you walked to Little Mill to get the train. We had Rutherford's buses and before that we had Little Adam's bus. He was the harbour master and he had a little bus and he called it 'The Ocean Maid.' He was going from here to Boulmer and something blew in the engine – he opened the doors and shouted 'every man for hissel.' He thought the engine had gone on fire.

He stole a lot of copper from a ship that came ashore and he put it in the floor of the bus, underneath the wood. The police came to look for it and he said 'it's no good looking there mind' and of course they did and he was fined for stealing the copper. He offered the police a lift and because the bus was too heavy to start, that's how they found the copper.

He was an old man when I knew him, and I met him in Annie Jane's shop and he was a great man for playing whist. They were playing whist in the house. He told Annie Jane he was going home to light the fire – he had a stove and he said 'I've only got one match, I tell you what, I'll strike it to see if it's a gooden.' He lived in a little hut on the pier. He was married, but his wife was in hospital (St. Georges.') She died when she was 84, but he was already dead by then.

Eva Archbold

Carol Grey

Eva never married, she was engaged to a gentleman but nothing came of it. She worked at the Store at Howick. She cycled to Howick and she told everybody that she made knickers last twice as long as they did because she 'turned them.' I don't know how she did it. Eva was a typical Archbold – she wouldn't spend a penny when a halfpenny would do. She was a housekeeper in Thropton for a little while. I can remember going to visit her, possibly on a Sunday. That was the only day we went out together. Mam told me that she was taking us along the rocks to see if there were any frogs and tadpoles and Eva asked 'what is the connection between frogs and tadpoles' and when told she said 'Do you know, I never knew that, I may as well have been brought up in a nunnery.' She was Secretary/Treasurer for the Hall and was one of the founder members of the W.I. She could keep you right on procedure.

Bella Archbold

Joyce Shaw

There were some real characters. The old lady that lived where Mrs. Davison lived, was Winnie Archbold's granny – Bella. When Matt Stephenson, who lived next door to Marjorie, got married - he would be in his 40's when he married – and he said to little Bella, who was a bit bad with her eyes – 'Bella, I've getten a good wife, she comes from Seahouses, they call her Eleanor White', Bella thought a bit and said 'she canna be that good or she would have been teken afore now'

Jack Archbold.

Billy Lumsden

There were 2 aviaries of canaries here. Jimmy Smailes had some and Jack Archbold. Now Jack was blind, and he had canaries up that garden. He had the feeders on the side, and he used to take the feeders down and blow into them to get the shell out. He could put it straight back. He was totally blind, so was his brother Roger. He used to put his fingers directly into the nests – he knew exactly where they were – to see how many little ones there were. He didn't show them, it was just a hobby. His old shed's up there now, it's covered in ivy.

Billy Bunk

Carol Grey

Billy Bunk got his nickname because he installed bunks into one of the tall fishing boats.

Fred Stephenson

Billy Bunk was in America or Canada for a while and one of his famous sayings was 'The only thing we're good at is murdering bloody folk.' He used to live up the cut between the kipper yards and the restaurant.

Neil Robson

Billy Bunk was a joiner by trade and they reckon he went away to San Francisco or somewhere and they were asking him what it was like and he said 'they've got tools out there you wouldn't know what to do with them, every kind of tool you can imagine.'

When I was a kid, our office used to be over there in the corner of the yard and there was the little alleyway up and Billy Bunk's house was at the top of the hill. Marjorie and I spent most of our childhood round here 'cause my mother used to work the machine and Marjorie's mother used to pack up kippers for posting. When we were about four, five and six years old, we were here all the time 'cause we weren't allowed to run wild and I remember one day, I think Marjorie was with me, his door was slightly open and I looked through the door and I said, 'come on, we'll go in and have a look', but Marjorie wouldn't come in. He had this great big high chair with wooden sides and a top on. I suppose it was a drafty hole to live in, and I looked around, he was fast asleep and he just opened his eyes as I looked and I went scarpering out, I was petrified of him. He was probably a canny enough fellow but he was a bit of a mystery man to us at that age.

The Butters family

Letter to Marjorie Lumsden with a copy of the picture of the bins on top of the pier. Dated 29.1.03.

'Many thanks for your card, I was very interested in the picture of the bins at the end of the pier, I am enclosing a photograph of a snap my brother, George took of the Spes Bona. I remember it well, even it's number, BK 123. It was one boat which always welcomed us aboard. I must call and see what else Mr. Oxley has of those years. We would like to visit Craster again this year and of course, would like to stay with you. Have you any vacancies in June or early July, we would want to stay for a week if that is possible, would you please let us know what dates are available and we will make our plans to fit. You will know that my sister, Helen, has died and I am the only one left of the Butters family of ten. We look forward to hearing from you soon.' (from Des Butters)

Marjorie Lumsden

Des Butters had two brothers that were drowned in the River Tweed, one walked with his head on his shoulder (Willy) and the other had something wrong with his leg (Albert.) They both worked, they worked at the crusher at the quarry. I can remember hearing about the Butters, going out to Muckle Carr in a bath, they were daring. It was headlines in the papers. Des Butters used to ride his bike along the top of the wall and he used to ride in the house, round the table, pick something up to eat and ride out, never off the bike. He ended up a Squadron Leader DFC and bar in the R.A.F. They all had good jobs, Gordon was chemist – they were all readers, like – George was more like his father. There was Jock. They were a close loving family, they idolised their mother and I can picture old Geordie sitting on the organ, his head on one side playing, they had an organ in the house – they lived in the bottom row of the Council houses.

Clippie (William Gibb Archbold, brother of Annie Jane Nelson and married to Liz Bell.)

Clippie Archbold (right) with Luke Robson

Eddie Grey

I remember Bill Archbold, Clippie as they called him – his nickname or bye-name – 'cause we used to play around about there, me and Dougie and Raymond, when we were younger and we used to run around his hut and he'd be mending the lobster pots and we used to shout 'Clippie' and he would chase us. If he caught you, he used to take the belt off and we got that. It wasn't often he caught us like. But he had a memory like an elephant, he never used to forget, he would get you a fortnight later.

When we were little we used to go along there, we were brought up on home-fed bacon, 'cause he kept guffies. He had pigeons, my dad kept pigeons as well, 'cause they were just opposite each other. If you were speaking to him and he didn't catch what you said he had a habit of saying 'What you say?' quickly, like. He used to speak sharply. He did everything quickly. When he was lighting his pipe he looked as though he was chasing the match to light it.

He was always mending lobster pots and crab pots, even when he was finished the sea. I can remember him knitting covers down there, for the lobster pots. He used to put a reef knot in. I used to knit one or two covers for him. He used to say 'Come here, I want you, will you knit some covers son?' I never knit very many, I was just in my early teens. He used to pay me £4 or £5 for knitting the covers. I never expected to get paid. We used to get some chases off him when we were young.

Neil Robson

Scottie, Jamesie and Clippie were all old men, when we were kids. They were retired from the sea. The kids were scared of Clippie. He could be quite nasty with them, but you just kept away from him. He couldn't catch you. He had pigs at the bottom sties behind where the joiners' shop is and we used to go and throw stones at them. You could see him, he had a chair under a bit veranda on his hut, and he would be dozing off and we would throw the stones and he would hear the squeaking and come out.

Mike Robson

I liked Clippie. He once set fire to the whin bushes when there was a football match and the game had to be abandoned. One night, I think he was drunk, he fell over the cat and his face was a right mess and Billy Lumsden wrote on his boat, right along the side in chalk, 'I tort I tor a putty cat.' He went mad when he saw that.

Bill Curry

The fishermen used to come up (to Howick Scar Farm.) The boats would be laid off in the winter time. Billy Archbold used to come across, Eric, and old Clippie - a little stubby pipe he had, he used to talk out of the side of his mouth. He would say, 'I'd have a farm the morn, but I've got neewhere to put it.' He used to lead the horse for Tom Grey onto the pier at Craster – a white horse – he would lead it with a cart. One day a visitor said to him 'what a lovely horse you've got there. What do you call it?' 'I haven't got time to tell you' he said. He always had a guffy in the sty, hens and pigeons. I remember him having a dog called Patch, and he used to come to the thresher. Rats used to come into the stacks in those days. Patch was a right good ratter. One day he chased this rat and it went into the bottom of the stack after we'd threshed it, and he went in and came out with the rat. Old Clippie would be sitting there with his pipe, puff, puff, puffing away.

My grandfather used to drink with them in the pub, and would say, 'I'm threshing tomorrow, do you want to give me a hand?' In those days we helped each other.

Crappy (John Willie Dawson)

Eddie Grey

I can remember John Willie, just mind. I would be about four or five at the time and he used to take me for walks down to the 'Shut.' I used to hold his hand and I can remember I loved the sound of his hob-nailed boots crunching in the gravel. I used to call them 'Clarty Boots' when I was little. I think his mother was my great aunt, she must have been my great grandfather's sister, I think. He originated from here then went to Blyth. They were lost in 1913, fishing out of Blyth, father and two sons. He went by the bye-name of Crappy. Eva Archbold's father, John was lost. He was one of the sons. The other son was called Edward. They were lost at a place, I think called the Sow and Pig Rocks at Blyth. They went to haul lobster pots and I think they were caught in a squall. They were lost in a coble called 'The Sisters' BK3.

Dodie Archbold

Eddie Grey

Clippie's brother, Dodie, was the harbour master. I can just remember Dodie. He used to sit on the north pier and there were always a few kids playing about and we used to fetch him broken bits of wood off the fish boxes, and he had a pocket knife and he would make you a little boat, with a matchstick stuck in it. There was a crane on the north pier and where the founds were it had places that filled up with water and we used to play with the boats in there. He was a character, like. I once got a licking off him, me and Raymond, for throwing stones into the harbour when they were hauling the boats up and he came down and picked up one of those weir bangs and leathered our bare legs with it. We came howling up the harbour, but of course we were back the next day, doing the same thing.

I remember he once made me a model coble, when my Dad was in the shop, I was only little, but I can remember him bringing it over wrapped in a bit newspaper. It was about 12 or14 inches long and it had a half deck on it, but it wasn't hollowed out for'ard like. It was solid. He'd carved it out of the solid. I think it was called 'The Violet' and I played for hours with it. I used to play in the bath with it – it used to float head down.

Sir John Craster

Joan Angus

I liked Sir John, he was an absolute gentleman as far as I'm concerned and accorded a lot of respect in this area. He was a great bloke. He had a sort of commanding appearance, you know. At one time, he was called the Squire, and people used to doff their caps when they met him. They owned the whole south side of the village at that time, going back a while. The Crasters have been at the Towers since 1197. They've been there a lot longer than the Percy family of Alnwick in this county.

Fred Stephenson

Sir John (Jock,) he was a character. He was the magistrate. He had a Humber Hawk and he phoned up at the garage to say it wouldn't start and he had to be on the Bench at Alnwick. There was a fellow called Sid Martin and Harold Reed had the garage and they had this ex-army wagon for a breakdown wagon, so they went over to the Towers and Harold walked over to open the bonnet and Sir John said he hadn't time for that. He wanted to be towed.

They went away over the Little Mill road and Jock shouted to ask Sid if he couldn't go any faster. So Harold put the foot down on the wagon and away they went, the car started and when it did Sir John banged the brakes full on. Sid was in the back of the wagon and the bumper bar flew past him on the end of the rope and Jock got out of the car and laughed and said 'Ha ha, good job we're all in a good fettle this morning.'

He was the most terrible driver in the world. In those days Little Mill crossroads used to go straight across and there was a sign 'Halt – Major Road Ahead', of course, Jock used to just go straight across.

Another day he came to the garage when I was working and heard this almighty crash – in them days the old pumps had the glass globes on the top. Sir John had gotten his petrol in, he went forward and he was reversing back to go back home, well, he didn't go far enough forward and he just backed straight back and the pump was lying flat on the ground. He got out 'Ha ha, I've never done that before.' He was a real canny fellow.

Sir John was too good of a payer. If he got a bill at eight o'clock, he paid it at five past. Well a good businessman didn't do that. He would phone for us to go over for a service, when you took it back for him he had to drive it back with you to the garage. You couldn't drive the car. He had to drive it. He used to go up the village in Embleton and out at the main road. He never stopped at the main road. You just had to shut your eyes. He never used to queue when he went to the kipper yard, it didn't matter who was there. You could get away with it in them days.

He was a laugh a minute. He was a grand fella. He used to cut the grass at the Towers but he was idle. He had a big sit-down lawn mower with a seat on the back and he had the wife with the barrow and instead of going along and back to where she was, he would shout at her – ' V darling' – to go along the other end with the barrow. She would have to tip it out as well, likely. One day the thing got away with him and he fell off it and the mower shot away into the woods and that was the end of Jock cutting the grass. Then he got the Coxon twins to cut it and he used to sit and watch them.

He was a grand fella, but nobody liked him on the Bench. They used to say 'who's on the bench, today?' 'Craster!' 'Oh, hell!' The punishment didn't always fit the crime, like. They reckoned once that somebody pinched a bicycle pump, or something, and was fined about £30. He was on the television one night and he said there were two kinds of people that poaches pheasants, one that's going to sell them and one that wants it for the pot, to feed the family. He didn't mind the feller that wanted it for the pot, but he was deadly with the ones selling them.

Mike Robson

Sir John wrote a book called 'Naturalist in Northumberland.' He was a great friend of Peter Scott, the naturalist. He was big on nature. We all got signed paintings by Sir Peter Scott, 'cos he used to film the birds coming in and he stayed at the Towers. He was a very close friend of Sir John.

Shafto Craster

Joan Angus

I knew Shafto Craster very well, because he used to come to my house and have a coffee, usually when I was washing. He used to be quite comfortable and just sit down in the kitchen and chat, because he used to take my third son, Paul, bird watching with Dr. Turner. Dr. Turner used to have a car, and they used to go to Budle Bay and Boulmer – all over the place. He had a lot of time for young people.

Shafto was a very keen, and well respected, ornithologist and botanist. He was asked by Northumberland Naturalist Society to lead walks along the coast between Boulmer and Newton to study birds and flowers and he did that regularly, at least three times a year, until he was too old to do it. He often worked with Dr Ennion who had an observatory at Monk House and it was Dr Peter Evans and Shafto who got the land for the Arnold Nature Reserve.

He was also in the choir, when I was in the choir at Craster Church. If Canon Granlund went on a bit with his sermon, Shafto used to rattle the change in his pocket, to remind Canon Granlund that the time was getting on, and he was desperate to get out and go for his tea. He was a great character and used to go about on his pushbike and everybody knew him. I liked him.

Billy Curry

Jack Train from Embleton was a road worker, putting in lines and cutting grass. He was good at the cuckoo sound. Shafto used to write about birds in the Northumberland Gazette and he said he'd heard the cuckoo in February. He was always the first one to hear it, but it was Jack Train he'd heard.

Fred Stephenson

Shafto was a different character from Sir John. He used to be like an ambassador for the vicar. He used to gan around all the houses getting cups of tea and that. He always went to the pub around 11 o'clock and he liked to have a have a cup of tea on the way. He loved it if anybody bought him a drink.

He played the organ in the church. He used to come down on a Friday with the hymns and ask what people thought of them. Mind, many a time the hymn would be ended and he started away on another verse. It was an old pedal organ and it was getting to the end of its days. If the vicar said somebody was sick, Shafto would go and visit. It was more 'cup of tea' orientated, mind. He was a character. There's no getting away from that.

Charlie Caisley

Billy Lumsden

In the war, he used to grow his own baccy, old Charlie. He had about 30 hives of bees as well. There's none now. When the baccy was ripe he used to get me to go up, he had one of these presses the printers use. He used to put the leaves in salt petre. He used to criss-cross the leaves, a little bit of rum sprinkled on and he had to tighten it down. He'd cut the sides off straight. It would be like that for about a month, and every now and then we'd tighten it, and this black juice used to run out of the sides. That's what he used to smoke.

Ralphie Dixon

Marjorie Lumsden

He was first Chairman of the Leek Club. He was a coal-cutter on the boats at Blyth before he came to Craster. He had a hard job learning to drive. He took seven tests and on the last one he told the examiner ' Mind, Ah divn't want to gan roond the world - ah only want to tek wor Nellie to Blyth.'

Edward Archbold

Marjorie Lumsden

Edward Archbold had a by-name of Jimmy Puffer. He's on the end of a football photograph. I asked my mother if she knew why he was called Jimmy Puffer. She said that somebody had told her that when he was a little boy, apparently he was delicate and when he was running he used to puff.

Eva France

Carol Grey

I can remember Eva France, the post lady. She took the papers as well. Sometime she had somebody came to inspect her to see how things were doing. One particular day the papers were left behind and as she was going round the country, on her bike, people were asking for the papers, to be told, 'Oh! There aren't any papers today.' She used to do a bit of decorating and I can remember – she was painting for Nancy Gray and Dad sold Luxor paint and the favourite colour was 'Dense White.' She ran out one day and she said to Nancy - 'Haddaway to Edward's for some paint. It's 'Dense White', and if you canna remember what colour just think of somebody thick.'

Dad sold Cadet cigarettes and Harry Archbold's wife, Lily, had come into the shop and she said 'Edward, I'd like 20 'Cadets.' Eva turned to Lily and said 'Lily, you're far ower aad for them .'

She would read everyone's postcards, she would hand them through the door saying 'the weather's fine and everyone's having a good time.' When it was Christmas time, of course, a lot of them were addressed to Mrs. Archbold, South Side, Craster, of whom there were more than one and she would give them to the right person 'cause she recognised the writing. She was as honest as the day. You could trust her with your life. She delivered the letters whatever the weather. It was a heavy bike with the grid on the front for the letters and parcel. She had a driving licence but she never had a car. These are the people you miss.

Eleanor Venus

The postwoman was Eva then, and we got the money from the Ministry of Agriculture then and she used to know what was in the envelope when she delivered it. She was coming up the bank one day as we were walking down and when we met her she said 'Oh Eleanor, there's a card for you', it was of the tulip fields and I thought somebody must have been to Holland and she said 'No, it's from Sir Ivan Sutherland and he's in the Norfolk Broads.' She was a character. She would post your letters and bring stamps. She started cleaning windows and I gave her an old Raleigh bike we had and she fixed it up for her window cleaning. Once when Doris and Wally's mothers were coming for the day, she told Doris 'you're getting company for the day.'

Bill Curry

Eva used to deliver the letters. She was the post mistress. She had a bike, and she went as far as Dunstan Hill in the north and our place would be the south, and she went to West Farm. George went to Spain, and this postcard came, and I can remember my mother saying, when Eva gave her the card, she said, 'my, your George is having a right time in Spain.' She'd been reading the card. She always knew everything.

Mike Robson

When Eva brought the post she always used to shout 'Post' just before she put it through the door and then shout, 'Thank-you' as she went away.

Betty Grey

Carol Grey

My mother was a nurse and of course, when she came to the village, everybody used to come for her when anything happened. I used to say that if she had had a pound for everyone she layed out and Dad had carried away – they would have been quite rich. If there was a knock on the door, we used to think 'who has died now?' Once Mary Annie was very poorly and it must have been a Saturday and I must have been going out and Mum asked me if Mary Annie dies tonight, would I help to lay her out. I wasn't keen, but there was nobody else to ask and I prayed that she would last the night – she did. My Mum didn't mince her words, what you saw was what you got. Brenda Ennis had a baby and she came into the shop for a tin of baby custard and my Mum said 'get away home and make some' – she never sold her anything. Once Dougie Hogg swallowed paraffin – it was in a Tizer bottle. Winnie brought him down to our house and I think she gave him milk to drink. She got on to the doctor and was told that Dougie must not go to sleep. She used to take fishing hooks out of people's fingers.

Granny's Bob (Robert John Smailes Dawson)

Marjorie Lumsden

His Granny brought him up when his mother died. He was only two and a half. He remembered – they didn't have funerals in the Chapel or the Church in them days – he remembered sitting on his mother's coffin while they were having the service, and after they took the coffin out of the house. There was a lady lived in the top house, where Christopher Dawson lived – I don't know her proper name, but he called her 'Margaret the Manty' – she was a dressmaker. His grandmother had already had seven sons and he made eight and he was probably spoilt 'cos her sons were grown up. Instead of calling him Robert John, which was his name, they called him 'Granny's Bob.'

I remember, later in life, he asked Jimmy (Shaw) to bring this pig's trough over on a barrow. It was very heavy. It was made of sandstone – they made them at the quarry opposite the car park, at Appleby's Quarry. He wanted that trough into our garden, when we moved into South Acres, 'cos we had a pig over there. We had two troughs. They are still there in the garden. He thought Jimmy was fit enough to do it. He was a young man, my father was 80+. He (my father) had a duck, called Casey, Jimmy (Shaw) took it over and it lived with the hens. I don't know where it came from, it laid eggs.

Billy Lumsden

His ears used to stick out and I said to him, 'How does your ears stick out like that Bob?' He says, 'it was the way my granny used to put my bonnet on.'

Marjorie Lumsden

Joyce & Jimmy (Shaw) had a friend here from Australia and he liked grandfather clocks and we had a one then, so Joyce said she would take him down to Robert John's to see the grandfather clock. I hated it. In he comes and Joyce says, 'Robert John, this is Bill. He's come to see your grandfather clock -Bill's Irish', and Robert John says 'Aye, there's good and bad in all kinds, he canna help that."

Hemp (William Gibb Dawson)

Marjorie Lumsden

Well, Hemp was married and had a little boy, which was my father. His wife was pregnant and when she was having the baby she took fits, so my father told me. They realised years later that she must have had very high blood pressure. She died having this baby and the baby also died.

He was only 32 then. He lived with his mother in the West End. They had the parlour end for their room. He went back to the sea about a week later and he was washed overboard. Fishermen in them days couldn't swim. He pulled himself up at the stern and Jack Hall was there when it happened. After that he never went back to sea. What they would say now was that he would need counselling. I think he had a nervous breakdown, what with his wife dying, and all that.

He never came out of the house again, from he was 32 till after I was born and then he would be 68. He was in the house for about forty years. He only came out the house when he was given his pension, which was 5/- and my mother said that if he wanted his pension, he would have to go and seek it. He went next door when it was dark with a coat over his head and although it was shut, the lady served him.

When I got to about a year old, he used to take me up the road in the pushchair and that was when he became normal again. To have been forty years in the house, I don't know how he was normal. They reckon that his face was like parchment.

He was late for the sea one day. They had certain berths and he bit through the rope, holding the boat and that's how he got his name 'Hemp.' There were seven sons that went to sea, him and his brothers. Above his bed he had the photo of his wife's grave, which is at Spittalford. They called her Elizabeth Archbold and she was sister to Joyce's grandfather, Joe Archbold. Hemp's actual name was William Gibb Dawson. I used to play the organ to him. I had no training, I was only five and he thought it would be a good thing if I was able to play this organ. He bought it from a man in Howick for £5, put it beside his bed and I used to have to play this certain hymn every night - 'Count your Blessings.' My daughter also was able to play by ear. The paraffin lamp was beside the bed. He was 84 when he died in 1941 – the day they bombed Pearl Harbour.

Jack Hall

Joyce Shaw

After Mary left school and went to the Farm, Kenneth at the yard asked me one day if I would like to work for him in the shop. I said I would, it was only for 8/9 weeks in the summer. I quite enjoyed it, you met a lot of nice people and it filled my time. One day, Kenneth came over to me and said 'Ha'ya seen that car over there – it's a Jaguar.' I said it was very nice and he said 'That fellow came all the way from London in four and a half hours.' While he was telling me that Jack Hall, who was a fisherman (Jimmy Hall's father,) lovely old man and he worked at the yard, he was the best tier up of parcels I have ever seen – he turned round and with the pipe in his mouth 'That's nowt. Wor Jimmy could do it in two and a half.'

He was a real character, a real old fisherman. He smoked a pipe. It was very short and instead of having it up, the bowl faced down. He would stand and tie up parcels of kippers and he made the boxes, everything was just perfect. He was a very particular old man about his work.

Neil Robson

It was good at North Shields. Jack Hall used to go with me Dad. He used to have a little pipe. He was a right character. He used to go with me Dad and Jimmy Straughan used to go with Ken. When I was a kid, Jack used to sit and teach me knots and everything in the wagon going to North Shields. I remember one morning the boats weren't landing till about 11 o'clock or so, he never went for a cup of tea he just stood outside with his pipe. We used to get the ice when the wagon came round and you got however many boxes you needed to cover the herring and Jack used to do that and I remember one morning the boats weren't coming in and I said 'Jack, are you not coming for your breakfast?' He says, 'Why no son. I always have my breakfast before I gan to bed, it saves getting it in the morning when I get up .'

He was 96 when he died. He used to come along in the winter and chop sticks. He used to make kipper boxes, and they were like porcupines as he got older, there were nails sticking out all over. He blamed the wood, he used to say, 'that wood's ower thin' and all that. When he was chopping sticks, we used to have to put cardboard at the windows to stop the glass being put out by the sticks.

Once we were going up to Edinburgh, Jack was with me, he didn't come every time, and it was absolutely pouring with rain and I went around this corner and skidded and we went down a little bit dip, there was no hedge, I think it was a potato field, just before Haddington and the wagon turned completely over and I was in the field. I looked over and said, 'Jack, are you all right?' He said nothing and I shouted, 'Jack, Jack are you alright?' He put the hearing aid back in and the pipe was upside down in his mouth and his hat over the side. He says 'what happened to us there?' I said we had skidded and we were all right. He said, 'We're in a ruddy field.' I drove along the field and there was a big ramp up onto the road and it was muddy and I couldn't get up. The farmer came along and he towed us up and I noticed Jack's hand was bleeding and I thought I'd better take him to hospital so the farmer's wife said she would run us along, which she did, and Jack went in and came out with this bandage on his arm and when I asked him what had happened, he said 'you know when we were hoying the boxes on at Craster before we left, I caught myself on a nail and the buggers have bandaged it up for me here .'

He was funny, 'cos Jimmy (his son) barred him from coming after that. He used to say 'I canna gan with you nee more, but ah'll meet ye up at the quarry ,' so I used to pick him up there.

Jenny Midge

Jimmy Shaw

Your grandmother was a character, when I first came here with you, before we were married, I had to go and be inspected and she said 'do you drink?' 'No', 'do you smoke?' 'No', and various things like that and then she said 'you'll do.'

Joyce Shaw

I think she was very concerned 'cause of me not having had a father for so many years and also being an only child. She wanted to make sure that I was going to get somebody who was upright. She also asked if he went to Chapel. If you went to Chapel, all sins were forgiven.

My granny had hens and a pig, everybody used to have hens and a pig. One New Year my father, who wasn't a boy at that time, he was a man and he black-leaded somebody's pigs. I think it was for a dare. My granny had her last pig in 1943. My grandfather died in that year and she had no more after that, she was then 78 and she lived until she was 85.

There used to be a prisoner of war camp along the back of the hills, they were Italians and they didn't come into the village at that time, but they used to come down – between Chapel Row and the way to the Castle was what we called 'The Chapel Field ,' which was where Scott the butcher's horse used to graze - to that wall and when we weren't here my granny says she used to give them a basket and ask them to collect sticks for her and she would give them scones.

As far as my granny was concerned – she lived in the top house – she never had a bathroom, hence, you went into the bait-house round the corner and put the set pot on to get the water, lifted the tin bath off the back and filled it with hot water and you got a bath and it was very cold in the winter.

I've heard my mother say that when I was a baby and they were staying here, my granny used to get up at half past four in the morning with my grandfather – that was when he went to sea. I wasn't a good sleeper and she would get me up, tie me into a wooden chair and give me a tin with some shells in. They went out and would maybe have a pot of tea and some bread or something and then when they came ashore about 9 o'clock in the morning they had what they called their 'second coffee', that would be a bit of home fed bacon and an egg, a proper fried breakfast.

My granny was quite a strict woman, quite severe. I can't say that she was ever severe with me, in fact, I loved her very much and I suppose she spoiled me. There was one thing she was very strict about, not just with me, but with most children in the village and there will be several people that can tell you this, she would not allow anybody up and down the Chapel steps. They were sacred, it was a place of worship and she allowed nobody to play there. She chased one girl who still lives in this village and she hit the back of her legs with a stick.

Marjorie Lumsden

Well you know what children are like, when they get a chase off somebody, they go back for another one won't they. Well we used to do that – it was dreadful really. She lived next door to the chapel in Chapel Row, and of course we used to play up and down the steps, jumping up and down them or sliding down the banister thing, and she used to chase us. Well of course we went back for more, and we used to put our tongues out – kind of delinquents in those days. Kids used to get into all sorts in those days, things that they'd get put into court for these days.

Joyce Shaw

My grandmother never got a widow's pension until the National Health Act came in, in 1948, when she got what everybody got, which was 26 shillings a week. In the 1940's, the boats were doing very well and the fishermen were doing well and I said to my grandmother that they appeared to be doing well and she said 'yes, but we did well in the First World War and they just have to save their money .' When my granny got her old-age pension in 1948 and we came here one weekend and she said to my mother 'fancy Polly, I've been to the Post Office and I've got 26 shilling for nothing .' She thought it was fantastic.

Annie Jane (Nelson,)

Joyce Shaw

Annie Jane, at the shop, was a character. Annie Jane – was originally an Archbold, but she married and became a Nelson. Her husband had been a fisherman, but was crippled with arthritis and walked with a crutch. That's how she came to open the shop because she had to be the breadwinner.

Annie Jane was a fantastic woman – if someone came and sat on the seat beside the shop, she would think nothing about asking them if they wanted a cup of tea and a biscuit – total strangers. She was President of the W.I. for years. Her daughter found her dead, sitting on the settee, with the Gazette in her hand. She was only in her 70's when she died.

Jimmy Shaw

That was our port of call on a Sunday morning, going over to Chapel, we used to call there and have a cup of tea.

Doris Clarke

The buses always stopped on the north side. They didn't come over here. They used to go down to the bottom of the bank and then back up, in front of Mrs. Nelson's house. She was the parcel office as well. I think that all of the drivers used to be pleased of her cup of tea in the morning, waiting for the first bus. She was very generous in that way.

Joyce Shaw

She was a very forthright and outspoken woman. When they were trying to get the lifeboat here in 1969 – it had been at Boulmer, but they had their big boat taken away and they didn't want an inflatable boat and the RNLI were cutting down and said we only warranted an inflatable (at Craster.) They first thought about putting the boat at Newton, then it was suggested that it came here – where the boathouse stands now. It stands on ground which is owned by North Side owners. They couldn't come to an agreement, Annie Jane was a North Side owner and there was a meeting which included her, Edward Garrett, Dr. Lishman, Billy Smailes and Willy Robson to decide about the boathouse and Annie Jane turned round and said to Edward Garrett and Dr. Lishman, 'My man, just 'tak the land, 'cause they'll never agree .' She didn't mince matters. Of course, the first boathouse was built and it was nothing more than a glorified garage.

Marjorie Lumsden

Every house on the North Side had somebody living in them (not holiday homes like now.) Things have changed a lot since then. If you were poorly – I had our Geoff at home and Annie Jane Nelson sent my dinner up home on a tray every day. I was in bed for ten days. She took all my washing away. I used to go for a bath to her house every week. We didn't have a bath and she had. This night, she had shut the shop at 8 o'clock and I was just ready to go up for a bath and there was a big thud on the outside door – she went to the door. She was mad 'cause she thought it was somebody wanting the shop. She went to the door and this lady said to her 'Please missus, I'm looking for the Castle, I want to see the Bloody Lady, ya knaa out about her?' Annie Jane said 'How the hell div aa knaa?', 'cos she was cross about being taken to the door at that time. She had a son, Ralph, he was a vicar. One night she was that mad, she had fallen out or disagreed with somebody and she said to me 'If it wasn't for our Ralph being in the Ministry, I would raise this bloody Raa.'

Annie Jane was well liked, very straight, she would tell the children in the shop, if they weren't well behaved. The shop was very busy - she had a tearoom before the War. Her husband was a total wreck with pains. They lived at Seahouses. He had been a fisherman and after the First World War he was invalided out of the Navy. He got this very bad 'flu and they thought he was going to die. Following that he couldn't walk - he used crutches. She used to go to Beadnell, where they used to collect limpets, with her creel, to bait the lines for other people, to make some money. She told me when she was at Seahouses, she was on the Parish - she had four children. When you were on the Parish, you got medication from the doctor free. She said Dr. McCaskey was the doctor and if you were on the Parish and you had a sore throat 'You got the same medicine for a sore throat as you got for a cut arse.'

Her father, who had this house on the North Side – he was a widower. He brought her here and had the idea that she could have a shop - there wasn't a shop on the North Side then – that's how she started. She was a proper slave. Her husband was so crippled that every morning she had to wash and dress him before the shop opened.

Billy used to go for a bath after me. One night he left his socks in the bathroom, by mistake and the next morning – 'cos he didn't have a lot of socks in them days – he went in the shop way and he says 'Annie Jane, I think I've left my socks in the bathroom .' She says 'No.' they're in the garden – I had everything oot the pantry to see what had gone off, so I threw them out of the bathroom window and they're on a rose bush in the garden.'

She was only 74 when she died. She died reading the Gazette on the settee, in her dinner hour. She died on 28thApril, 1973. Joyce (Shaw) looked after the shop when Annie Jane went for an operation.

Raffa. (Ralph Martin Archbold)

Billy Lumsden

Just after the war when his sons, Harry and Jack came back, they were both away in the Army, Raffa bought a boat, a new coble, and he had netted a salmon. The bailiffs came up and took the net off him and he had to go to court, and he had to go to Newcastle. He said to the magistrates, 'I had two sons away to the war and I sat all the war knitting them nets, and that 'b' there come up and took them away. That's not right you know.' You know what the magistrates said? 'case dismissed.'

Another time he reckoned he'd seen the Loch Ness monster out there. This was on the radio, on the B.B.C. Telling them what it was like, all these big humps. When he was finished, they started to play 'It's a sin to tell a lie.' He was a character.

He used to play the melodeon on the end of the pier on a Sunday morning. The boss used to give him corn for his hens 'cos he kept the key for the gate, and he used to come up and get the corn. He only had half a dozen hens. He came this time, and says 'I've got no corn for my hens .' I says 'Well, mind, there's none at the farm because we're waiting for the harvest starting.' 'Well I divn't knaa what I'm ganna do.' So I went to the boss and says, 'Ralph Archbold's up here for some corn for his hens, but I says, we haven't got any.' The boss says, 'I've got some of the pellets I bought in Alnwick, give him a stone of them and tell him that 2 ounces a day is quite sufficient for a hen.' So I went down and says, 'he's given you some of what he feeds his hens on, but you've got to give them very little, because it's good stuff.' The hens must have been ready to lay, because he came back two days after. He says 'that's grand stuff - I was getting no eggs at all, and I got two yesterday.' He'd walked all the way to tell us that. He says, 'I've never known stuff like that .'

Billy Curry

Ralph Martin Archbold once said to a visitor who was stroking his dog: 'if ye want a dog to stroke, get yer own dog.'

Fred Stephenson

Ralph Martin Archbold. Raffa was a character. You used to laugh at his voice. He got a new fireplace with an all night burner and he said 'They burn bloody soil, never mind anything else .'

Joan Angus

He used to come in the shop and ask for a bag of tattie peelings, when he wanted a bag of crisps or 'one of those cakes with lather on' when he wanted a cake with icing on.

Andy Robson

Bill Curry

There was a fellow drove a wagon for Michael Robson's father, Willie Robson. You called him Andy Robson. He used to get himself full of drink and I've even seen Willie come looking for him in his pyjamas, with his trousers on, on top of his pyjamas. He used to live in a caravan in the Quarry, just where those pine lodges are now. He used to be tramping back at nights and I used to pick him up and take him down, and drop him off there. No bother at all. Even when I was courting, I used to pick him up when I was coming back from Embleton. I never left him, 'cos I used to think that somebody could knock him over, 'cos he was all over the road, full of drink. He could be full of drink, but he would get in and say; 'O it's you Billy, are you all right?' Then he would never say another word. Just drop him at the quarry. The next night if I saw him at the pub, he wouldn't say anything, but there was always a pint. He always did that.

One night I was in the Bell, and he landed in. It was about half past ten on Sunday night, and the fellow who had the Bell in those days was called Geordie Naseby, 'Popeye' we used to call him 'cos he always smoked a pipe. Alan Robson's married to his daughter. Andy came in this night and said have you seen anything of Jimmy Simpson. 'No, I haven't.' 'Do you think I could have a pint of beer?' 'No you cannot, have you seen the time, its half past ten. We're closed. If you come back at 11 o'clock in the morning you can have a drink then.' The pub was full - a good few folk in. He went out and came back a few minutes later, and says 'George – you might give me a pint just to be going on with, just until the morrow.' He was a character. What a bloke.

When he drove for Willie, he used to lead the pipes out of the pipe works. There was a fellow called Pickup who was the boss man at the pipe works, and he used to call everybody Bill. These flat wagons, he used to put planks, batons along the middle, and he used to roll the pipes on – 'cos they used to have collars on, and it used to keep the pipes level. He also put wood chocks in, and nailed these wood chocks in, there were no straps in those days. He just put these wood chocks in, he nailed them in. Once Pickup was on the wagon, putting the chocks in and he missed the thing and hit his thumb with the hammer, and he chucked the hammer away. He said, 'Where's the hammer, Bill?' Andy says, 'Well you chucked it away, down the yard there.' Pickup says 'Well go and get the b----- thing', and Andy says, 'I'm not going to get it, you chucked it away so you get the damn thing.' So in the end Pickup went and got it. He nailed it on and they reckon after that, Andy and him were the best of buddies, 'cos Andy had stood up to him. He was just a bully to start up with.

Scottie Archbold

Ada Archbold

My Dad was called Scottie, because when the Scots fisherfolk used to come in, they used to wear the galasses over the top of their clothes. That was so they could pop over the side when they wanted to go to the toilet. My Dad was only a lad, about 14 or 15, helping down at the herring and he started wearing his galasses over the top and that's why they called him Scottie 'cause he was watching the Scotsmen off the boats.

Neil Robson

Scottie was Dougie Hogg's grandfather. I used to play with Dougie and we were playing along Heugh Wynd kicking a ball backwards and forwards and Scottie came out and he said 'give us a kick of your ball, son.' He took this big howk at it and it went right through Sid Wilson's greenhouse and he went running into the house like a school kid. It was my ball, I remember that. Sid came steaming out – 'who was that?' We said it wasn't us. 'Who was it then?' Dougie said, 'It was me grandda.' 'Don't talk stupid, lad!'

Alfie Shell

Lena Shell

I met Alfie at the dance at Longhoughton, in the hut where the N.A.A.F.I. is now. It had a lovely dance floor, people came from all over. We had Taylor's Band, there was Mr.. Taylor and the daughters, all family members. They had the paper shop in Alnwick. We were married in 1933 at Longhoughton church.

Alfie was in the Navy during the war, H.M.S. Windsor, he was the officers' cook. He was a butcher, worked for Mr. Pitt at Embleton and from there he went to the Store and from there he went to Scott's. The killing shop and the hunger house were in Whin Hill. He was 93 when he died. The hard work didn't do him any harm. He was a hard man, tough as leather.

We moved to Heugh Crescent when Connie was two and a half and then we moved to Heugh Road and I lived there for 60 years. I've always lived where I could see the sea, but if I moved away tomorrow it wouldn't bother me. I would like to live in the hills. I worked at Eglingham for a while. Alfie wouldn't have moved for anybody. When Lavinia Green was married, her man was a butcher down in Lincoln, and she asked if we wouldn't fancy going, there was a manager's job, but Alfie wouldn't budge. He wouldn't even go to Alnwick. He never ever bought a pair of trousers, a pullover, or nothing. I did everything for him. He wouldn't go anywhere.

Jamesie Smailes

Neil Robson

Jamesie Smailes was another character. That was Billy Smailes uncle. I bought his house on the north side in 1976, so it would be about 1975 when he died. As a kid I remember being petrified of him. He was the harbour master and he used to give you wrong for throwing stones in the harbour. He kept canaries up where Peter Humble lives now and he had a lovely strawberry bed. Once me and Allie Grey were up pinching his strawberries. Allie was always little and he was under the nets passing them back to me and I must have had a woolly hat on, or something, and I was putting them in my hat and I felt something on my ear and over me mouth, and then Jamesie's hat, he always wore a flat cap, came down and Allie was putting them in Jamesie's hat and he said 'I've got enough now.' I can still remember Allie's face.

We all had pocket knives in those days, the fishermen always had knives and as kids we had them. Eddie gave his knife to Jamesie Smailes to sharpen 'cause he reckoned he could sharpen knives better than anybody in the world (he wasn't a modest man you know) and he brought the knife back to Eddie and said, 'what do you think of that.' Eddie says 'it's not bad.' Jamesie said, 'Not bad? Gi's it here.' He got the knife he'd just sharpened and went like that … three or four times on the brass weight on the balance scales in the shop and took the edge off the knife and said, 'you'd better do it yesel.'

Fred Stephenson

Jamesie Smailes, he was a great man for going to the pictures at Alnwick and of course Vincent Morris was a practical joker and he went to the kiosk one night, Jamesie just lived two houses up the street and Vincent went into the telephone kiosk. Now there was a fellow called Sanderson, was in charge of the Corn Exchange picture house in Alnwick, and Vincent phones up Jamesie from the kiosk and says, 'It's Mr. Sanderson here, there's a tremendous picture on tonight.' Vincent put the phone down and stood in the kiosk and not long after Jamesie comes running by to catch the bus into Alnwick to see the picture.

Mike Robson

When we were kids we used to kick the ball around beside the telephone kiosk and this day it went over the wall and into Jamesie's garden. He came out and we thought he was going to pass us the ball, but he walked away towards the harbour and he kicked the ball into the harbour and it went out to sea.

Matt Simpson

Joan Angus

Matt Simpson used to work at Little Mill. He delivered everything to Little Mill and there were some coffins came one day and he couldn't spell it so he just wrote down 'one large box.' He told me that during the First War you couldn't get tobacco, so he said they used to sweep up the horses dirt, dry it out and smoke it.

Charlie Varnum

Joan Angus

Charlie Varnum was a little man who wore leather gaiters up to his knees. He was bow legged. He used to walk to Alnwick with a box of fish on his back. He smoked a pipe. He told the most awful stories. He lived at the top of the bank where Doherty's live. You had to go down two steps to get into his house. We used to sledge down the bank to the lonnen and he used to come out and put ashes on it to stop us. We used to sing 'Charlie, Charlie, Chuff, Chuff, Chuff went to bed with three little ducks' and he used to chase us. He was married, with a family. He wasn't a fisherman – he sold fish. The bank is still called 'Charlie Varnum's Bank' by some older residents.

Fred Stephenson

Charlie was about five foot tall and he used to go around Embleton with two boxes of kippers on his back and he would walk there and they would weigh about two and a half stone each, that's five stone. Now that's heavy on your back when you leave Craster, but when you get to Embleton – just imagine it. Now, I think Clippie used to sell kippers as well. One of Charlie's favourite sayings was, 'Don't buy your kippers off Clippie. He smokes them in the netty.'

Old Mrs. Wilkinson

Joan Angus

The Reading Room was originally built for the men to read their papers in. The women didn't go there. During the war there were whist drives in the Hall. I went to a whist drive in the Hall recently with Scott Grey. They were talking about the whist drives that used to be and they got on about old Mrs. Wilkinson. She used to live where the Biott's live now. She had a kist full of stuff that you could borrow for fancy dress. She used to wear a hat with a big veil on it and she smoked. She never had a cigarette out of her mouth. Winnie Hogg was on about her this night at the whist drive – evidently the net on her hat took fire and George Norris, who was an avid whist player, tried to put it out with his whist card and it caught fire as well. Mrs. Wilkinson had brought a cake that night for a prize and Winnie said ' I won the cake. When we got it home we couldn't get into it with a pick it was so hard, so we gave it to the pig and it broke the pig's teeth.' It was a typical one of Winnie's stories. I never laughed so much as I did at that story. Winnie's father used to be the same. People came just to hear him talking.

Benny Williams

Mike Robson

Benny used to work up at the quarry. He used to fight in the boxing booths. He would work all day and then go to fight after work. They were tough fellers. After the second round when he was battered and covered in blood, he still would go on to the third to get the money. Them fellers used to 'knock up' in the quarry. They used to smash the stones. It was a hard job. It was piece work and they got paid more the more they knocked up. It was a skilled job mind, 'cause they had to know where to hit the stone.

I can remember being at the garage and Benny looked over the top and asked what I was doing. I was trying to shape a piece of whinstone and he stood at the top and laughed and told me to stop and he went away up home and brought this hammer down. I had been chipping away at the stone for ages trying to get it into shape and he just took one look at it and he could see the seam and he hit the stone and it was like putting a knife through butter. They used to make these kerbs just perfect out of the whinstone.

Bob – the wire-haired terrier

Carol Grey

We had a dog called Bob, a wire-haired fox terrier. The children used to tease him by wiggling their toes in front of him. He learned to pull their laces out, which was great fun. I can remember Auntie Eva holding on to the end of the Post Office wall saying, 'Carol, get him off, get him off.' She was wearing those old-fashioned black laced-up shoes and Bob had whipped the laces out of them.

Dad used to tease him, too. When the shop was closed he would run into the shop hotly pursued by Bob and he would run up the ladder that led up to the store room above the shop. There was Bob jumping to reach dad and dad laughing, just out of reach. No wonder Bob was temperamental! He would let you in the house, but not out. It used to be a race as to who could get to the post van first, Bob or the postmen. In those days the postmen came in to collect the parcels and carry them in a postbag. Sam Appleton, one of the regular postmen had two pairs of trousers ripped and little Jimmy Sanderson, another of the regulars was terrified of him.

Mam and I were the only one's who could pick him up, but you had to tell him first that you were going to pick him up. Eddie used to say the next dog we had after Bob was going to be big enough to bite their a***s not their ankles. So after Bob came Marcus, the Labrador.

Tramps who came to Craster

Edna and Gladys Simpson

There were a lot of tramps came to Craster, there was Charlie Smart, Killiecrankie, Nellie the Sweep, the Sea King, old Tom Fox the scissor grinder. He wasn't a nice person - his family were not nice. Charlie Smart used to collect bottles and rabbit skins and he would gather brambles while he was here, he was a relative of the Smarts who had the White Swan Hotel in Alnwick. He used to stay in the hemmel opposite the quarry, you knew when he was there - you could see the smoke coming out the chimney. The Sea King came every year. He came from the south and went north, he was a big man and wore oilskins. The man from Killiecrankie used to sing. One I can remember him singing, he used to sing 'When you played the Organ and I sang the Rosary.' Old Tom Fox used to waltz Mrs. Taylor round the square.

Winnie Hogg

There used to be a tramp that used to come to where the Bark Pots are now, the little quarry. It was all crusher dust. We used to sit there with the lads. We didn't use to throw sods like they did at some of the other tramps. This tramp used to take his glass eye out, wash it in the stream. Then he used to dry it on a hanky and put it back in his eye. At that time I'd never seen anybody with a glass eye. When I told my dad about it, he started to laugh and said, 'well it's a glass eye.'

There was another one used to come he was called Charlie Smart. He came regularly, and some of the big lads threw sods at him. They got pulled up at school by the teacher Mr. Blackburn. If you said to him, 'tell us a story Charlie', he said 'there was a man, went up the tree, and then fell down and sh—hissel.'

Nellie the Sweep

Violet Hall

Nellie the Sweep had a pram she pushed around, and she was frightened of the thunder. I can remember her knocking on the door at the Scar Farm and she came in the house while it thundered. She used to sleep in the barn sometimes.

Marjorie Lumsden

Nellie the Sweep was the nicest one of the tramps; she was a gypsy really, pushing the pram. She used to sleep in the barns around the place. She had children; one of her daughters lived in Alnwick when I worked there. They were very dark, looked gypsy like. She was a lovely woman; she used to sell needles and pins.

I'll tell you a tale about her. There was a person in the village called Belle Straughan. She told me when she lived on the farm, Nellie the Sweep came every year and stopped in the barn. This particular day she (Belle) had been married about 10 or 11 years and never had had any children. This day Nellie came to the door. They used to give her a sandwich and a can of tea. She said to Belle, 'You're with child.' She said, 'I never knew, but sure enough I was.' She told me that 'cos she used to come and bait lines with my mother, in the bait house. I remember her telling me about this. 'Would you believe that', she said, 'she must have seen something in my face, because I didn't know myself.' She stayed a lot at Dunstan Hill when Willie Haddon was there. She had her places where she went. She had a pram and all her worldly goods were in this pram. In the winter she went in a house.

Judith Browell was the same age as my daughter. They were walking along the pier road, and she had a doll in a dolls' pram. Annie Jane Nelson at the shop was stood looking over the wall and she said to me, 'come here and look at this.' Judith had a kettle and a pan tied to her pram, a dolly's kettle, you know. Annie Jane said. 'Look at that – Nellie the Sweep.'

Part Three: Context
Medieval Craster, Craster Tower & the Craster Family

by Mary Craster

The name was spelt Crawcestre until around 1500. It means Crow's earthwork (Crawe Ceastre) in the Anglo Saxon.

There is a small Iron Age fort on top of the south heugh, but the medieval village was nowhere near the shore. It lay back from the sea, on the hill where the Tower now is. The name is more likely to have come from another prehistoric settlement, now entirely disappeared, amongst the trees at the top of the hill, where the rooks still nest.

Here the early Crasters are likely to have built their first, timber hall-house.

Before the Norman Conquest Craster was one of nine townships (now villages or hamlets) within the parish of Embleton. It was later split between the barony of Embleton and the Vescy Lordship of Alnwick. Henry I granted it to John Vesconte, son of Odard, who held his barony from the King for three knight's fees. In 1166 John had split this responsibility for military service by granting part of his lands to three tenants. One of these was Albert de Crawcestre.

Albert is not an Anglo Saxon name (he may have come from the Rhineland;) he married Christiana from the North Riding of Yorkshire, and his son William succeeded to the Craster part of her estate.

In 1255 the sole heiress of Baron John Vesconte conveyed her barony to Simon de Montfort, Earl of Leicester, one of the greatest nobles of the realm, and with this went the services of John of Crawcestre.

When Simon de Montfort rebelled against Henry III and was eventually defeated at the Battle of Evesham in 1265, his lands were forfeit to the Crown and were granted to Edmund Plantagenet, Earl of Lancaster.

This did not involve forfeiture for the tenants. By 1278 all tenants with estates worth over 20 pounds were in duty bound to become knights and entitled to a coat of arms. This was not necessarily a welcome privilege, as it involved providing a fully armed and mounted knight for 40 days a year, as well as agricultural services. In 1296 the then Craster, Sir Richard, had to provide:

> Feudal service for ½ a knight's fee;
>
> Homage for his holding;
>
> Attendance as a freeholder at the Earl's manorial court at Stamford;
>
> Payment of certain rents to the Crown;
>
> Rent for a mill-pond and water-mill on Howick Burn;
>
> Help in cultivating the fields of the Earl's demesne;
>
> Providing 6 ploughs (drawn by oxen), 12 horses for harrowing; and
>
> 12 men for reaping and 12 carts for a day's carting of hay and corn.

In that year a Scots army under William Wallace invaded Northumberland and caused great damage in this area, burning the Earl's manor at Stamford and much of Embleton and Dunstan.

In 1301 Sir Richard Craster sued Richard Wetwang of Dunstan over the right-of-way by which Wetwang was taking his carts to cut seaweed, used as a fertiliser. (This manorial privilege was still bringing in revenue to the Crasters in 1737.)

Richard named his son Edmund after his feudal lord and for the next 200 years nearly all the eldest sons were confusingly called Edmund.

Thomas, Earl of Lancaster, son of Edmund, was an ambitious & powerful man. He it was who began to build the great Castle of Dunstanburgh in 1313.

The road to Dunstanburgh ran along the inland, western side of the Heugh (still visible) and up through one of the two gaps, Big & Little Shand.

The castle promontory was turned into a near island by a great ditch dug in 1314 along the low lying ground to the west, extending from Embleton Bay to the head of the harbour which ran inland below the Castle on the south side. The entrance to this depression is now blocked by rocks and shingle banks. (A recent survey suggests that the entrance may have been further along). There is a record of three of Henry VIII's ships sheltering there in

1514. After the defeat at Flodden, the Scots were no longer a threat, and the castle fell into disrepair.

By the mid 14th century a pele tower had been built attached to the old hall-house at Craster. It is first mentioned in the list of border strongholds in 1415. An elegant pointed arched door led through into the tower on the ground and first floors and a circular stair led up in the thickness of the wall at the SE corner; there were four storeys.

In 1344, two years before the Scots defeat at the Battle of Neville's Cross, near Durham, the second Sir Edmund Craster was Collector for Northumberland charged with raising militia against the Scots invasions and funds to repair the destruction they caused. This proved a very long drawn out job (13 years) largely due to the depredations of the Black Death. The plague carried off most of the inhabitants of Newton in 1379. In 1384 further damage was caused by a Scottish army.

In the Wars of the Roses, the Crasters supported the Yorkists, although their lands were held from the Duchy of Lancaster. They seem to have accommodated successfully, however. In 1489 the then Edmund Craster was appointed Constable of Dunstanburgh Castle for life by Henry VII.

An amusing side light – in 1506 Edmund Craster testified that one Bertram Dawson was Embleton born and bred; he was a draper in York, and his business was falling off as his broad Northumbrian speech caused him to be 'sinisterly deformed that he should be a Scotchman born.'

All this time and until the late 18th century, Craster village was still at the top of the hill, immediately north and east of Craster Tower. A map of 1723 shows an E – W road with 12 houses in 2 rows on each side of it still to be seen in the pasture, running straight down the bank next to the Tower. The present road did not exist and there was nothing by the sea apart from the little cove where the fishing boats were beached.

The 16th century was a disturbed and unruly period, with constant feuds and cattle reiving on both sides of the Border. In 1521 one Richard Storey was killed by Jasper Craster. In 1598 a later Edmund Craster was arbitrator to settle a feud between Storeys and Hebburns. Despite all this, the Crasters managed to increase their property and obtained various outlying farms, let to tenants. One Thomas Craster, who had a tannery business in Alnwick, was appointed guardian to his great nephew until he succeeded to the family property. At Thomas' death in 1557 he left 3 beds, 1 cupboard, 5 brass pots and 10 pieces of pewter, as well as his stocks of leather. Even the comparatively prosperous had very few personal goods and chattels in those days.

Yet another Edmund, who died in 1594, left a widow Alice, who moved into the still habitable portion (possibly part of the Constable lodging?) in Dunstanburgh Castle. She ran a farm within the Castle (18 plough-oxen, 32 cattle, 3 horses, 145 sheep and 12 pigs). She was evidently quite well off and at her death her personal possessions were listed as a bed (perhaps a 4-poster) 2 truckle beds, 2 tables, 2 chairs, 7 stools, 2 benches, a cupboard and a chest; also a silver salt cellar, 6 spoons, 18 pewter vessels & 3 trenchers, kitchen utensils, 2 spinning wheels, bedding and bed – and table – linen.

Her grandson John received a university education at Cambridge. In his days, the Greys came to live at Howick Tower, and so as to make their estate more compact, arranged to exchange with John, various scattered Craster holdings, including Howick Mill, for the Howick land to the west of Craster; this now represents the greater part of Craster West Farm.

During the Civil War, the Crasters supported the king's party, but somehow managed to avoid sequestration of their estates.

Between 1666 and 1675, Craster Tower was enlarged; the old timber hall-house on the East side was replaced with a two storey stone manor house, and a new front door was made on the South side of the pele tower, opening on to a courtyard with a well, which is still there, under the later dining-room floor. Beyond the front door courtyard was a formal garden; it was just outside this garden that in 1680 a maid saw a younger son, Thomas, leaving after having killed Edmund Foster in a duel.

In the next generation, the eldest son (another John) went to Merton College, Oxford, (the college has the gift of the living of Embleton). He became a barrister at Gray's Inn, London.

In 1724 stables and coach-houses were built on the north side of the Tower and the old village, with a 'home farm' yard behind them (now the site of the Stable Yard Farm Shop). One imagines the old village may have been in the process of moving down to the sea. In the mid 18th century, Dunstan Hill Farm and Craster West Farm were built. John Craster married Catherine Villiers, daughter of a former governor of Tynemouth Castle. She became lady-in-waiting to Queen Caroline, wife of George II; two of her court dresses are to be seen in the Victoria and Albert Museum in London. John became an M.P and collected quite a reasonable and very typical country gentleman's library at the Tower, although he lived much of his time in the South and the Craster property was rented to a cousin, Daniel Craster. John's son, George, married Olive Sharpe, daughter of a neighbour at Gray's Inn and in 1760 they set off on an extended Grand Tour of Europe; South France, Rome, Florence, Venice and back to Paris. On their return they decided to enlarge and modernise Craster Tower, building a Georgian wing with pedimented front door on the South courtyard. A kitchen-garden was also constructed with its North wall backing onto a row of cottages at the southern edge of Dunstan (thus warming the garden wall). These form the present Cottage Inn. The Summer House on the SE point of Craster haven was also built as a picnic house for the Craster family. Olive's health was not good and she died, childless, on a visit to Paris in the winter of 1769. George returned to the North, but died a few years later.

The property eventually passed to Daniel, son of the cousin who had rented it from John the barrister. He was a keen farmer and interested in the agricultural improvements of the later 18th century – such as the cultivation of root crops for feeding livestock in the winter. He was succeeded by his son Shafto, who was squire for over 50 years and did much for the village in charity, medical assistance and so on. He built the school in Dunstan and laid out tree plantations round the Tower gardens. He it was that completed the removal of the village to the sea. It was known as Craster Seahouses as late as 1828. In 1822 he built Craster Square on the hill behind where Robson's Yard now is, as housing for the fishermen. This was pulled down in 1962. A water reservoir was also built and coastguards' cottages (the castellated) building on the hill above Bark Pots tea rooms.

The road past the Tower on the North side of the house was moved further away, making the Avenue, from the Pillars at the new cross-roads and leading through the sham Gothic archway and down the bank.

On Shafto's death in 1837, the estate passed to his sister's husband, Thomas Wood of Beadnell (whose mother had also been a Craster). Shafto's only daughter, Francis, was furious at not inheriting and removed herself to Preston, taking all Shafto's family records, furniture and furnishings, and even the rockery from the garden!

Thomas Wood employed the architect John Dobson of Newcastle to modernise the Tower extensively, renewing and moving the fireplaces and chimneys to the internal walls (the house suffered from damp – it still does, despite Dobson's efforts), adding a second floor to the old East wing and turning it into domestic offices and servants' quarters. He also built a laundry, bakery, brewery and dairy around an internal courtyard behind the NE side of the house; these were pulled down in 1969. He added a handsome bay window to the East side of the South wing, with a good view to the sea, for which a ha-ha was constructed in the east garden wall.

Thomas Wood took up residence in 1839 in the newly refurbished house. He took on the name of Wood-Craster (the Wood was subsequently dropped). He bought Craster South Farm back from Lord Grey.

On his death in 1867 the little Anglican church of St. Peter the Fisherman was built in the village in his memory; it was at first intended as a Sunday school, but became a chapel-of-ease to Embleton, which remains the parish church. The Memorial Hall, next door to it was built in 1887 and inaugurated as a men's reading room in 1889.

The last member of the family to live in the Tower as a single house was Sir John (1901– 1976). He served a term as High Sheriff of Northumberland and was Chairman of the Associated Sea Fisheries Committee of England and Wales from 1949 – 1970. He was very knowledgeable on wild birds being a member of the Home Office Advisory Committee on the Wild Birds' Protection Act. He took great interest in the creation of a national reserve on the Farne Islands. The Arnold Memorial Reserve below Craster Heugh was set up in 1973 in memory of Dr. Lawrence Arnold on land sold by Sir John Craster to the Northumberland Wildlife Trust.

A fine double window - the last work of Leonard Evetts, a notable designer of stained glass, was placed in St. Peter the Fisherman in 1998, in memory of Sir John's twin brother and sister, Shafto and Phyllis Carr-Ellison, who lived for many years at the Bogie, Craster South Farm.

During World War II, the army was quartered at the Tower. There was a camp of Nissen huts in the NE corner of the grounds, to the left of the present North drive.

In 1965, Sir John sold a large part of Craster Estates, Craster Harbour and the West Farm only being retained, and left eventually to Oswin Craster (his cousin). S & A Grey are the tenant farmers. South Farm was sold to Howick Estate, except for the Bogie and Keeper's Cottage, now belonging to children of Phyllis Carr-Ellison. The Tower itself was bought by three Craster cousins, who employed the Edinburgh architect, Schomberg Scott, to divide it – very skilfully – into 3 separate, self-contained dwellings, two of which still remain in the ownership of members of the Craster family.

With acknowledgements to Oswin Craster, and detailed articles on the history of the Craster family written by Sir Edmund Craster, published by the Society of Antiquarians of Newcastle upon Tyne.

1865 Sketch map of Craster.

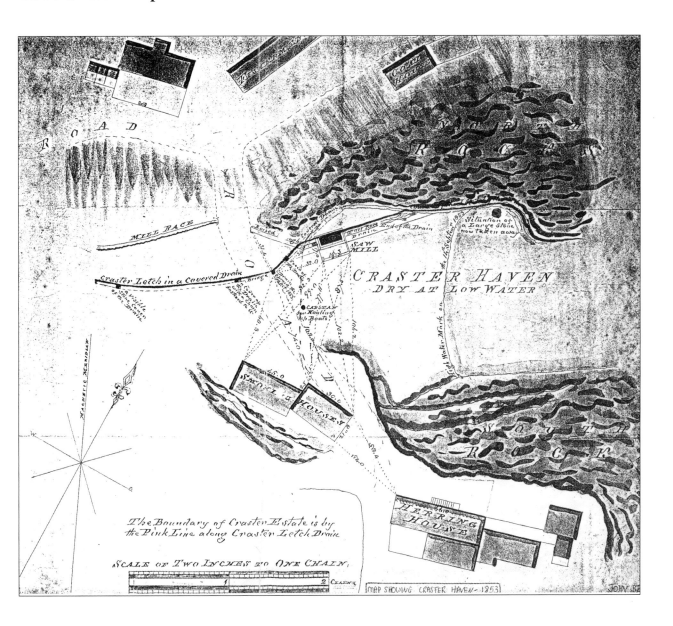

Map of Modern Day Craster

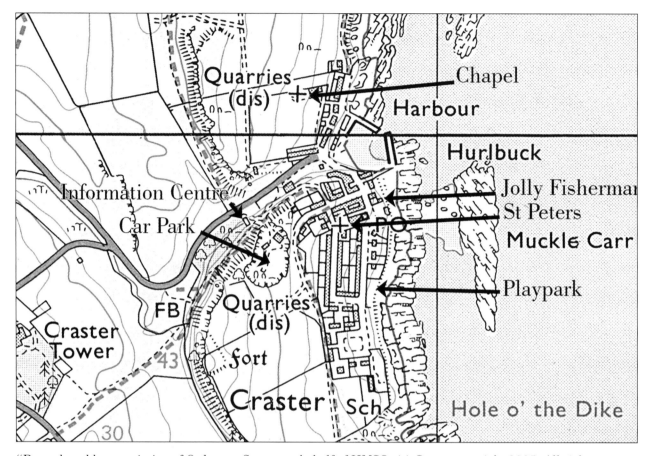

Glossary

Bark	preservative made by steeping tree bark
Bagie	turnip
Callant	young fellow
Cran	measure for new-caught herring = 28 stones
Fleet	set or group of pots or lines
GPS	global positioning system
Gansey	fisherman's heavy woollen sweater, knitted in various distinctive local patterns
Guffey	pig - (local fishermen considered the word 'pig' to be unlucky)
Howk	dig or hook-out
Lipper	a white-capped wave
Lonnen	path or lane
Mash	mesh of nets
Minging	stinking
Pellet	float for fish-nets
Poss	to agitate in a wash tub with a poss-stick
Prog	tool for poking or pulling wool through cloth to make floor mats (proggy mats)
Scen (skyen)	to shell bait such as limpets
Set pot	vessel for heating water
Shoot	to cast lines, nets or fleets of pots
Shut	chute or channel for tipping rubbish
Spelk	splinter
Swill	basket for holding lines for baiting
Sheer- legs	apparatus for lifting weights, consisting of three spars spread out and tied at the top, from which a block and tackle was hung
Tenter	rame for attaching tenter-hooks on which split herring are hung for smoking
Wear	seaweed matted on the beach
Wear bangs	long pieces of kelp, seaweed